Online Surveys FOR DUMMIES®

by Vivek Bhaskaran and Jennifer LeClaire

WILEY

Wiley Publishing, Inc.

Online Surveys For Dummies®

Published by
Wiley Publishing, Inc.
111 River Street
Hoboken, NJ 07030-5774

www.wiley.com

Copyright © 2010 by Wiley Publishing, Inc., Indianapolis, Indiana

Published by Wiley Publishing, Inc., Indianapolis, Indiana

Published simultaneously in Canada

For general information on our other products and services, please contact our Customer Care Department within the U.S. at 877-762-2974, outside the U.S. at 317-572-3993, or fax 317-572-4002.

For technical support, please visit www.wiley.com/techsupport.

Wiley also publishes its books in a variety of electronic formats. Some content that appears in print may not be available in electronic books.

Library of Congress Control Number: 2010926854

ISBN: 978-0-470-52796-2

Manufactured in the United States of America

10 9 8 7 6 5 4 3 2 1

WILEY

About the Authors

Vivek Bhaskaran is a software developer, the founder of Survey Analytics, and creator of their flagship product, QuestionPro. He had been developing easy-to-use software that drives results for over ten years. In 2002, he brought these principles to QuestionPro and created the most user-friendly yet powerful survey tool in the industry. More info about Vivek can be found at: http://researchaccess.com/vivek.

Jennifer LeClaire has been chronicling the Internet since 1997. She has witnessed the rise, fall, and resurrection of Dot-com Land, the emergence of the social media phenomenon, and the birth of online survey software. Jennifer's tech news credits include *NewsFactor, E-Commerce Times, Information Week,* and *Inc.com,* among others. In fact, tens of millions of readers rely on Jennifer for straight-up business and technology news and insightful special reports each year.

Jennifer is also a veteran business news journalist, with credits including the Associated Press, *The New York Times,* and CBS and ABC News. Jennifer is a weekly guest technology analyst on CBS Radio's KMOX, where she shares the real news behind technology headlines with millions of listeners nationwide. Jennifer is also an active blogger on AnalyticsInsider.com.

Jennifer is a member of the American Society of Authors and Journalists and the Public Relations Society of America. Jennifer's personal Web site is www.jenniferleclaire.com. She also heads Revelation Media Networks, an integrated marketing communications firm.

Dedication

This book is dedicated to my parents, Ranganathan and Vasantha Bhaskaran. If it hadn't been for them pushing and challenging me, I would never have written my first computer program in basic, which I'm sure led to me developing Survey Analytics.

— Vivek Bhaskaran

This book is dedicated to my daughter, Bridgette, who sits for hours at her laptop and creates online surveys just for fun. Her inquisitiveness and her creativity in asking questions — and getting responses — on just about any topic at the age of 12 should inspire us all.

— Jennifer LeClaire

Authors' Acknowledgments

Between the two of us, we've developed and taken plenty of online surveys, but writing a book that applies those skills and that knowledge is an entirely different story. Blair Pottenger is the project editor of this book and deserves a hearty round of applause for his careful reading, incisive comments, and patience. Blair is a pro who shows no signs of cracking even under deadline pressure. Whatever you throw his way, he catches it and runs with it. Thanks, Blair!

We tried to make the copy editing job easy for Virginia Sanders and John Edwards, but we appreciate their keen eyes. They made us look good by ridding our pages of unclear techie stuff and a few typos along the way. With an entire new language to learn over a few short months, we're convinced Virginia and John could copy edit books about almost anything techie and beyond.

Many thanks to Steve Hayes for launching this project and cultivating its first seeds. Steve held our hands through the beginning stages of developing the outline and sample chapter. His advice and experience in the publishing arena made this project an experience to remember (a good one!).

Every single pair of eyes and hands that played a role in bringing this book to fruition should be congratulated. This is an important topic for online businesses large and small and the editorial team deserves a place in the online surveys hall of fame for deciding to make this complex topic understandable to anyone.

Publisher's Acknowledgments

We're proud of this book; please send us your comments at http://dummies.custhelp.com. For other comments, please contact our Customer Care Department within the U.S. at 877-762-2974, outside the U.S. at 317-572-3993, or fax 317-572-4002.

Some of the people who helped bring this book to market include the following:

Acquisitions and Editorial

Project Editor: Blair J. Pottenger

Executive Editor: Steve Hayes

Copy Editors: Virginia Sanders, John Edwards

Technical Editor: Paul Chaney

Editorial Manager: Kevin Kirschner

Editorial Assistant: Amanda Graham

Sr. Editorial Assistant: Cherie Case

Cartoons: Rich Tennant
(www.the5thwave.com)

Composition Services

Project Coordinator: Lynsey Stanford

Layout and Graphics: Carl Byers, Kelly Kijovsky

Proofreaders: Rebecca Denoncour, Cynthia Fields

Indexer: Joan K. Griffitts

Publishing and Editorial for Technology Dummies

    Richard Swadley, Vice President and Executive Group Publisher

    Andy Cummings, Vice President and Publisher

    Mary Bednarek, Executive Acquisitions Director

    Mary C. Corder, Editorial Director

Publishing for Consumer Dummies

    Diane Graves Steele, Vice President and Publisher

Composition Services

    Debbie Stailey, Director of Composition Services

Table of Contents

Part II: Building Compelling Surveys............................. 75

Chapter 5: Preparing to Build Your Survey 77

Chapter 6: Developing Questions that Get Responses 89

Introduction

Online research can be exciting, revealing, and an exercise in greater
profitability for your company — or it can be arduous, time-wasting,
and downright frustrating. Your experience depends largely on the tools you
use to conduct your online research . . . and the knowledge you have about
how to use those tools. Consider this book a tool to help you streamline your
online survey building and promotional processes.

Maybe your boss is pushing you to leverage Web 2.0 in your marketing research
activities. You might be the director of a nonprofit trying to get new fundraising
ideas. You might even be a human resources manager polling employees about
their experience with the new benefits plan. Whatever your research needs,
Online Surveys For Dummies is the book you've been waiting for. Online research
gives you an advantage both over your competition and with your internal
operations, and that's critical for companies doing business in the 21st century.
In fact, from entrepreneurs to mega corporations, the value of online surveys
is becoming increasingly apparent, and corporate usage of them is increasing.
What you don't know about your customers might be hurting your chances for
success. And what you don't know about your employees, supporters, students,
or other constituents might damage relationships.

Online Surveys For Dummies is your A-to-Z guide to understanding how online
surveys work and how to use online survey software to get the answers you
need for your organization. Indeed, this book helps you unleash the power of
online survey software. It takes you step-by-step through the process of using
tools to discover new insights about your customers and how they view your
products and services. We dare say that by the time you're done reading this
book, you'll have confidence in your abilities to use this practical software
to get results — and confidence to share these abilities with others in your
organization, too.

About This Book

Online Surveys For Dummies takes the mystery out of online surveys. You find
out what you need to do to make online survey software work for you. You
discover the basic functions of developing and sending surveys, as well as
the more advanced tools to measure the response rates of your online questionnaires so you can make future adjustments.

In this book, we show you how to

- ✔ Understand online surveys
- ✔ Select your target audience
- ✔ Prepare effective online questionnaires
- ✔ Track respondents
- ✔ Create multilingual surveys
- ✔ Send your survey to the masses
- ✔ Avoid spam complaints
- ✔ Analyze your survey results
- ✔ And much more!

Readers of this book get a special bonus: A free three-month license to QuestionPro. To access your free account, go to http://questionpro.com/dummies to find out more.

Foolish Assumptions

You know what they say about people who make assumptions, but because you hold this book in your hands we have to presume a few things about you, such as

- ✔ You own a company, are planning to launch a new venture, or are running an organization that needs answers.
- ✔ You know how to use a Web browser.
- ✔ You're willing to invest a few hours to gain valuable insights into customer preference and behavior.

Of course, if you bought this book we have to figure you're more than a little hungry for customer data — or that you're working for someone who is. Because this book deals with online surveys and how to use them to glean revenue-generating insights that thrust you toward your organizational goals, we have to assume that you can take action on what you ascertain from this book.

This book can't do all the work for you — you have to understand your business model and your organization's specific needs. However, this book does help you get the answers you need and show you how to analyze response data so you can take steps to improve your bottom line.

How This Book Is Organized

This book won't put you to sleep. To the contrary, it wakes you up to new opportunities in data mining. This book is organized like your traditional reference manual — you can start with any chapter in the book and get the information you need on the spot. You don't necessarily have to read the chapters in order like you would an action thriller or a mystery novel. However, you certainly can and may read this book in order, cover to cover, if you choose to do so.

This book is divided into five parts: the basics, how to build surveys that get results, distributing surveys to target audiences, drilling down into the results, and the Part of Tens. If you want to jump right in and try your hand at an online survey, read Chapter 3. If you need some insights into developing questions, read Chapter 6. If you're ready to discover how to analyze your results like the pros, skip ahead to Chapter 13. You get the idea. You can return to this book again and again when you need to refresh your memory on some aspect of online surveys.

With that said, the topic of online surveys is complex, and each chapter builds on the others as you strive to gather and analyze the insights you need to improve your customer service, develop new products, enhance employee relations, or achieve whatever other purpose you have for launching an online survey. Yes, you can skip ahead to Chapter 4 and start the process of comparing and contrasting online survey software vendors. If you don't understand the common terminology in the online survey software world, however, you might not have a clue what you're really looking at. We recommend that you take the time to read the entire book from cover to cover and then use it as an ongoing reference guide as needed. We believe that you'll better understand how to develop questions, interpret the answers properly, and use the right metrics to travel down the path to success.

Part I: Getting Started with Online Surveys

In this part, we give you the keys you need to start the online survey software engine and keep it humming. Like a foreman setting out to build a skyscraper, this part of the book lays a strong foundation that supports your efforts as you develop the questions on which your online survey success hinges. Why are online surveys important to your market research efforts? What types of surveys can you conduct online? What's the difference between a rating scale and branching? What the heck is branching? You find out the basics of online surveys: how they can benefit you, how to speak the language, and how to choose the best software for your needs, whether it's a free tool or enterprise-class software.

Part II: Building Compelling Surveys

In this part, we help you understand how to build surveys that compel responses. We show you how to determine your survey objectives, discover the timesaving power of templates, and offer you insider secrets on developing questions that get responses. There are so many different types of questions you can ask that it might just make your head spin. But don't worry, we break down the most common question types as well as the rarest question types, and we offer guidance on when to use which ones. It's easy to shoot yourself in the foot with online survey questions, so we take the time to help you avoid question-development mistakes that can lead to survey abandonment or leave you with responses that don't fulfill your objectives. We also get into the technical aspects of actually using the software to build an online survey, from basic surveys to complex questionnaires.

Part III: Distributing Your Survey to Target Audiences

In this part, we take you one step closer to getting the insights you crave. Before you do anything else, you need to select your target audience. We show you how to do that as well as address other aspects of preparing to launch your survey to the masses. There are various nitpicky details you need to be aware of when you launch an online survey, like tracking responses, collecting anonymous responses, and how to publish your survey. We cover all that, as well as the critical aspects of complying with spam laws. So much hinges on your online survey e-mail invitation that we've dedicated a whole chapter (Chapter 11) to showing you how to create compelling copy, how to convince people to take part in your survey, and how to follow up. We also get into some of the technical aspects of administrating your survey from the back end (Chapter 12).

Part IV: Analyzing Your Online Survey Results

If knowledge is power, then online survey software offers the thrust of a jet engine. Reviewing your results lets you see your organization through the eyes of your audiences. We show you in Chapter 13 how to dive headfirst into your online survey reports to get real-time results while the survey is still in progress; how to review participant stats so you can see who is taking your survey (male or female, ages, and so on); and even how to analyze open-ended answers with a view toward gleaning insights that multiple choice questions just can't offer. In Chapter 14, we offer information for the brave at heart, daring you to get advanced with survey analytics functions like banner tables, grouping, and segmenting. Finally, we get into some technical mumbo jumbo you need to know, such as exporting your raw data (Chapter 15).

Part V: The Part of Tens

All *For Dummies* books have The Part of Tens. Chapter 16 shows you ten ways to increase your response rates. In Chapter 17, you discover ten common survey mistakes that can water down your success — if not completely derail your hard work. (Of course, we also show you how to avoid these mistakes along the way.) Finally, we leave you with Chapter 18, which provides ten best practices for online surveys so you can make the most of your efforts before you ever officially launch your questionnaire.

Appendix

Don't forget to check out the appendix, where you can find an online survey glossary that'll serve you well, regardless of which vendor you choose.

Icons Used in this Book

Like all *For Dummies* books, this book uses icons to highlight certain paragraphs and to alert you to especially useful information. Here's the lowdown on what those icons mean:

A Tip icon means we're giving you a valuable tidbit of information that might help you on your journey or provide some extra insight into the concepts we're discussing.

When you see the Remember icon, take note. That icon means we're offering information that's worth remembering.

The Technical Stuff icon alerts you that you're about to enter the geek zone. If you'd rather not venture into that realm, then simply skip it. But if you want to know every last detail, you'll love these sections.

The Warning icon does just that — it warns. It helps you avoid common mistakes, misconceptions, myths, and pitfalls. The bomb symbol sort of gets your attention, doesn't it? Be sure to look for it so you don't do more harm than good as you wade through the world of online surveys.

Web-Based Software: Get In The Know

In a Web 2.0 world, it's no longer necessary to download and install every piece of software. New technology and new business models are seeing the software industry evolve to embrace Web-based services. Online survey software falls into that category. Web-based software offers plenty of benefits — it saves you time, slashes your paperwork, and reduces errors. Web-based software offers you anywhere, anytime access to your data. (That means you can launch a survey from your laptop while you're at the pool!) With Web-based software, the administrative duties — including security — fall on the shoulders of the vendor. You have less risk all the way around. These are the key reasons why Web-based software is taking the world by storm.

Part I

Getting Started with Online Surveys

The 5th Wave   By Rich Tennant

"Our customer survey indicates 30% of our customers think our service is inconsistent, 40% would like a change in procedures, and 50% think it would be real cute if we all wore matching colored vests."

In this part . . .

The basics of online surveys are, well, anything but basic. Knowing the ins and outs of online survey software might not be as daunting as understanding complex computer programming languages, but it's not quite as easy as firing off a document in Microsoft Word, either. The online survey developer is one part marketer, one part investigator, and one part statistician. The good news is you can glean valuable insights into what your target audiences like and don't like, want and don't want, without being any of the three.

This part starts with the basics. We begin by explaining what online surveys are, who should use them, and the types of online surveys. You also need to have an understanding of a new language — the language of online survey software. That's why we spell out the ABCs of online surveys in clear terms that anyone can understand. You discover the differences between various question types and how to distinguish between the different types of measurement scales.

This part of the book also gives you an opportunity to try your hand at online surveys. We show you how to find free tools to experiment with, create and send a sample survey, and review your results, including reading real-time survey reports and interpreting open-ended comments. Finally, we set you on the shining path to online survey insights by reviewing some of the online survey software options available on the market today.

Chapter 1

Understanding Online Surveys

· ·

· ·

Surveys aren't merely a luxury — they've become a necessity for almost all types of research. Whether it's a *satisfaction survey* (a survey designed to measure consumer satisfaction) that your boss is insisting you complete by noon or a complex public health study that'll help you earn your Ph.D., Web-based surveys have emerged as the most affordable window into the world of your clients.

Online surveys are a tool for electronically collecting survey data from your target audience via the Internet. If your mind is rolling over and over with questions about online surveys, never fear; the answers are here within this book. If you come from the old school of market research, your brain might start reeling when it sees all the modern technology available for surveyors today. But your brain will soon thank you because tapping into the power of online surveys makes your life so much easier.

How so, you ask? Instead of using your brain power to crunch numbers, for example, you can use it to dig deeper into meaningful insights that drive results and make you look like the Superman (or Superwoman) of your organization. Using online survey software reporting tools, you can slice and dice your data in more ways than one to answer questions from many different angles.

In this chapter, you're introduced to the wonderful world of online surveys. If you're still wondering what an online survey is, you can get your answer here. If you want to know who should use online surveys, we have that covered, too. We even show you some of the basic types of surveys so you can get a taste of what's possible in this digital world of market research. We also talk about additional survey methods that complement online survey software. We wrap up the chapter with a discussion on the standards of the market research industry.

Surveying 101

Before we get into the world of online surveys, you need to get a quick foundation on surveying, its history, and why it works. (That's why we call this section "Surveying 101.") Merriam-Webster defines a *survey* as "questioning or canvassing people selected at random or by quota to obtain information or opinions to be analyzed." In simpler terms, a survey is a poll.

The first known survey conducted in the United States was the U.S. Census of 1790, but most of the survey industry's growth came after World War II. According to the Council of American Survey Research Organizations, in the first part of the 20th Century manufacturers didn't have to be concerned about marketing because items like soap were made a batch at a time and sold door-to-door. There were no colors, fragrances, or performance differences. Soap was soap, and consumers were glad to have it. Manufacturing advances led to better products, more choices, and the need to conduct market research. Surveys offered a way to discover what consumers liked — and didn't like.

How surveys work

Here's how surveys work: Just as a doctor takes a sample of blood for a blood test (notice we say a *sample;* he doesn't take all your blood), a market researcher ask questions to a small sample, or subsection, from a large group of people. This method makes surveys a time-efficient and economical way to conduct market research, as it would generally be improbable to examine the entire population.

The key to accurate surveys is getting the proper representation of *demographics* (population characteristics) to represent the *target audience* (the primary group that something is aiming to appeal to) as a whole. If you want to know whether your new soap fragrance might be a hit with consumers, you need to sample a *cross section* (a sample that represents the entire population) of your target audience, whether that's broad or narrow. If you're targeting women, for example, then you want a broad spectrum of ages. If you're targeting elderly women, by contrast, then your spectrum would be narrower.

Surveys are proven to work time and time again. Just about everything you see in the store is a product of market research — from childproof caps on medicine to the location of shopping centers to, yes, new fragrances of soap — and that market research included surveys in some way, shape, or form.

What is an online survey?

Just as there are many ways to skin the proverbial cat, there are many ways to conduct a survey. You could go door-to-door with a pen and pad, stand outside your local grocery store with a pen and pad, make hundreds of telephone calls, or do mass mailings through the post office. Or you could do it the easy way — with an online survey. An online survey is just that: a survey that collects data electronically from your target audience over the Internet (see Figure 1-1).

An online survey gives you the best of all survey worlds. It's the easiest way to distribute and collect information. It's the fastest way to create customized surveys based on different target demographics. It's an anonymous way to get feedback from customers, clients, and partners about products, services, marketing campaigns, and just about anything else. In short, online surveys give the survey creator and the survey taker ultimate flexibility, freedom, and convenience.

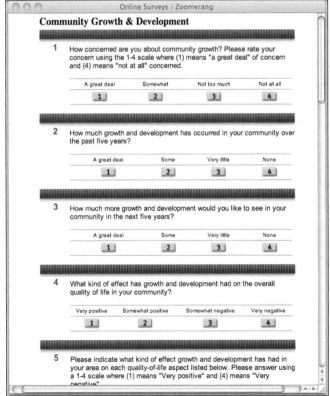

Figure 1-1:
A
Zoomerang
online
survey.

What you need to know about online software

The way people buy software has changed dramatically over the years. Sure, you can still go to your favorite big-box computer retailer and purchase a box with a CD containing your program of choice — in most cases, anyway. But online software, or Web-based software, is dramatically changing the face of the industry. As its name suggests, *Web-based software* is software that's hosted on a Web server. That means you access it through your favorite Web browser.

The inherent advantage of online software is the ability to access it anytime, anywhere, from any computer. As it relates to online surveys, using Web-based software means you can launch a survey from a hotel room in Hawaii just as easily as you can from your desk in Des Moines. You can also track your responses along the way and analyze the results.

Web-based software has some potential disadvantages, however. If the Web server on which the application is hosted gets overloaded, the software might not be available or it might run slower than you'd like. Some people also point to the security risks with online software. The bottom line: Check out the track record of your online survey software company. Even the best companies have seen their servers crash, but a pattern of downtime or security breaches should raise a red flag.

Examining the Need for Conducting Surveys

You picked up this book, so we figure you're fairly well convinced that you need to conduct surveys. We're also pretty sure you've decided that online surveys are at least one vehicle you want to use to find the answers you need.

Of course, surveys aren't the only way to get information. You could use existing data from other sources to answer your questions, such as market research reports from major firms. You could also hold focus groups. You could even rely on technologies like Web analytics to determine customer interests. (Check out *Web Analytics For Dummies,* by Pedro Sostre and Jennifer LeClaire, (Wiley Publishing, Inc.) for a good read on the nearly endless data-mining opportunities available through Web analytics software.)

For some, however, a survey is the best answer for getting, well, answers. There are many reasons why you might want to conduct a survey. Here are a few:

> ✔ **Surveys uncover marketplace potential.** If you want to know whether your customers would buy a new product you're considering manufacturing — or a new service you're thinking about launching, a new employee benefit you're mindful of adding, or some other addition to your offerings — then conducting a survey is one of the quickest ways to determine whether your target market is receptive to what you have to offer. The

survey can also help you hone in on the details around your products, services, and programs that your target audience appreciates most.

✔ **Surveys help determine weak spots in customer service.** Do you have new competition coming into the marketplace? You'd better shore up your customer service and product offerings now before your competitor steals your unhappy customers. It might be time to do a customer satisfaction survey to determine where your weak spots are. You might discover that your call center personnel are aggravating your customers or that your packaging really annoys them. Or, you might find your customers are loyal and you shouldn't change a thing. Better to find out now.

✔ **Surveys reveal public opinion.** You don't have to be Gallup (a well-known polling company) to run a public opinion poll. If your organization is about to make a decision that could impact the community — like bull-dozing a public park to build a self-storage facility or erecting a statue in the town square — you'd better get the public's opinion, or else you might find out the hard way that you don't have the public's support. In other words, if your decision making is driven by public reaction, surveys can reveal the information you're looking for.

Most online survey companies provide you with templates based on the type of survey you want to conduct (see Figure 1-2). These templates even suggest question types that are common to your objectives to give you a head start.

Figure 1-2:
The QuestionPro template library.

Deciding If Online Surveys Are Right for You

For all the virtues of online surveys, they admittedly are not the best solution to every information-seeking mission. Sometimes you need to be in the thick of the action to get the results you need. Sometimes you need to send out paper-based surveys because your target audience just isn't online. And sometimes telephone surveys are the best approach. We take a look at your offline options later in this chapter. For most companies, however, online surveys are a viable option for gathering opinions, reactions, and other feedback.

Before going any further in this book, take a look at the following sections, which discuss the benefits and drawbacks of online surveys.

Understanding the benefits of online surveys

Consider these benefits when determining whether online surveys are the right vehicle for your information needs:

✔ **Save time:** If you want to save time, online surveys are a good choice. Paper-based surveys can be time-consuming to develop, distribute, and analyze. Online surveys have a broader geographic reach so you don't have to put employees on the street — or on the phones — to survey the land.

✔ **Save money:** Online surveys are the top choice when money is an issue. Online surveys are perhaps the most cost-effective method to conduct surveys because after you develop the questions and launch the survey, it's up to the respondents to do the rest. You don't need to pay for envelopes to stuff, buy stamps, hire pollsters, or bankroll call centers.

✔ **Assistance developing questions:** If you need help developing questions, online surveys are again a winner. With paper-based surveys, you're on your own. Online survey vendors like QuestionPro offer templates and other helpful tools to help you design surveys that yield the types of answers you need to move your organization closer to its goals.

✔ **Quick feedback:** Online surveys offer real-time responses, which allow you to get quick feedback. This means you can get play-by-play action on the answers as they roll in. What could be more fun that a live look at the results?

✔ **Creation of charts and graphs:** If you need to create charts and graphs, online surveys can help. Paper-based surveys demand your data input and analysis skills. Online surveys offer analysis tools that do the number crunching for you.

> ✔ **Ability to change the content of the survey:** Online surveys give you the flexibility to change the course of your survey midstream. After you print paper-based surveys, you're stuck, but with online surveys you can change questions, delete questions, and add questions as you discover the need.

Knowing the drawbacks of online surveys

Online surveys are a great alternative to expensive mail or telephone surveys. However, you should know about a few caveats to online surveys. Ask yourself these questions to determine whether online surveys have too many drawbacks for your particular project:

> ✔ **Are you trying to survey a representative sample of the general population?** Remember that not everyone is online. What's more, not everyone is receptive to online surveys. Studies show the demographic that responds to online survey invitations is generally biased toward younger, more computer-savvy people.

> ✔ **Are you averse to risk?** Several technical glitches can derail your online survey. The respondent's browser might crash, and she might be too frustrated to restart the survey from scratch. What's more, programming errors can cause error messages. Power outages might keep respondents from finishing the survey.

> ✔ **Are you concerned about accuracy?** Online survey respondents can lie about their age, though this possibility exists with other forms of surveys as well. Lying about gender is another possibility, one that's avoided through in-person and phone surveys. If the respondent doesn't fully understand the question in an online survey, he has no one there to explain it to him.

Table 1-1 lists some of the pros and cons of online surveys.

Table 1-1	Pros and Cons of Online Surveys
Pros	*Cons*
Save time	Everyone is not online
Save money	Technical glitches could cause errors
Help developing questions	Respondents may not give accurate answers
Quick feedback	Could take weeks to tally responses
Charts and graphs	Need design skills to create accompanying art
Ability to change questions	

Looking at the Types of Online Surveys

There are many different types of online surveys, but most of them fall under four basic categories: customer satisfaction, customer loyalty, market research, and human resources. The following sections take a more in-depth look at each of these four types.

Calling on customer satisfaction surveys

Customer satisfaction surveys set out to determine whether your customers are satisfied with your products and services. The goal is to measure the customer perceptions of how well your organization delivers on its critical success factors. Those factors typically include service promptness, staff responsiveness, and understanding the customer's problem. Armed with this information, you can shore up your customer service efforts.

Customer loyalty surveys

Measuring customer loyalty is critical in an ultracompetitive marketplace, and online surveys can lend a hand in doing so. It's been said that acquiring a new customer is about ten times more expensive than servicing an existing customer. By conducting customer loyalty surveys (see Figure 1-3), you can identify customers who promote your company, customers who are passively satisfied, and customers who are most likely to abandon you in favor of a competitor. Then you can decide how to respond to each customer type.

Market research surveys

Market research surveys are what most of people are familiar with. These surveys attempt to determine what flavor of toothpaste consumers would like to see on the market, how the interior design of a vehicle could better serve them, or whether they'd eat some new strange spice on a potato chip. Market research surveys are one of the driving forces behind product innovation. Smart companies don't launch new products without doing market research first, and online surveys play a part in that research.

Human resources surveys

Human resource surveys can come in multiple forms. The most common are employee satisfaction surveys and employee exit surveys. Employee satisfaction surveys focus on things like work hours and benefit plans. Employee exit surveys gather information about people who are leaving the company, either through resignation or termination. Both survey types are vital for large and small companies that believe employees are the lifeblood of a company.

Augmenting Online Surveys

Sometimes you can't always reach your respondent online — getting a survey to someone who doesn't own a computer will always require some additional steps. However, there are many methods to bridge the gap between reality and online survey software: mail surveys, telephone interviews, in-person interviews, and drop-off surveys.

Making the most of mail surveys

When it comes to surveys, conducting your interviews via traditional mail has its advantages. You can select your sample from a database of mailing addresses that target specific demographics by neighborhood. So if you want to reach affluent consumers only, mail surveys would let you do that. By the same token, if you want to reach consumers with children, mail surveys might also help you narrow the field.

This survey type can be costly, though, because of printing and postage. Typically surveyors send out an advance letter, followed by the survey, and finally a follow-up postcard reminder to those who didn't meet the deadline.

A thank-you postcard is also in order. That's up to four separate mailings for one survey, and you still have no guarantee you'll get an answer.

After all the paper surveys are collected, responses can be transcribed using an online survey tool. The analytical tools that are included for free in most online survey software can then be leveraged.

Talking up telephone interviews

Telephone interviews can also narrow the field through directories listing databases. But few people like to be bothered at home with unsolicited phone calls. Telephone surveyors often are mistaken for telemarketers. The benefit to telephone surveys is that you can get more rapid responses than with mail surveys. The surveyor can also manually input respondent answers into a computer using online survey software while conducting the survey, so the results can be tabulated fairly quickly.

Facing up to face-to-face interviews

In-person interviews are a good option when you have personnel on hand that can go out into the communities, in front of grocery stores, in malls, or door-to-door with a clipboard and survey form in hand. Surveyors may obtain lists of suitable demographic areas (or just seek responses from people who seem to fit their profile) and ask qualifying questions to ensure they are surveying the target audience. This survey type can be tedious because those answers then have to be entered into a computer at a later time, but for live events such as voter polling this is the best solution.

Dealing with drop-off surveys

The drop-off survey is not often used these days. It combines mail surveys with in-person interviews. The surveyor visits potential respondents door-to-door and drops off the survey, and the respondents then mail the surveys back to the surveyor.

Searching for Standards

Online surveys are still an emerging segment of the market research industry. Although Fortune 500 companies are using online survey software regularly, it's a newer area and one with far fewer industry standards. For example, some companies refer to online surveys as *Web surveys*. Some companies call them *e-surveys.* Others call them *electronic surveys* or *Internet surveys.* The good news is you can employ research quality best practices across all types of market research, from paper-based surveys to telephone surveys to focus groups and beyond. The Marketing Research Association (`http://mra-net.org`) and the Council of American Survey Research Organizations (`www.casro.org`) offer strong standards guidance.

Making friends with the Market Research Association

The Marketing Research Association (MRA) was formed in 1954 as an outgrowth of the Trade Problem Discussion Group of the American Marketing Association's (AMA) New York Chapter. MRA is a self-managed, not-for-profit organization that provides programs and services for members to do the following:

✔ Enhance their professional development

✔ Stay connected with the marketing research community

✔ Gain insight into information about trends occurring in the industry

✔ Network with fellow researchers

The MRA offers a Respondent Bill of Rights, for example. The Respondent Bill of Rights is a document that describes the principles governing the researchers' responsibility to respondents. The group also promotes Survey Non-Response Metrics. Response rates and other non-response measures are thought to be important indicators of survey performance. Historically, the survey research profession has been divided in a consistent method of calculating these metrics. MRA recommends researchers use this guide to determine the appropriate formulas for calculating and reporting survey non-response. The most reputable companies in the online survey software world belong to the Marketing Research Association, but you don't have to be a member to glean from its resources.

Counseling with the Counsel of American Survey Research Organizations

Founded in 1975, the Council of American Survey Research Organizations (CASRO) represents over 300 companies and research operations in the United States and abroad. CASRO promotes a rigorous code of conduct that enhances the image of survey research and protects the public's rights and privacy. CASRO requires members to adhere to the CASRO Code of Standards and Ethics for Survey Research, a tough, internationally cited set of standards that has long been the benchmark for the industry.

The Code of Standards and Ethics for Survey Research sets forth the agreed-upon rules of ethical conduct for survey research organizations. Acceptance of this code is mandatory for all CASRO members. The code has been organized into sections describing the responsibilities of a survey research organization to respondents, clients, and outside contractors as well as in reporting study results. If you want to make sure your surveys hold the highest integrity, reviewing the CASRO code of standards is a must.

Chapter 2

Steering Clear of Common Terminology Confusion

*J*ust like your car, your online survey software has a dashboard, of sorts, that displays important information about your survey. Instead of oil, temperature, and gas, though, it offers information about how many people have taken your survey, the responses they've offered to your questions, and how many people have quit the survey before finishing it. You might think of your online survey dashboard as the control center for your market research. You have a lot to comprehend in order to put your survey results into an action that pays dividends — and it begins with understanding online survey terminology.

Of course, most online survey software dashboards are far more complex than even an especially high-tech car dashboard. The more sophisticated the software is, the more difficult it is to navigate the charts, graphs, and other data that unlock the secrets of respondent preferences and opinions.

If you don't understand the terminology that describes the various online survey attributes, you could be in for a bumpy ride as you continue down the market research road. If you can't discern what the data means — and doesn't mean — your results aren't worth the Web they're displayed on.

Indeed, you have a lot to master about graphs, charts, symbols, and terminology as you venture into the world of online surveys. You won't find this info in your friendly dictionary, and little progress has been made toward industry standard online survey language. Even though some vendors and researchers use similar terminology, it can and does vary widely.

Think of this chapter as your study guide that defines common signs, symbols, and flashing lights on the road to successful online surveys. With definitions, acronyms, and the like, you can be sure to choose the right tools and use them well.

For even more definitions and descriptions of the language and terminology of online surveys, be sure to check out the appendix at the end of this book.

The ABCs of Online Surveys

What is abandonment? Why is drop-out analysis important? What does TURF analysis mean? With synonyms, acronyms, and words like *dashboard* that have different meanings in the online and offline worlds, you need to know the ABCs of this tech terminology if you want to make the most of your online survey software demands. Like English, some terms have synonyms, so one online software vendor might define *variables* as hidden questions, another might define them as hidden fields, and another might define them as custom variables. The different vendors are all talking about additional information — such as participant names — that's passed to the survey to create a more personalized survey experience.

Online survey software vocabulary is extensive. The good news is that the language is pretty stable. Unlike many emerging technologies, the vocabulary is well defined. Still, you have to take the time to review and understand the common nouns, verbs, and adjectives that characterize the creation, distribution, analysis, and reporting of online surveys. When you do, you'll be well on your way to understanding — and unleashing — the power of online surveys for your business.

A word by any name . . .

People who are trying to learn English often complain that the language has too many different meanings for the same words. These words are called *homophones.* In the world of online survey software, you'll run into your fair share of homophones. Respondent, multiple-choice question, and e-mail reminder are fairly self-explanatory terms. But there are also synonyms galore. With no industry standard for online survey software vocabulary, terms used in Software X could mean something very different than terms used in Software Y. Take interval scale questions, ordinal scale questions, and check box questions as examples. All three terms have to do with specific question types — but they all have at least one synonym. In other words, what one vendor calls an ordinal scale question, another vendor might call a rank order scaling question. What one vendor calls a check box question, another vendor might call a multiple-select question. You get the idea. As you choose your software vendor — and as you begin to decipher data — be sure you're speaking the same language as your application.

Questions, Questions, and More Questions

An online survey is all about questions and answers, right? After all, you can't analyze answers if you don't first ask questions. There are dozens of different question types you can use in your online survey. If you don't understand what's what, you might end up confused — or confusing your participants. And when your participants get confused, they typically abandon your survey. That means all your hard work was for nothing. So take a moment to do a quick review of the myriad of question types you can ask. You can dive deeper into the when, where, and how of using these question types in Chapter 6.

- ✔ **Check box questions:** Also known as *multiple-select questions,* check box questions let users choose more than one answer for a question.

- ✔ **Closed-end questions:** These are questions that can be answered with "yes/no," a specific piece of information, or a predefined list of answers (for example, multiple choice).

- ✔ **Constant sum question:** A question that permits the collection of *ratio* data, meaning the data is able to express the relative value or importance of the options. (For example, option A is twice as important as option B.)

- ✔ **Dichotomous questions:** These are questions that offer only two possible answers. Generally a yes-or-no question, such as "Have you ever purchased a product or service from our Web site?" The respondent simply chooses Yes or No.

- ✔ **Double-barreled question:** A question that combines two or more issues in a single question. An example of this type of question would be, "Do you like rocky road ice cream and do you think your friends would buy it?"

The following are not good questions to ask your respondents as they make it difficult for the respondent to gauge what you're measuring. We want you to know about this type of question so you can avoid this type of writing yourself.

- ✔ **Filter question:** A question that helps you determine whether a respondent is qualified or experienced enough to offer the insights you need in your online survey. This term is also called a *contingency question.*

- ✔ **Multiple-choice questions:** Questions with answers that consist of three or more mutually exclusive options. These questions can allow the respondent to choose just one option (single select) or more than one option (multiple select).

- ✔ **Multiple-select question:** A question that allows participants to select more than one option.

✔ **Open-ended question:** A question that seeks to explore the qualitative, in-depth aspects of a particular topic or issue.

✔ **Rank order scaling questions:** Questions that allow people to rank a certain set of brands or products based on a specific attribute or characteristic.

✔ **Rating scale questions:** Questions that require a person to rate a product or brand along a well-defined, evenly spaced continuum. (Figure 2-1 shows a rating scale question.)

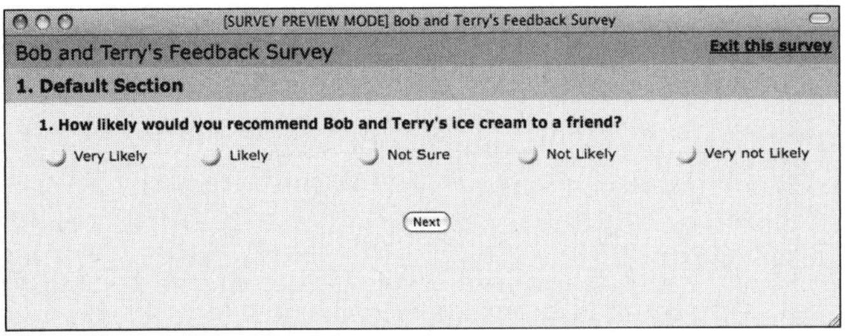

Figure 2-1:
A Survey Monkey rating scale question.

✔ **Semantic differential scale:** A scale that asks a respondent to rate a product, brand, or company based on a seven-point rating scale that has two bipolar adjectives at each end.

✔ **Staple scale question:** A question that asks a respondent to rate a brand, product, or service according to a certain characteristic on a scale from +5 to –5, indicating how well the characteristic describes the product or service.

Are you forcing the issue?

When it comes to question types, some are more innocent than others, and some are more influential than others. Some of your questions might be *quantitative* (question types that include multiple choice, rank order, and constant sum), and others might be *qualitative* (questions that explain perceptions or opinions by using text instead of numbers). Then there's the all-important *pivot question* (a question you use to segment the rest of the survey). Whatever you do, you want to avoid *question bias* (wording that influences the respondent to answer with a preference toward a particular result). You can avoid question bias by using *leading questions* (questions that suggest the answer or reveal the interviewer's opinion). Also known as a *trick question*, a loaded question contains an assumption of agreement. Some questions demand *mutually exclusive responses* (responses for which the respondent can't choose more than one answer). And, you can even force the issue with a *forced response*, which requires the respondent to answer your thought-provoking question before he or she can move on to the next question. Don't you feel powerful?

Understanding Participant Actions

Some terms, like *abandonment* and *opt-in,* describe what a consumer did with regard to your online survey. *Survey abandonment* means just what it says — the participant left your site in the midst of the questionnaire. Terms like ballot stuffing, by contrast, might stir images of political corruption. But in the online survey software world, *ballot stuffing* is when an individual responds to your survey more than once. The meaning is the same as it is in terms of voting, but the motives and the consequences are far different.

Take a moment to review this list of the most common terms describing participant behavior in your online survey or with your survey invitations.

- ✔ **Affirmative consent:** The practice of someone deliberately choosing to receive e-mail from an organization. Also called *opt-in.*

- ✔ **Completed:** The number of respondents that have gone through the entire survey and clicked the Finish button on the last page of the survey. This count is important because it signals when you have a large enough sample to conclude your survey. (A *sample* is a group of people who fit a particular demographic and are willing to take your survey.)

- ✔ **Completion rate:** Represents the number of completed survey responses divided by the number of started survey responses. This metric is telling. If your completion rate is low, you might be doing something wrong in your questionnaire. Perhaps it's too long or the questions are too confusing. You need to take some time to reflect.

- ✔ **Drop-outs:** The number of respondents who start the survey but do not complete it. If your completion rate is low, you have a high drop-out rate. Again, you need to get to the root of the problem.

- ✔ **Response rate:** The proportion of those who actually participate in a survey. If you send out 1,000 online survey e-mail invitations and only 10 people responded, your response rate is 10 percent. And, we dare say, your e-mail invitation probably wasn't too compelling. For more information on how to boost response rates, check out Chapter 16.

Pay for play surveys

Here's a concept you need to understand early on in your quest to hunt down relevant insights that'll drive your organization forward: paid surveys. Taking paid surveys online has become big business for stay-at-home moms and others looking to earn a quick buck. People touting themselves as paid survey gurus have even written books to teach consumers how to tap into this revenue stream. These gurus promise consumers they can make as much as $1,200 a month taking surveys from the comfort of their own homes. The bad news is that a lot of scammers out there have burned survey respondents, putting legitimate *panel companies* (the companies that gave you the list of people willing to participate in surveys like yours) a bad name. So, as you contemplate partnering with panel companies that help you find participants, proceed with caution. Make sure the panel company is reputable, or it might taint your survey . . . and your good brand name.

Online Survey Diversity

Maybe you plan to conduct only customer satisfaction surveys over and over again. You might not plan to launch any other type of survey — that is, until you understand what you can do with online survey software. Sure, you can launch simple customer satisfaction surveys all day long. But you can conduct many, many other types of surveys. Really, the possibilities are almost limitless. Here are some of the most common types of surveys that companies are conducting today:

- ✔ **Attitude research surveys:** Surveys conducted to obtain information on how people feel about certain products, ideas, or companies.

- ✔ **Customer satisfaction surveys:** Surveys that seek to determine whether your customers are satisfied with your products, services, and even your customer service.

- ✔ **Customer loyalty surveys:** Surveys that seek to determine how loyal a customer is to your brand.

- ✔ **Employee attitude surveys:** The goal of these surveys (see Figure 2-2) is to collect information about the general feelings of an organization's employees. They usually include a series of multiple choice options grouped along one or more dimensions of the organization.

- ✔ **Employee exit interviews:** Surveys that seeks to determine an employee's reasons for joining the company, the department or business unit in which the employee worked, and the reasons for leaving the company.

- ✔ **Tracking studies:** Surveys that track consumer behavior over long periods of time.

- ✔ **Transactional surveys:** Surveys that measure the customer's satisfaction in relation to a particular transaction.

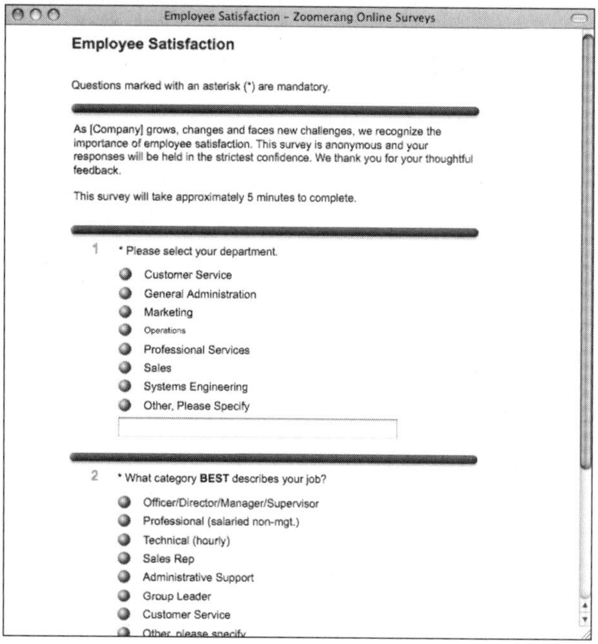

Figure 2-2:
An employee
attitude
survey using
Zoomerang.

✔ **Relationship surveys:** Surveys that measure the satisfaction of customers who have an ongoing relationship with your organization.

✔ **Shopping cart abandonment surveys:** Surveys that seeks to determine why people abandon shopping carts and registration pages, giving you the opportunity to make improvements to your site.

Analyzing Survey Analysis Terms

Analyzing data can be fun for some and intimidating for others. Sure, the colorful charts and graphs are pretty to look at and can tell you a lot. But if you don't understand the underlying analytical methods, you might not be able to put your results into action. Remember, the whole point of conducting your online survey is to get actionable insights that drive your organization to the next level. Here are some common survey analysis terms you need to become familiar with:

✔ **Basic frequency analysis:** An analysis that offers an overall insight based on percentages and averages.

✔ **Conjoint analysis:** A popular marketing research technique used to determine what features a new product or service should have and how it should be priced.

✔ **Cross tabulation analysis:** An analysis that offers insights into how two variables interact and a distribution of how users responded to both of them.

✔ **Data cleaning:** The process of detecting, correcting, and removing data from your online survey results that's inaccurate, corrupt, incomplete, or irrelevant.

✔ **Drop-out analysis:** An analysis that tracks at what point your participants dropped out of (meaning they quit before finishing) the survey.

✔ **Frequency analysis:** Calculates how often a particular answer option is selected.

✔ **Grouping and segmentation analysis:** An analysis that lets you create filters to group respondents based on demographics or responses.

✔ **Real-time summary report:** Provides basic statistical analysis on your survey questions as completed surveys come in (see Figure 2-3).

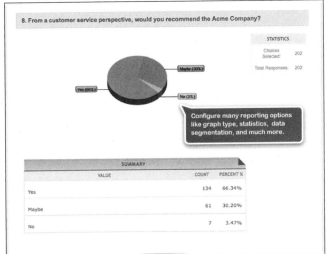

Figure 2-3:
A Survey-
Gizmo
summary
report.

✔ **Simple frequency analysis:** An analysis that compares the values of the fields you specify and creates a report that lists each value for those fields along with the number of times each value occurs.

✔ **Spotlight report:** A report that lets you share the survey results with the respondents so they can see how their answers compare with the rest of the respondents' answers.

✔ **Started:** Total number of respondents who have started the survey.

✔ **System variable–based filtering:** Grouping surveys based on variables.

Making sense of market research lingo

If you're doing market research, it only makes sense to take the time to understand market research lingo. You might want to measure metrics like *aided recall*. Also called *awareness,* this is a technique used to aid memory, like showing the respondent a picture or words alongside the possible answers to your question. The common categories of awareness include top-of-mind awareness, unaided awareness, and aided awareness. Top-of-mind awareness is the Holy Grail of awareness metrics because it means consumers think of your company first when they're in the market to buy the kinds of products or services you sell. Unaided awareness is also desirable because it means people thought of your brand without being prompted.

✔ **Time-based grouping:** Creates segments of data based on time, such as when the survey was completed.

✔ **TURF (Total Unduplicated Reach and Frequency) analysis:** A statistical model that you can use to answer questions such as "Where should we place ads to reach the widest possible audience?" and "What kind of market share will we gain if we add a new line to our model?"

Untangling Technical Terms

There's no need to attend a technical institute to take full advantage of online survey software, but you do need to untangle a few technical terms if you want to fully understand what you're looking at — not to mention what you're looking for. Take a few minutes to review these complex technical terms spelled out in plain language and you'll be rattling off these acronyms with the best tech geeks out there:

✔ **Cookie:** A small piece of text stored on a user's computer by a Web browser. In the online survey world, a cookie helps the software recognize a participant who might have started a survey but ran out of time before finishing it and closed their browser. When the participant logs back in, the cookie recognizes them, allowing them to finish the survey. By the same token, cookies can signal and block repeat users. If you don't want people to take your survey more than once, cookies can be a key to stopping ballot stuffing.

✔ **E-mail firewall:** A piece of hardware or software application that's programmed to identify and block e-mails that appear untrustworthy. This is important to understand when you enter the world of sending online survey e-mail invitations. You might need to ask your participants to *whitelist* you (put you on a list of e-mail addresses that are known, trusted, and explicitly permitted) so you don't get *blacklisted* (put on a list of e-mail addresses that are automatically marked as "SPAM"). A blacklist is also known as a *blocklist*.

✔ **Hosted solutions:** Web-based software that requires you to log on to an Web site in order to create, launch, and analyze your reports. Most online software vendors offer hosted solutions, but some still offer an install-your-own model where you purchase the software and install it on your machine. Hosted solutions are also referred to as *on-demand solutions* or *software as a service (SaaS)*.

✔ **JavaScript:** Not to be confused with the Java programming language, JavaScript is a scripting language developed by Netscape. It can be embedded into the HTML of a Web page to add functionality, such as validating data or responding to a visitor's button clicks.

✔ **Radio button:** A circular button on a Web page that can be selected by the respondent to mark a choice.

✔ **RSS reader:** A software program that aggregates data from Web sites.

✔ **Widget:** A mini Web application you can put on your Web page, blog, or social media site that allows you to embed information.

Chapter 3

Trying Your Hand at Online Surveys

In This Chapter

▶ Starting your survey with free tools

▶ Getting a feel for what's offered

▶ Conducting a sample survey

▶ Sending survey invitations via e-mail

▶ Reviewing your survey results

*O*nline surveys are easy to use and can offer your company insights into new markets, current customers, or future product lines. With online surveys, you're poised to tap into a wealth of information that will position your organization to compete more effectively in whatever market you serve.

Of course, like most other things in life, a learning curve is associated with using online surveys and all their glorified technological bells and whistles. But don't let that intimidate you. Once upon a time, you had to figure out how to use Microsoft Word, remember? Now you're a whiz.

How does navigating online survey software compare, you ask? If you can use word processing software, you'll be comfortable with online survey software. Armed with some new online survey terminology (covered in Chapter 2), you're now ready to try your hand at online surveys. In this chapter, we examine both free and paid online survey tools and discuss how to use these tools to create an actual survey.

Getting Started

You've most likely encountered online surveys before. Sometimes they pop up when you land on a magazine Web site, asking for a quick minute of your day. Other times you receive an e-mail with a link from a company that wants you to rate its customer service based on a scale of one to ten. You've probably seen companies using online surveys for all sorts of purposes. But where do you start? How do you get your feet wet with online surveys?

If you're ready to begin your journey into the world of marketing research, start with the freebies. There's no sense in subscribing to sophisticated enterprise online survey software that might cost hundreds of dollars a year before you determine whether you (or someone in your organization) can develop the skills to create an effective online survey. Of course, with this book in hand, you have everything you need to develop the skills — but why invest in a pricey subscription when you're just starting to get your feet wet?

You have two options: Choose a free online survey software tool or a 30-day free trial with a more robust online survey software tool. If you're serious about pursuing online surveys as a marketing research strategy, the free tools only take you so far. If you go for the free trial, keep in mind that you'll eventually have to pay a monthly fee in order to continue using the software. The following sections look at a few of the options in both categories. (We dive deeper into the tool types in Chapter 4.)

Finding free tools

You might determine that you'll never need more than what the free online survey tools have to offer, or you might not have the budget to subscribe to a more professional service. That's fine. The freebies can get you up and running and can take you a long way down the road to information, especially if you're running smaller surveys.

SurveyMonkey.com (www.surveymonkey.com) is one of the most popular free online survey tools available. You can also find numerous free survey tools at www.freeonlinesurveys.com, www.esurveyspro.com, and www.surveygizmo.com. If those options don't cut it for you, go to www.google.com (or your search engine of choice) and type **"free online survey tools"** in the search box. You'll come across a handful of options on the first page.

Free survey software companies have limitations in terms of the number of respondents, the types of reports, the templates, and other features that they offer. But if you're a guerilla marketing aficionado, the freebies might suit you well. The free online survey software companies typically offer paid upgrades so you can add on the features you need. Table 3-1 lists some of the big differences between free and paid online survey tools.

Table 3-1	Major Differences Between Free and Paid Tools	
Feature	*Free Survey Software*	*Paid or Subscription Survey Software*
Response limit	Yes: Normally capped around 100 responses a month	No: Either unlimited or capped at a much higher number
White label	No: Unable to remove survey software branding (logos, brand name)	Yes: All or some branding removed
Survey/question limit	Yes: Usually allows for 10–20 surveys/ questions.	No: Unlimited surveys and questions
Branching/skip logic	Yes: Basic branching (the ability to jump or skip over questions based on a particular answer)	Yes: Complex branching (similar to basic branching, except more advanced logic can be used)
Spreadsheet data export	No	Yes: Allows you to export data to an Excel file.
Question types	Basic question types (multiple choice, open ended text, and so on)	Advanced Question Types (extraction, file uploads, and so on)
Survey templates	None or limited	Yes
Live support	None or limited	Yes: Live support provided via phone, e-mail, and/or chat

Finding free trials for paid tools

If you want an online survey solution that's a little more robust (and often more professional-looking) than the freebies, opt to get started with online surveys by enrolling in a free trial from a company that offers advanced tools.

Companies like QuestionPro (www.questionpro.com), Vovici (www. vovici.com), and KeySurvey (www.keysurvey.com) offer 30-day free trials to people who know they need advanced features and want the support that comes with enterprise-level online survey software. You can find additional resources by typing **online surveys free trial** into your favorite search engine.

Table 3-2 takes a look at some of the features of paid tools.

Table 3-2	Notable Features of Paid Tools		
Feature	*Vovici*	*QuestionPro*	*Keysurvey*
Install on your own server	Yes	No	No
Security integration methods	Password upload, panel integration	Facebook, password upload	LDAP
CRM integration	Salesforce, Oracle CRM	Salesforce	Salesforce
Enterprise workflow management	Yes	No	No
Panel management solutions	Yes	No	No

Using QuestionPro as our example for this chapter, if you want to take advantage of the free trial, you need to offer up some basic information through an Internet form and agree to the terms of service. (Figure 3-1 shows the form for QuestionPro.) From there, you can jump right in to creating a new survey from scratch or using one of the templates in the company's template library.

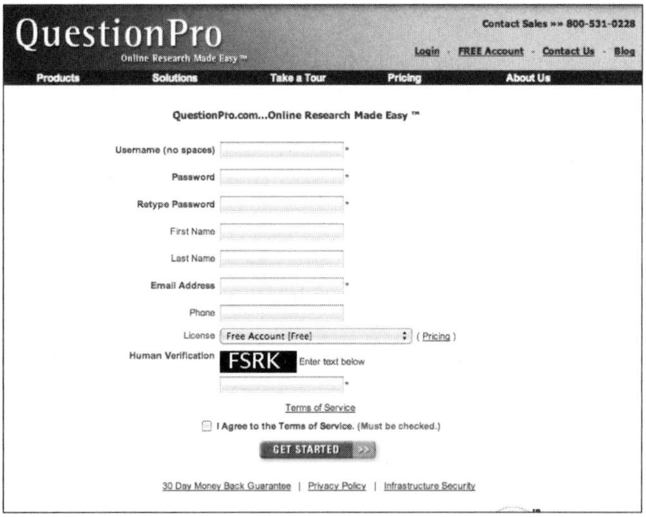

Figure 3-1:
The QuestionPro free trial signup form.

Discovering What's Offered

Before you dive in to survey development, use some of your time to get some quick education on the specific features and functions that your online survey software company of choice has to offer.

Although the fundamentals of online surveys are the same, each vendor offers its own buttons, links, features, and functions. You need to get the lay of the land, so to speak, before embarking on your survey journey or you could end up driving in circles and wasting plenty of gas in the process. You can get up-to-speed quickly through virtual tours, online tutorials, and free webinars, as we describe in the following sections.

Taking virtual tours

The quickest way to get up-to-speed on the overall workings of an online survey tool is to take the virtual tour. *Virtual tours* are typically video presentations that walk you through the capabilities of the software with a voiceover and screen shots that demonstrate the software in action. Most of the larger online survey software companies offer them for your perusal.

Browsing online tutorials

Online tutorials can also help you get the lay of the land. QuestionPro, for example, offers a searchable knowledge base, how-to articles, and video tutorials to help you grasp the basic concepts that allow you to shorten the learning curve. Whether you like to read, listen, or dive in and figure things out as you go with the help of an article or two, online survey companies offer training alternatives.

Leveraging free webinars

Webinars — live meetings or presentations given online by using Web conferencing tools — can be an efficient means of discovering more about the online survey software of your choice. These Web-based seminars are like attending a traditional seminar but there's no travel expense. Webinars go deeper than virtual tours or online tutorials by providing live instruction on specific topics, such as "QuestionPro 101" or "Analyzing Your Data."

Conducting a Sample Survey

When you're satisfied that you have the lay of the land, it's time to conduct an actual sample survey. This is where the fun begins! This exercise shows you the power of the software you're using and also helps you become more familiar with the hands-on possibilities of online surveys. Reading and watching videos about online surveys are one thing — experiencing the fun for yourself is something entirely different.

You have a few different options for sample surveys. You can conduct a sample survey based on a real need within your organization and kill two birds with one proverbial stone. Or, you can choose something quick and easy just to become more familiar with the tools. We recommend the second option. Although using online survey software isn't rocket science, your introductory session with online surveys is hardly the time to release a survey to the masses. If you make any silly mistakes, it could make you look, well, silly.

If you don't want to feel like you're wasting your time completely, you have a third option: Send a survey to internal workers around a genuine informational goal. You might ask employees about their thoughts on a new health-care program or proposed dress codes. In this way, you gather valuable information that can actually help your company breed more loyal employees, and if you make a mistake in the survey, your secret is safe with them.

Creating a new survey

Creating a new survey is a process that requires you to choose survey layouts and options and to add questions. Don't worry; it doesn't take long at all. And when you're done, you'll be well on your way to gaining the insights you need into the issues you choose.

You can create a survey from scratch or use a template. Using a template might save you time because it gives you preformulated questions, but to get the full effect of learning, try starting from scratch.

The examples in this book use QuestionPro. If you don't have an account with QuestionPro, you can easily sign up by visiting http://questionpro.com and then clicking Free Account in the upper-right corner. Follow the instructions to create your account.

This book includes a free upgrade to more features within QuestionPro. To upgrade your license, first make sure you've created a free account, and then follow the instructions at http://questionpro.com/dummies.

Choosing survey layout and options

After you've logged in to QuestionPro, click the Create a New Survey button to open the Create Survey Wizard. The wizard takes about a minute to complete and serves as the foundation for your survey. This is where you choose the name and theme for your survey. Don't rush through this — put a little bit of thought into how you name these items. Your survey name should be descriptive enough for you to remember what it's about when you see your list of surveys. The URL should be short and descriptive.

The Create Survey Wizard has three steps, as shown in Figure 3-2. The steps are as follows:

1. **Complete the Survey Name.**

   This is where you name your survey. Again, you should choose a name that describes the purpose of the survey. For example, if you're doing a customer satisfaction survey, name it such. In this case, we'll enter the name "Sample 1" in the Survey Name text box.

2. **Select your Layout/Options.**

   Select a theme for your survey from the Survey Theme drop-down list. As you select themes from the list, you can preview the look and feel of the layout in a box to the right. You can customize the theme later if you change your mind. In this case, we're choosing the Ocean theme.

3. **Facebook Connect.**

   QuestionPro lets your survey respondent log in with their Facebook login ID to take the survey. For this is example, we'll uncheck the box titled Enable Facebook Connect on this Survey and then click the Finish button in the bottom-right corner of the wizard window.

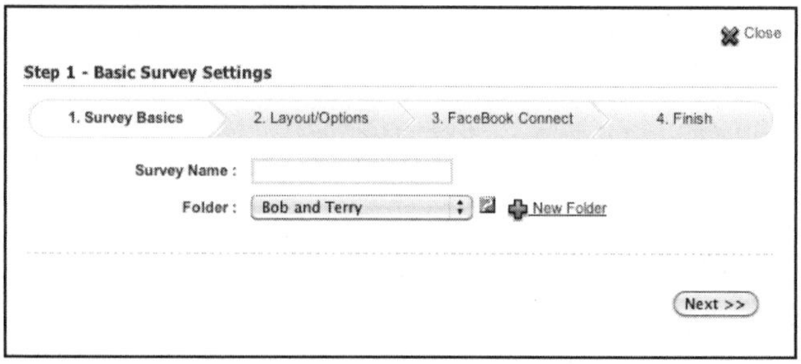

Figure 3-2:
The Create Survey Wizard dialog box.

Close

Step 1 - Basic Survey Settings

| 1. Survey Basics | 2. Layout/Options | 3. FaceBook Connect | 4. Finish |

Survey Name :

Folder : Bob and Terry   New Folder

Next >>

Adding questions

After you've laid the foundation of your survey, you can start building it with questions. Immediately after you complete the Create Survey Wizard, you're ushered to the Edit Survey page with a box named "Add a Question to This Survey". You can watch a video tour by clicking the link on the right, or you can skip it and get right to adding questions by clicking the button.

You have many different question types to choose from (as described in Chapter 2). For now, just choose from the basic question types. Here are the steps to follow when you're ready to start adding questions:

1. **Select the Standard Question Types option.**

   It's the first option listed.

2. **Indicate the question type.**

   Click the drop-down list beneath the Standard Question Types option and select one of the following:

   - *Multiple Choice*

   - *Open-Ended*

   - *Matrix Table*

   - *Presentation Heading*

   - *Miscellaneous*

   For the purposes of these steps, select Multiple Choice (see Figure 3-3) and click the Next button. You'll now be on the screen that lets you insert your question and answer text.

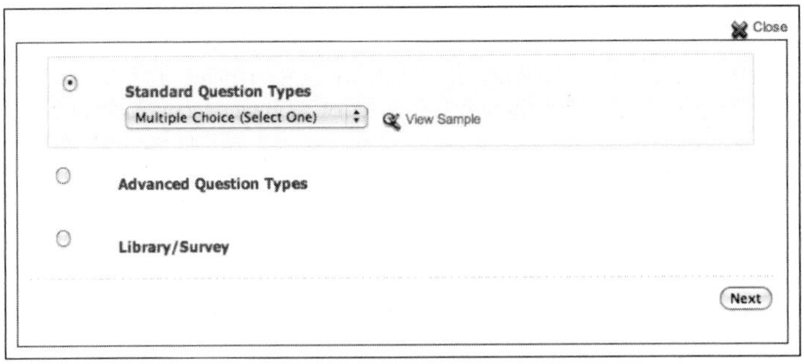

Figure 3-3:
Selecting
your
question
type.

3. **Add a question and the answer(s) for it.**

   Enter the text for the question in the Question Text box (see Figure 3-4) and your multiple choice options in the Answer Choices box. You can select standard answer sets (like yes, no, or maybe) from the drop-down list above the Answer Choices box. You can also select the Other option and choose to let the user type a different response that offers more detail.

Did you mess up? Decide you want to use a different type of question? Don't worry. Just click the Start Over arrow in the bottom-left corner of the dialog box, and you can get a free pass to start writing a fresh question.

Figure 3-4:
The
Question
Text dialog
box.

4. **Continue adding questions.**

To add additional questions, click the Add New Question link at the bottom of the question. You can continue adding questions along these lines until you're satisfied that you've covered all your bases. Go ahead and add a couple of more questions just so you get the full swing of adding them.

You can also add intro text to your questions by scrolling to the top of the page and clicking the Add Intro Text button in the top-left corner. Intro text is used as an introduction to the survey and gives a quick summary of what the survey is about. It helps the respondents understand what they're getting themselves into before they spend too much time on the survey.

Adding in a bit of introductory text can do more than just give your respondent the warm fuzzies — it's actually a proven way to increase the response rate for your survey. People are bombarded with surveys day-in and day-out. Letting people know who you are and why they're getting the survey is a great way to keep them from closing the browser window and ignoring your survey.

Sending Sample Survey

It's time to pat yourself on the back. You've just created your first sample online survey. But don't plan a party just yet. Only about one-third of your work is done. You still need to send your survey so you can get the answers you're looking for. Most online survey software companies offer at least two options for making your survey available to your target audience: linking from your Web site and sending an e-mail invitation. More advanced possibilities include publishing your survey as a pop-up; we take a closer look at pop-ups in Chapter 9.

Linking from your Web site

If you decide you don't want to track your respondents, you have the option of publishing your survey with a link. Creating a link is simple — most online survey software companies provide a unique link to your survey. In QuestionPro, go to the My Surveys section and click through to Send Survey. That's where you'll find your unique Survey Web Address. You can share this link with your survey respondents (via a link in an e-mail or posted on a Web page, or even to a social networking account like Facebook or Twitter). You might want to try this out just to see how it works, if you have the capability.

Creating and sending an e-mail invitation

If you don't want to wait for people to stumble onto your survey (or if you want to cover all your bases), you can choose to send an e-mail invitation directing respondents to the survey. Here's how to do it with QuestionPro:

1. **Click the Send Survey tab to go to the Send Survey page (see Figure 3-5), and then click the Send Email Invitation link in the left navigation bar to create an invite.**

   You'll then have the option to create an e-mail invitation.

2. **Click the Create New Email List button to launch the create email list dialog box.**

3. **Enter a name for your e-mail distribution list next to Enter a Name and then click the Create New List button.**

   This will open a screen that will allow you to type in e-mail addresses.

4. **Under Add Email Addresses, enter the e-mail addresses of the people you're like to send an e-mail to — one per line — as shown in Figure 3-6.**

   You might want to use these exact same recipients again in the future, and saving them as a distribution list allows you to do so without having to enter all of their e-mail addresses again.

5. **Click the Upload button in the lower-right corner to upload your e-mail addresses into your new list.**

   The next screen will give you an overview of all the e-mail addresses that have been uploaded.

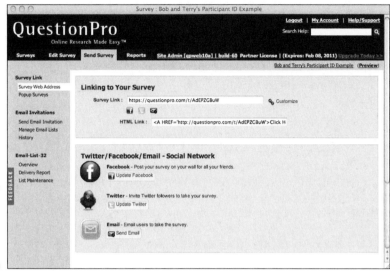

Figure 3-5:
The Send
Survey
page.

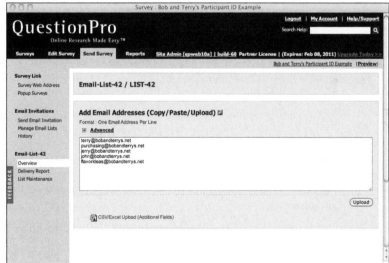

Figure 3-6:
Adding
recipients
to the e-mail
invitation.

6. **Click the Finish button in the lower-right corner once you've reviewed your list.**

7. **After you create your e-mail list, you arrive at a screen that tells you how many people are on your list and lets you add more e-mail addresses if needed. If you're satisfied with your list, click the Send Email button.**

8. **You then land on the overview page for the e-mail invitation. Here you can review the e-mail invitation and also edit it if needed. Once**

you're ready to send out the email invitation, click the Send Email Invitation button.

Don't worry — the e-mail won't go out right away. You'll have a confirmation screen that'll ask you one more time if you want to proceed.

9. **Delete or keep existing data.**

This next screen will ask if you'd like to keep any existing responses that you've collected in your survey, or if you're like to clear out all the data and start fresh. Since this is the first time we're sending the survey, we'll choose the "Keep Existing Data As Is" option, and then click the Proceed button in the bottom-right corner of the screen. The e-mail invite for your survey is now e-mailed to your respondents. Success!

Reviewing Your Results

Whether or not you like stats, you'll appreciate all the options online surveys offer to help you make the most of your market research. Beyond the answers themselves — such as how many people prefer your brand of jelly — you need to keep tabs on how many people are actually taking your survey, how many only make it halfway through, how many never open the e-mail, and other telling statistics.

For even more info on reviewing your results, see Part IV.

Reading real-time survey reports

Using QuestionPro as our example, it's time to read the Real-Time Survey Report. This is where you view overall statistics for all questions in your survey as they come in. That means if you check the stats at 8 a.m., you can see the results as they are at 8 a.m.; if you check them later that same afternoon, you see the results as they are at that time.

Let's take a look at the real-time summary report. After you're logged in to QuestionPro, follow these easy steps:

1. **Click the My Surveys tab in the navigation bar at the top of the page.**

   Your surveys are listed on this page.

2. **Click the title of your survey to select your survey.**

3. **Click the Reports tab at the top of the page.**

   You're taken to the Reports page.

4. **Click the Real-Time Summary link in the left navigation bar. This will launch the Real-Time Summary report.**

The statistics of your survey appear, including how many times the survey was viewed, how many times it was started and completed, the completion rate, how many people dropped out after starting, and a myriad of other stats to keep you busy. Don't close this window — we continue discussing this information in the next section.

Previewing participant stats

You use the Real-Time Survey Report to view participant stats with QuestionPro's software. This is where you find the completion and drop-out rates, e-mail list statistics, and meta-analysis.

This report is an important one to view because it offers information on *validation errors* (errors that occur when users don't respond to required items). If this number is particularly high and a lot of respondents are starting the survey but not completing it, it usually means respondents get frustrated with the strict validation requirements. You might want to rethink your questions.

Likewise, on the meta-analysis front, you'll want to pay close attention to the Drop-Out Analysis (shown in Figure 3-7) that tracks at what point your participants dropped out of the survey.

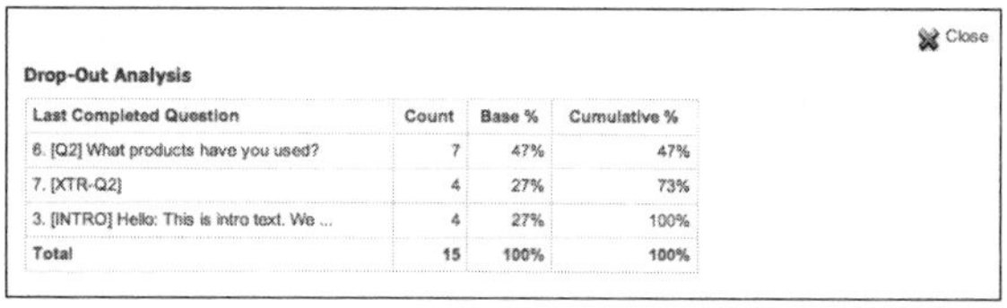

Figure 3-7:
The Drop-
Out Analysis
window.

❌ Close

Drop-Out Analysis

Last Completed Question	Count	Base %	Cumulative %
6. [Q2] What products have you used?	7	47%	47%
7. [XTR-Q2]	4	27%	73%
3. [INTRO] Hello: This is intro text. We ...	4	27%	100%
Total	15	100%	100%

Reading open-ended comments

If you've included *open-ended questions* (questions that seek to explore the qualitative, in-depth aspects of a particular topic or issue) in your survey, you obviously need to review the text responses manually and take them into consideration based on general trends you find in the responses. To do so, click the Reports tab. Under the Reports section in the left navigation panel, click Open-Ended Text. You find a list of each open-ended text question and the responses for your reading enjoyment, as shown in Figure 3-8.

03/03/2008	7680008	[Yes] Through a University Research License partnership, Spalding University has embraced QuestionPro as the choice for survey development. Being responsible for training, I can say students, faculty and staff have all picked it up quickly, going beyond simple surveys to include branching, tracking and reminders. QuestionPro has provided me a powerful tool that is indispensable to the Office of Institutional Effectiveness. I would recommend QuestionPro to anyone insterested in research.
03/03/2008	7680065	[Yes] It has been very useful for multiple training events and statewide surveys. Recently used it internally for a staff development report.
03/03/2008	7680218	[Yes] Cannot at this time, since we've just signed recwently.
03/03/2008	7680335	[Yes] yet, to actually complete a survey, but the survey creation is intuitive.
03/03/2008	7680647	[Yes] "Easy to use and very flexible, allowing me to be creative with its application."
03/03/2008	7680794	[Yes] I have found QP to be very easy to use.
03/03/2008	7681010	[Yes] The software is very easy to use and continues to improve as time goes on. The results are fabulous!
03/03/2008	7681452	[Yes] very convenient once you master the system
03/03/2008	7681912	[Yes] I'm still learning about it, but it should prove to be helpful.
03/03/2008	7682970	[Yes] QuestionPro is sufficiently flexible to allow us to recruit for both qualitative research projects and to survey for quantitative research projects.
03/04/2008	7702440	[Yes] We love the ease of functionality of this online survey product. We conduct all of our job seeker and employer CS surveys online!
03/04/2008	7706651	[Yes] Just created and sent out first customer service survey... Very impressive... "We didn't know what we didn't know... We DO NOW... We had our head in the sand, luckily we are doing fine but did find some neturual customers... Thanks... Great Product/Service.

Figure 3-8:
The Open-
Ended Text
Viewer.

Downloading an Excel report

Some folks are hooked on Excel reports. If you fall into that category, online survey companies have you covered. If you want this type of report or you just want to use it as a backup, you can export the raw data from your survey to an Excel file format or Comma Separated Values (CSV), which Excel can also read.

You can generate raw data within QuestionPro in a few easy steps:

1. **Click the Reports tab.**

   Under the Reports heading in the navigation panel on the left, you see a subheading called Export Data.

2. **Download the data file.**

   To do so, in the section titled Raw Data Export, click the Download button.

3. **Open the file in Excel.**

   Your Web browser will download the file to your computer. You can then open the file in Microsoft Excel.

Chapter 4

Online Survey Tools You Can Use

*Y*ou can find dozens of online survey software vendors on the market — and the industry is still young. Chances are good that the world of online survey software will see some consolidation and some newcomers to the scene in the years ahead. The task of wading through the scores of online survey software tools on the market today can be daunting for even the most experienced market researchers. That same task can be frustrating for people who are just beginning to understand the lingo. And it can be absolutely maddening for newbies.

Unlike many other software segments, choosing an online survey software tool isn't merely a matter of brand name or even price. Though those factors should certainly play a role in your decision, you have several distinct options in the online survey software world: limited-response freebies, install-your-own, response-based models, and enterprise-class tools that offer unlimited responses.

Each one of these segments offers upsides and downsides. In a nutshell, freebies are great if your budget is zero, but enterprise-class tools are where the power is. Install-your-own programs are ideal for organizations that are ultra-concerned about privacy, and response-based models are a must-have for companies that need to purchase a panel of targeted survey respondents.

Which one do you choose? The answer: It depends. It depends on your specific needs. It depends on the size of your company. It depends on how many online surveys you're going to launch. It depends on how much you want to spend. What's certain is this: If you want to conduct market research cost-effectively in the 21st century, you need to use online survey software as part of your research mix. With the rise of the Internet as an e-commerce and information-seeking platform, online surveys allow you to find respondents where they spend a lot of time — online.

Of course, that's just the nutshell. Finding online survey software tools that work for you means cracking that nutshell. Before you begin reviewing online survey software vendors, you need to understand the ins and outs of these classes of applications. In this chapter, we review the pros and cons of the various types of online software setups you can choose. We also survey (pun intended) the online survey software landscape to give you an overview of what's available in each category.

Before You Begin . . .

You wouldn't rush into a marriage, so don't rush into a commitment with an online survey software vendor. Take your time to compare apples to apples, so to speak, and capabilities to capabilities. Because the ability to analyze the data you collect is vitally important to the cause, you want to make sure the vendor you choose has the features, functions, and technologies to serve your needs in the long-term.

You can't possibly know whether a vendor has what you need until you know what you need. The best way to do that is to start out with a free tool and become familiar with the baseline functions. It's quite possible that the free-bie tool has everything you need and more. If not, it won't take you long to figure out what's missing.

 Plan to take several weeks to choose your online survey software vendor. If you're looking at free or low-cost solutions, you need to ferret out which software meets your business requirements. Online survey software tools all have similar functions, but some are more advanced than others.

That might mean reviewing vendor Web sites or even picking up the phone and calling them. If you're looking at an enterprise solution, however, the vendor might work up a proposal to win your business. Either way, you'll need to put on your investigator's cap and check out the vendor's history, stability, track record for innovation, implementation and support offerings, contract terms, and, of course, pricing. Always ask for client referrals, and don't jump on the low-price bandwagon just to save a few dollars — inaccurate results might cost you well more than a few dollars in the long-run.

Before you set out on this four-pronged trail, take inventory of your supplies and outline a clear map of your specific needs. You might be impressed with the bells and whistles a certain program class has to offer, but your budget might not allow you make that much noise.

If your budget looks like a goose egg, don't fret. There are some attractive options that cost little to nothing. In addition to the free applications, there's a fair selection of feature-rich, hosted applications in the intermediate budget range (between $15 and $30 a month).

Most corporate- and enterprise-level solutions worth using are going to cost you a pretty penny upfront. On the low end, you can spend between $100 and $500 a month. If money is no object — meaning you can fork over thousands of dollars without blinking — don't hesitate to check out the enterprise-level solutions used by Fortune 500 companies. Pricing for these solutions isn't usually listed on the company's Web site, so you need to set up a call with a sales representative to get a quote.

Some people swear by the adage "you get what you pay for." Of course, to a certain extent, that is true. But with so much competition in the online survey software market, you can find helpful tools at any price point. Decide how you want to access your online survey software, determine what options you need, and then begin your search for a provider that meets those needs.

Don't Forget the Freebies

Before you invest a single penny in online survey software, why not take some of the free programs for a test drive? You might find that these tools give you a nice view of the landscape.

The advantage of free tools is clear: They're free. There are plenty of free tools out there. There is a downside, though, and it can be dark: Free tools don't pack the same informational punch as paid tools. Free tools don't usually offer any support, either. That means you're on your own in a sea of data. No one is there to hold your hand, explain a metric, or help you interpret the results of your online survey. (Of course, that's what you have this book for.) Still, you should at least give the freebies a try. Who knows? You might catch on quick and begin leveraging the tool for more profits.

Before you can begin using the free tools, you need to know where to find them. And as you begin to use them, you should go in knowing what to expect — and what not to expect — or you might wind up frustrated. You wouldn't expect a Hyundai to perform the same way a Jaguar does. Similarly, you can't expect a free tool to perform the same way an enterprise tool does. What you can expect a free tool (and a Hyundai) to do is get you on the road so you can see some pretty views.

Finding free online software tools

If you want to explore the free landscape, your task is easy. Just go to your search engine of choice and type in **free online survey software**. You'll get a number of results that can get you started. A few survey software tools, however, have achieved a solid reputation in the freebie market. The following are some companies that offer free tools and have a solid reputation in the industry.

FluidSurveys

www.fluidsurveys.com

FluidSurveys (see Figure 4-1) has one goal in mind — to help you build and launch online surveys with advanced features that are convenient and easy to use. What's unique about FluidSurveys' online survey software is the drag-and-drop interface. The drag-and-drop interface allows you to click an object on the computer screen and drag it to a different location on the screen. This is a popular feature in today's software, and FluidSurveys is using it as a competitive differentiator. The company also offers other advanced features such as piping, skipping, branching, multi-condition logic, data extraction questions, 3D matrices, looping, role management, cross-tabs, and export into various formats. FluidSurveys offers various pricing levels, from free to $400 a month for an enterprise package. The free package offers unlimited surveys, with 20 questions per survey and a maximum of 100 responses per survey.

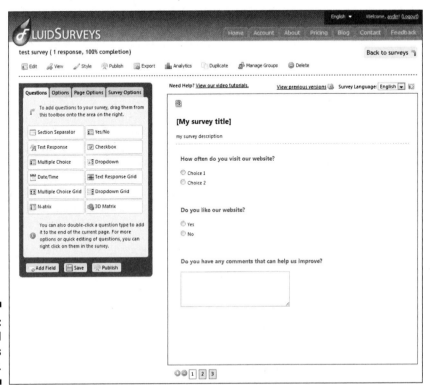

Figure 4-1:
The Fluid
Surveys
editor.

PollDaddy

www.polldaddy.com

PollDaddy offers free accounts that let you create both online surveys (see Figure 4-2) and quick-and-dirty online polls that you can post on your Web site, blog, or social network. The company pushes two messages: simplicity and flexibility. This is definitely a hot option for the social media–savvy online survey builder because you can customize the look and feel of your PollDaddy questionnaire to match your Web site, social networking profile, or e-mail campaign. You can also tap into the power of features such as conditional branching. You can even insert HTML code directly into the survey, which is vital if you're a multimedia type who loves to add photos and videos to your online survey. As far as question types, you can choose from 11 common scenarios. PollDaddy even lets you create multi-question, multi-page surveys with its free software. And on the analysis front, PollDaddy offers real-time reporting capabilities that won't keep you in suspense. If you need to export your data, you have a few format options: XML, CSV, or via e-mail through an RSS feed. Support for foreign languages is also included with this powerful freebie.

Figure 4-2:
Creating a
PollDaddy
survey.

QuestionPro

`www.questionpro.com`

QuestionPro (see Figure 4-3) bills its online survey software as a one-stop solution for managing feedback via the Web. The software lets you run everything from simple Web surveys to large, complex, international market research. QuestionPro's free Web-based account requires no additional software or hardware, offers the ability to create surveys with unlimited responses, and has a complete set of advanced tools for conducting online research. In addition to the free account, QuestionPro offers a $15-a-month basic license and an enterprise class license for $99 a month — both include unlimited responses, questions, and surveys. This survey software includes a full suite of tools for creating surveys, sending e-mail invitations, and analyzing survey data.

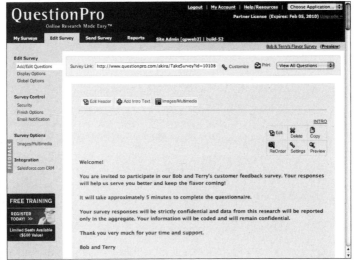

Figure 4-3:
An example
of the
QuestionPro
software.

SurveyGizmo

`www.surveygizmo.com`

SurveyGizmo's online surveys software tool (see Figure 4-4) is designed for market research, job applications, marketing campaigns, blogs, landing pages, contact forms, sales tracking, and lead generation. The free account offers 250 responses per month, no ads or page redirects, free webinar training, support via forums and tutorials, branding control, and multi-lingual capabilities. You can even embed your surveys into Web sites and blogs. SurveyGizmo never deletes your data and lets you export it in various formats. Beyond the free account, SurveyGizmo has levels ranging from $19 a month to $599 a month for enterprise users who need sophisticated features and the ability to collect and analyze up to one million responses.

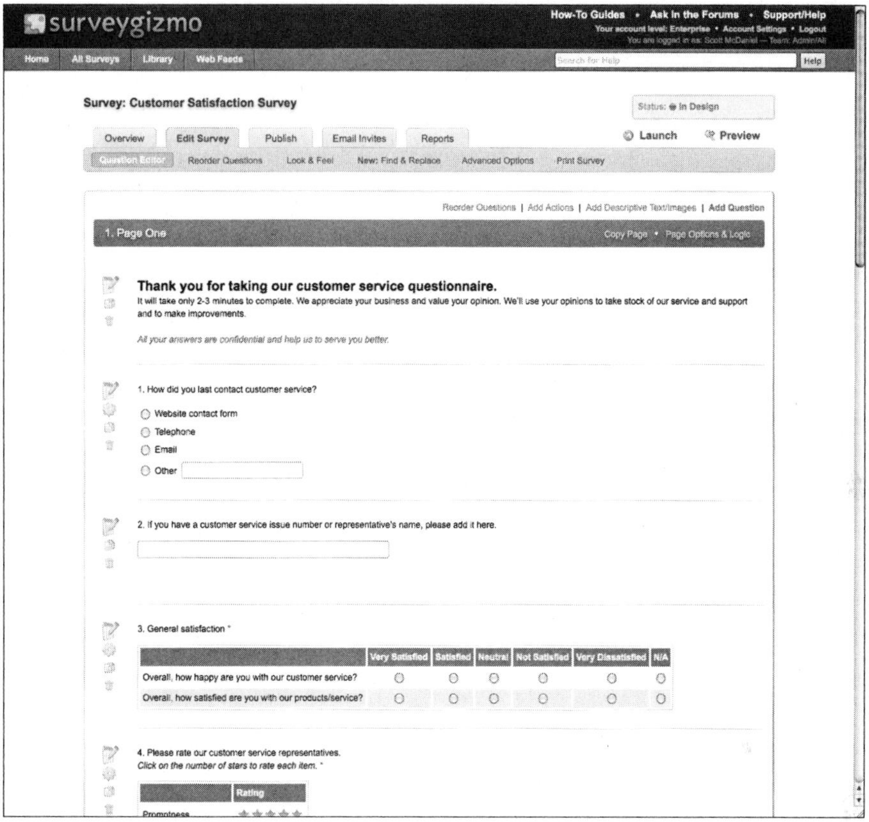

Figure 4-4:
A Survey
Gizmo
survey.

SurveyMonkey

www.surveymonkey.com

SurveyMonkey is a tool for the beginner of beginners. The company prides itself on making it as easy as possible for people to create online surveys. At the same time, however, this freebie offers some compelling features like multiple-choice, rating scale, and open-ended text questions. (See Chapter 3 for more on these features.) Although some free online software tools offer cookie-cutter templates, SurveyMonkey lets you customize the layout of each and every question type by changing the color, size, and style of any individual element (or you can fall back on the good old-fashioned templates if you really want to). No matter what language your respondents speak, you can create a survey in their native tongue with SurveyMonkey. You can also validate your responses in advance, add a logo to your survey, randomize or sort your question choices, save your survey as a PDF, collect responses in various ways, and analyze your responses (see Figure 4-5).

Figure 4-5:
A Survey
Monkey
online
survey
software in
action.

Zoomerang

www.zoomerang.com

Zoomerang's (see Figure 4-6) tagline is "easiest way to ask, fastest way to know." You can sign up for a basic account (a limited version of the full-featured online survey tool) for free. Dubbed Zoomerang Basic, the free account offers an unlimited number of surveys with up to 30 questions and 100 responses each. Zoomerang Basic also offers access to over 100 survey templates. Some of the features included are cross-tabulation, skip logic, filtering, and customizable surveys, images, logos, and links. The results never expire, and you can download them to Excel and create charts. You can upgrade to Zoomerang Pro for more powerful functions. That'll cost you $199 a year. You can also choose a Premium account for teams and power users for $599 a year. This would be considered an enterprise-level tool complete with multi-user sharing, a management dashboard, unlimited phone support, deployment to mobile phones, and other features.

What to expect from free analytics tools

Free tools often have very simple user interfaces that any beginner can quickly understand. At the entry level, you get quite a bit of mileage out of your online survey investment, especially considering you aren't making an online survey investment! Free online software is a massive temptation for marketers who see the possibility of putting budgets currently assigned to tool sets into more market research. You can expect a wide spectrum of functions and feature sets among the free tools, but at the baseline they all show you responses in real time, offer most of the question types, and offer fairly decent reporting tools. (We discuss question types in Chapter 2; Chapter 6 discusses them in even greater depth.)

Figure 4-6:
The
Zoomerang
text analysis
tool.

What not to expect from the freebies

Free tools are great solutions for infrequent online survey users. But when your market research needs to grow, these solutions might no longer be effective. Basic metrics are about all you get with most of the free online software tools. So if you want to engage in complex market research of special survey types, don't expect to find that option in your freebie tools. Also, don't expect to get any type of customer support with most of these tools. All the free licenses offered are limited by the number of the responses that can be collected, typically over the course of a month, and the software provider's brand or logo appears on your survey.

All the freebie survey vendors offer some level of branding on their surveys. The size and level of the branding ranges from obnoxious to discreet: survey URL branding (for example *mygreatsurvey.surveygizmo.com* or *mygreatsurvey. questionpro.com*), survey vendor logo in the header and/or footer, or even a sign-up form as part of the respondent Thank You page at the end of the survey. Generally, the free tools provide an upgrade path to a paid license that removes some or all of the branding from your survey. What's more, most enterprise-level online survey vendors even let you use a URL that you control (*mygreatsurvey.mycompany.com*, for example).

Grasping Install-Your-Own-Online Survey Software

There is a class of tools many refer to as *install-your-own* online survey software. As the name suggests, you can install these tools on your own server. That means they aren't hosted by a SaaS (Software as a Service; sometimes also referred to as ASP, or Application Service Provider) — you aren't renting the software, you're buying it! As such, you're responsible for maintaining it.

There are, however, some inherent advantages to the install-your-own model. Namely, privacy. If you install the online survey software on your own server, you might be able to better secure the privacy of your respondent's personal information. Some organizations might have no other choice but to go the install-your-own route because of privacy mandates around storing data on third-party servers. Others, such as research institutions studying human subjects, tend to take this extra precaution.

But there is downside to the install-your-own model. As we already noted, you have to maintain it yourself. If something goes wrong, you might or might not be able to fix it internally. That means investing in technical assistance from the company that sold you the software or from some other company. What's more, install-your-own software requires a major investment in hardware and software licensing fees — unless you use open-source software. Licensing and support fees for open-source software are typically much less than *closed-source,* or proprietary, software.

The following sections take a look at some of the install-your-own online survey software available to you.

Checkbox

www.checkbox.com

Checkbox Survey Solutions (see Figure 4-7) offers scalable survey solutions for Web, mobile, and desktop environments. The company targets professionals who need to design, implement, and analyze online surveys. You have three options with Checkbox. You can opt for the server software, subscription-based hosted software, or professional services. Checkbox Survey Server installs on your own server infrastructure. This means you have full control over your survey software environment. Software licensing plans range from $3,350 for the Professional Edition to $6,850 for the Enterprise Edition. The company also provides the option to lease the install-your-own software, which offers all the standard features of sophisticated online survey tools you can find on the market today.

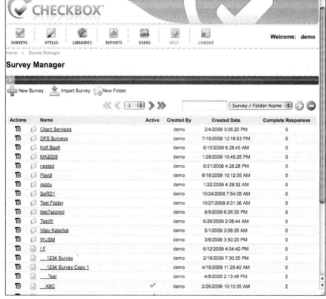

Figure 4-7: The Checkbox survey administration screen.

chumpsoft

www.chumpsoft.com

chumpsoft offers free installation of its install-your-own software, dubbed phpQuestionnaire (see Figure 4-8). The software builds multi-page surveys with an unlimited number of questions and answers and real-time results reporting, all fairly standard feature sets at this level. Some of the features include conditional page branching, cross-tabulation of survey results, multiple language support, e-mail verification of participants, CSS and template customization, and more. The cost is surprisingly low at just $199. A lite version is available for only $59. The company recently launched a hosted product called SurveyFactory with prices ranging from $9.95 a month to $149 a month.

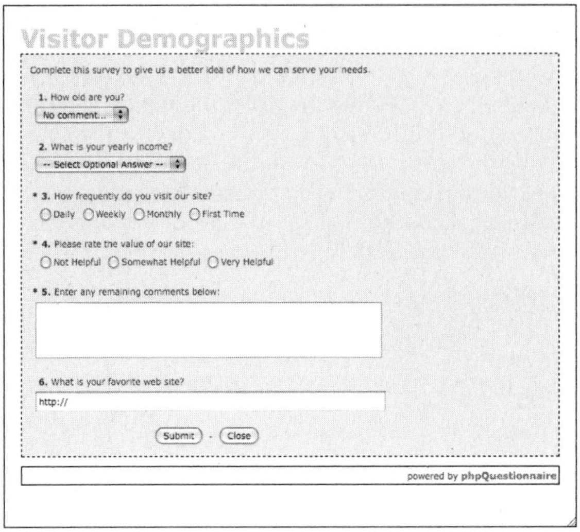

Figure 4-8:
A demo-
graphic
survey
built using
phpQues-
tionnaire.

Confirmit

www.confirmit.com

If you need to design surveys with multiple question types, complex logic for routing, and customized branding options, Confirmit (see Figure 4-9) is a solid product that gives you plenty of options for layout. You can even add images to your online survey. Like many other online software tools, Confirmit offers support for any language in the world. If you need question libraries and template libraries to speed up your online survey building, Confirmit has you covered. One interesting feature of Confirmit is the ability to schedule alerts for any online survey feedback that you need to be imme-diately aware of. If you get a negative response on a customer service survey, for example, Confirmit e-mails you so can reach out to that customer immedi-ately. If you want customization, Confirmit has plenty of it. You can purchase this software as a hosted or an install-your-own solution. The company does not disclose pricing on its Web site.

Inquisite

www.inquisite.com

Inquisite Survey (see Figure 4-10) is another enterprise-grade, install-your-own feedback management software tool. This tool is easy to use, with drag-and-drop question capabilities. You can also tap into a shared ques-tion library and change the look and feel of your survey on a whim with the Inquisite template toolsets. When you get ready to send your survey,

Inquisite Survey offers an invitation wizard, segmentation options, fatigue management, random sampling, and data import tools. You can also manage user roles, launch authenticated or unauthenticated surveys, and tap into sophisticated analytics reporting such as answer grouping, charting, auto-tabulation, and drill downs.

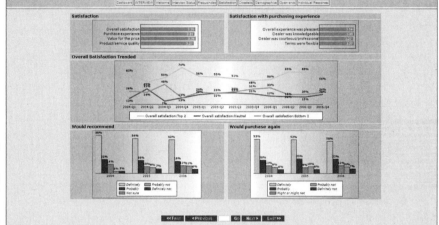

Figure 4-9:
A Confirmit survey report.

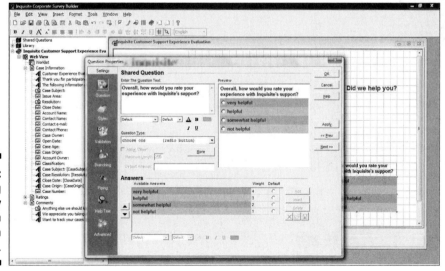

Figure 4-10:
Building a survey question with Inquisite.

LimeSurvey

www.limesurvey.org

LimeSurvey (see Figure 4-11) is an open-source, free, install-your-own online survey software product. The company recently launched a hosted service but is best known for its install-your-own model. LimeSurvey describes itself as "the leading open source tool for online surveys." The features list is too long to include, but some of the key features are unlimited surveys, questions and participants, multi-lingual surveys, integration of pictures and movies, 20 different question types, e-mail invitations, reminders and tokens, template editors, statistical and graphical analysis, and much more. The hosted tool is more limited, allowing only 25 responses per month. LimeService charges bandwidth fees if you exceed that number.

Figure 4-11: Collecting survey responses using LimeSurvey.

REDCap

www.project-redcap.org

REDCap Survey is another free, open-source, install-your-own online survey software program. The REDCap Consortium, which manages the software, includes 60 active institutional partners from CTSA, GCRC, RCMI, and other institutions, and it supports two secure, Web-based applications (REDCap and REDCap Survey). The difference between REDCap and other online survey software is its focus on data capture for research studies. This software is not for your average online survey builder, but if you have research-intensive needs this is a strong fit. You can create and design surveys in your Web browser and engage potential respondents by using a laundry list of notification methods. You can easily export participant responses to Microsoft Excel or to common statistical analysis packages (SPSS, SAS, R, Stata). REDCap Survey (see Figure 4-12) lets you choose from the standard question types and offers plenty of advanced features aimed at its target audience of sophisticated researchers.

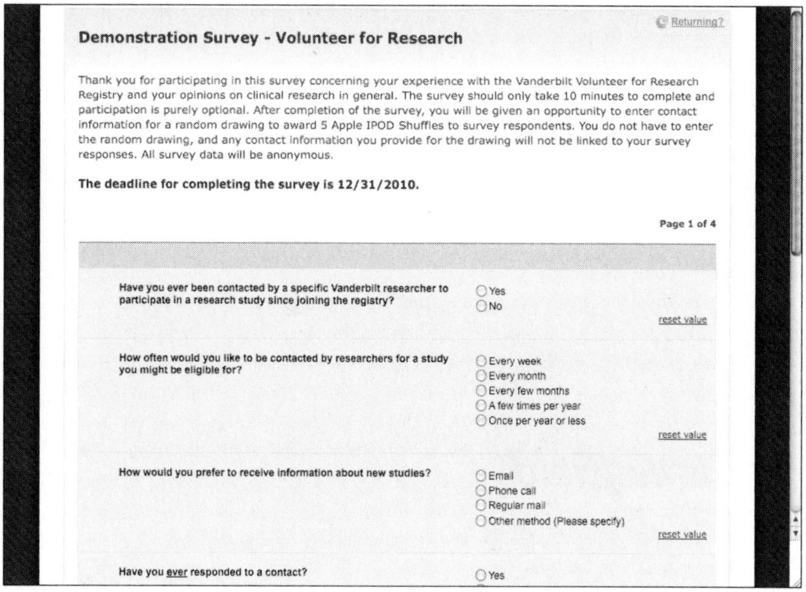

Figure 4-12: An example of a REDCap survey.

SPSS

www.spss.com

SPSS (see Figure 4-13) offers a family of statistical products, and the most famous is a statistical package (known as PASW Statistics) for hardcore number crunchers. SPSS also offers a family of PASW data collection software packages that you install on your own servers, including Data Collection Author, Data Collection Author Professional, and Data Collection Interviewer Web. What's unique about the SPSS software is its multi-channel functionality. With this tool, you can create a survey and deploy it across multiple channels, from Web sites to telephone surveys to mobile devices. SPSS has made a name for itself with its intelligent wizards that guide you step-by-step through the survey building process. On the analysis end, SPSS offers tools that help you prepare for reporting during the survey creation stage.

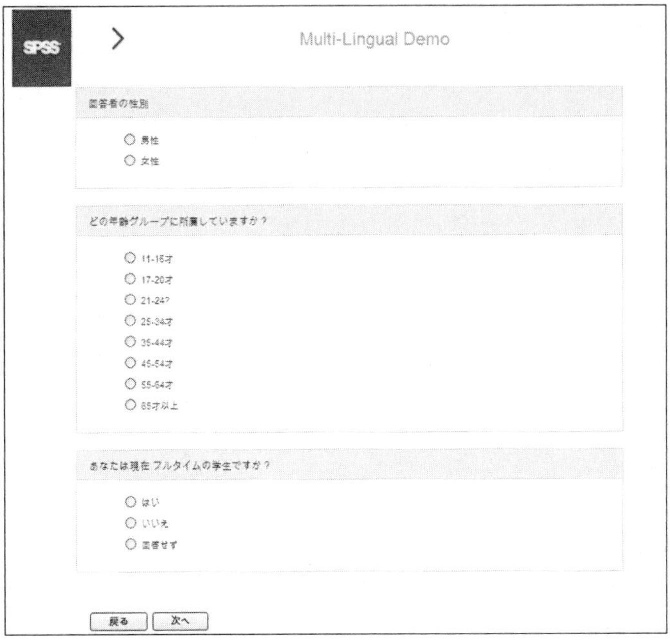

Figure 4-13:
A Japanese
survey using
SPSS.

This is highly sophisticated software — it's not for the faint of heart!

SurveyGold

www.surveygold.com

SurveyGold (see Figure 4-14) promises it has the best value in online survey software. You'll have to be the judge of that. Here's what we can tell you: You can get an individual license for $159 and tap into additional discounts if you're a non-profit, government, or academic staff member, or a student. SurveyGold survey software installs on your computer's hard drive. With it, you can create surveys that you respondents can take online or that you can print out to conduct paper surveys. SurveyGold aims at the occasional survey author, so if you aren't planning on launching surveys very often, this might be the only tool you need. On the analysis side, you can view graphs and cross-tabs, means and weighting indexes; publish reports via Word, PDF, or HTML; and create views of respondents based on responses and data ranges.

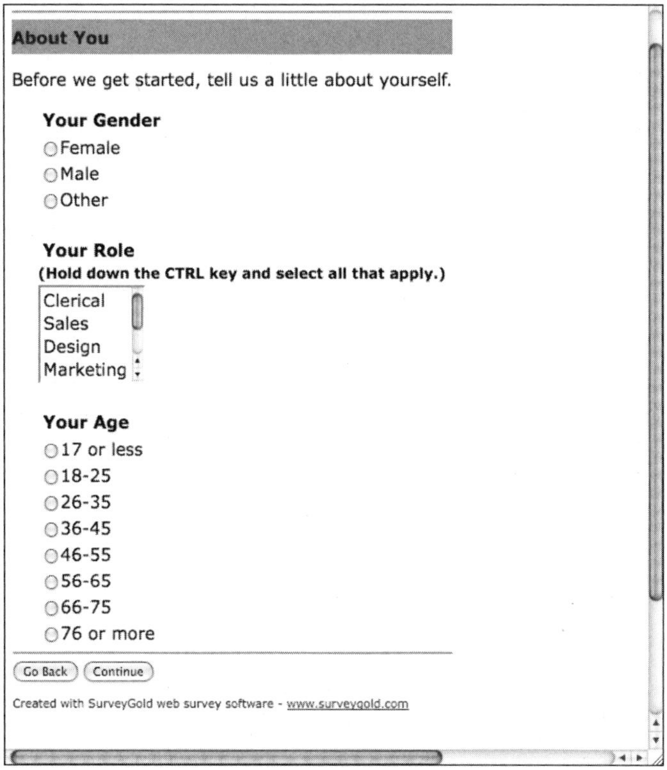

Figure 4-14:
A set of
demo-
graphic
questions
using
SurveyGold.

Vovici

www.vovici.com

Vovici (see Figure 4-15) offers an install-your-own option. This company targets large organizations, so if you aren't working for a major enterprise that's doing tons of surveys this probably isn't the best option for you. But if you're employed by a large enterprise and you need to work with online survey software that will integrate with your legacy systems, this is a strong contender for your online survey dollars. The Professional version lets you create and deploy surveys on the Web directly from existing Microsoft Word documents. Like most other enterprise-level online survey software, you can tap into features such as hierarchal questions, branching logic, e-mail triggers and alerts, hidden questions, data piping and custom end pages. If you have a team working together on the online survey project, Vovici has some strong collaboration tools that let you work on developing and analyzing the survey together. The company does not disclose pricing on its Web site.

Figure 4-15:
The Vovici
Survey
Wizard.

Hooked on Hosted Solutions

Offered by any one of many SaaS providers on the market, hosted online survey solutions are gaining momentum over install-your-own applications. *Hosted solutions* are called such because the data is stored on the SaaS provider's server instead of the shared server provided by your Web host or the dedicated server in your offices. Hosted solutions require you to log in to an SaaS provider's Web site in order to create, launch, and analyze your reports. Hosted solutions have plenty of pros and cons that you need to understand before you can make an intelligent decision about your intelligence-gathering tool of choice. Here are a few pros and cons to consider:

- ✔ **Survey software on demand:** Also called *on-demand solutions,* hosted solutions are all the rage — and for good reason. The online survey software vendor does all the technical heavy lifting. There's no downloading, no installing, and no maintenance. The vendor also gets to deal with all the troubleshooting if something goes wrong. That means you don't need to know how to do anything except create, launch, and analyze your online surveys.

- ✔ **Keep your cash flow flowing:** Hosted applications can also help regulate your cash flow. SaaS providers let you rent the application for small monthly payments — payments range from about $10–$99 a month for intermediate tools and $150–$500 a month for enterprise-level tools — as opposed to handing over a large, one-time fee to actually purchase the software and call it your own.

- ✔ **Anytime, anywhere access:** Hosted online survey software solutions don't tie you down to one-computer access. That means if you're the type that gets sudden impulses to check how many responses your current online survey has received since you launched it this morning, hosted solutions accommodate you with Web-based reports that can be accessed anywhere there's an Internet connection.

- ✔ **Less Control:** When times are good, you can sit back and relax while your hosted online survey software provider deals with the headaches of keeping everything running 24/7. However, when something goes wrong, you aren't in control. You have to wait in line with everyone else while the problem is getting fixed. If your survey project requires complete control over the survey software, hardware, and its data, hosted online survey software is not for you.

- ✔ **Data Privacy:** Due to privacy or security reasons, some online survey projects require that the survey response data be collected on your own servers. With hosted solutions, the survey response data is stored on the vendor's servers. Thus, these types of security restrictions prevent you from using a hosted solution.

Response-Based Pricing on a Budget

Response-based pricing is just what it sounds like: A pricing model that's based on how many responses you generate. This is a lesser-used model in today's online survey world, but it still exists. Typically you have a limit on the number of responses you can receive, and after you reach that limit you have to pay per response. It's sort of like leasing a car. You can buy the miles you think you're going to use upfront. If you miscalculate, though, it can be costly.

Most companies that offer this option also offer an enterprise-level solution with unlimited responses. If you're wondering why someone would want to pay per response, consider the upside: If you know you aren't going to go over the allowed limit, you might be able to save money by going with licenses that offer a set number of responses because they tend to be less expensive than the higher-end licenses.

SurveyMonkey, SurveyGold, and Checkbox are among the companies listed in earlier sections of this chapter that offer response-based pricing models. But a few other reputable vendors are also worth exploring. In a nutshell, these tools don't lack any of the groovy features that you've read about so far — the difference is the model. With some response-based pricing models, there's no cost and no obligation until you use the tool. With others, you pay a monthly fee whether or not you use the tools, but you pay extra if you exceed your response cap.

Hosted Survey

www.hostedsurvey.com

As its name suggests, Hosted Survey is a hosted survey software application. The company specifically targets researchers, evaluators, and organizational improvement specialists. You can do more with Hosted Survey than just create online surveys; you can conduct 360 feedback reviews for human resources purposes and develop a host of other types of online question-naires for opinion polling, training and education, membership associations, and the like. With Hosted Survey (see Figure 4-16), your first 50 responses are free. Hosted Survey offers a pay-as-you-go model. If you're only conducting surveys from time to time, this might be a good solution for you. But it's also suitable for organizations gathering feedback, conducting ongoing market research, and running organizational improvement programs.

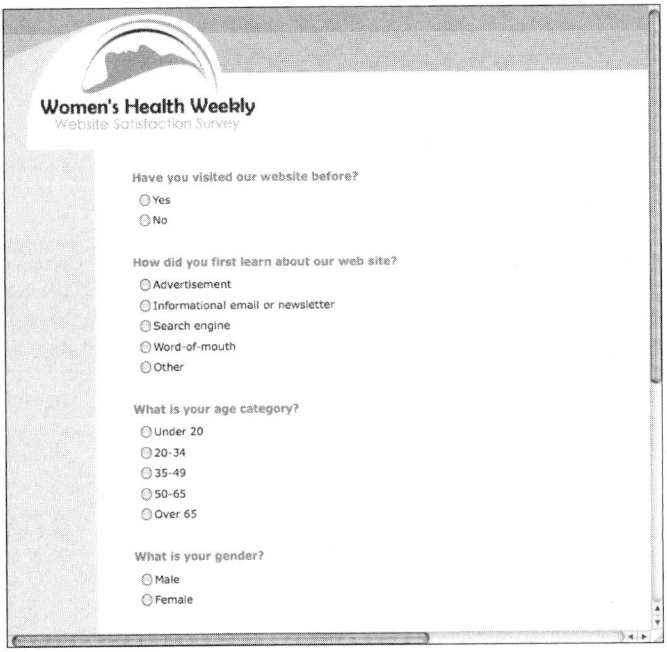

Figure 4-16:
An example
of a
Web site
feedback
survey using
Hosted
Survey.

InstantSurvey

www.instantsurvey.com

InstantSurvey Pro isn't for casual online surveyors. The company targets business users that want to build and manage deep respondent lists and leverage advanced analysis tools. If you need to make custom presentations and in-depth reporting, this tool is worth exploring. If you're developing mul-timedia surveys, InstantSurvey (see Figure 4-17) has you covered with audio, video, and image capabilities. And if security is a concern, InstantSurvey offers enhanced security with an optional SSL encryption. You'll pay $1,000 a year for up to 500 responses, $1,500 a year for up to 1,000 responses, and $2,500 a year for up to 10,000 responses.

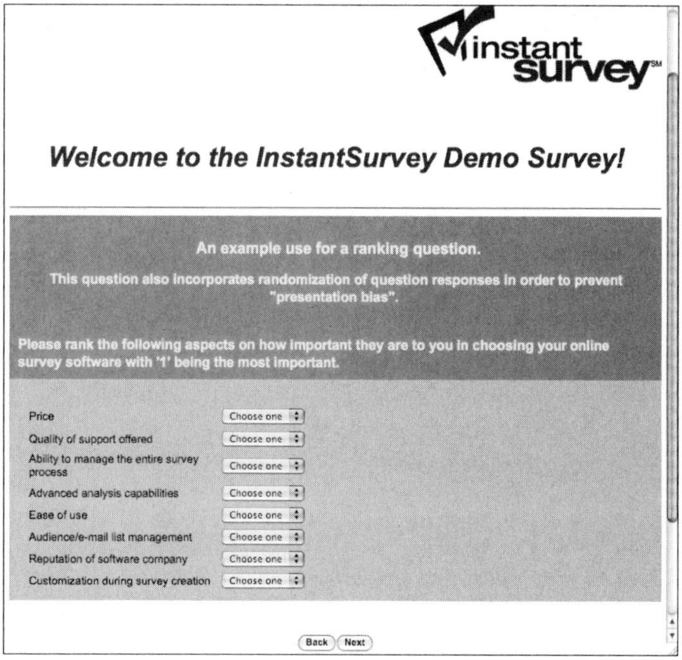

Figure 4-17:
A survey
built with
Instant
Survey.

Mineful

www.mineful.com

Mineful (see Figure 4-18) offers on-demand market research software that
lets you do what every other online survey software lets you do — collect,
analyze, present, and share data. Mineful's software mimics the look and feel
of a desktop so it's intuitive for most computer users. The software features
a questions wizard, drag-and-drop functionality, and the ability to view and
sort data based on fields you determine. You can also analyze, report on,
and share data. Mineful bills its software as an enabler of business decisions
rather than a polling software. The company offers a free plan with three surveys and 25 responses a month, a Personal plan with unlimited surveys and
1,000 responses a month, and a Business plan with unlimited surveys and
unlimited responses.

SurveyMethods

www.surveymethods.com

SurveyMethods (see Figure 4-19) is on a mission to provide a user-friendly survey tool. The company focuses heavily on survey builders that need to create customer satisfaction surveys, customer loyalty surveys and other surveys that help drive revenue and profitability. One attractive feature for the enterprise is the ability to integrate SurveyMethods software into most CRM or ERP systems. This software has all the usual functions and features for creating, launching, analyzing, and publishing your online survey results. The company does offer a free version, but the surveys can't be accessed after a year of usage and you can only get 500 responses during that year. The Professional Edition runs $39 a month and offers up to 5,000 responses a month.

Survey Galaxy

www.surveygalaxy.com

Survey Galaxy (see Figure 4-20) offers all the usual online survey software bells and whistles, but the company puts a strict cap on how many responses you can receive. You can get fully hosted services, and support for multiple languages. You can even pull data into other third-party applications for more granular analysis. If you're waiting for the catch, here it is: If you go over 4,000 responses a month on your enterprise-level account, you pay a few pennies each for them. One interesting feature about Survey Galaxy is the Snap Poll, a way to pose quick questions to audiences in situations where you don't need a longer survey. You can do that for free as long as you don't go over 2,000 responses in a month.

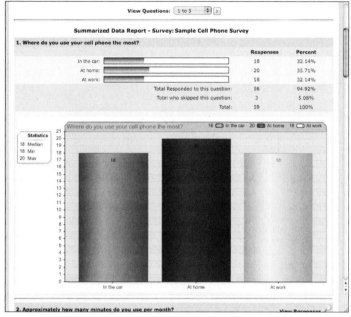

Figure 4-19: A set of demographic questions using Survey Methods.

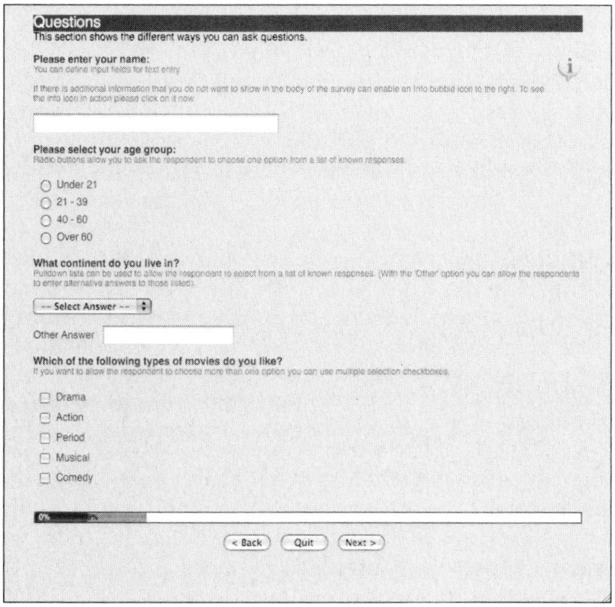

Figure 4-20: A survey built using Survey Galaxy.

Unlimited Responses for the Masses

Unlimited responses. Those two words are music to your ears if your organization has a large audience base or needs to conduct online survey research on a large scale. The online survey software vendors that offer unlimited survey responses also tend to offer higher-end, more feature-rich tools. These are what you would label enterprise tools. Although you can find enterprise tools in the install-your-own and response-based categories, the unlimited responses model is where the industry is headed.

The downside is that the unlimited response online survey software tools tend to cost more than their response-based counterparts. Because there's no limit on the number of online survey responses you can receive in any given month, the company has to pre-plan for bandwidth and other technical capacity issues it might face if you decide to survey the entire world about global warming — or even a whole state about a political issue. The point is that unlimited responses mean unlimited responses, and the online survey software vendor has to take that literally and invest in the technology infrastructure to make good on the offer.

Deciding whether to use unlimited response tools

If you aren't sure how many responses your online survey will get — and you don't have a predetermined limit on how many you want to receive — then unlimited response vendors are a good choice. If you choose a response-based pricing model, you might rack up a big bill if every one and their brother — and their brother's sister and their sister's friend and their friend's cousin and so on — find out about your survey and take it. You can set up your online survey software not to exceed a certain number of responses with a quota tool, but if you forget you might pay through the nose . . . and the ears.

Enterprise-level tools typically also offer a collaborative user model or multi-user license scheme. That means you don't have to be the only one in your organization to create, launch, and analyze surveys. You can share the market research responsibility among your colleagues. Some online survey software vendors offer every member of your organization an individual account for creating surveys and, in some cases, editing the same survey at the same time. That's just part of the power of enterprise-level tools.

Understanding the power and price of enterprise tools

Enterprise-level tools can do everything the freebies and mid-level applications can do — and much more. Because they're targeting larger companies, enterprise-level tools are heavily focused on metrics that demonstrate return on investment (ROI) on the analysis end. You can usually slice the data six ways from Saturday, Sunday, and Monday.

Enterprise-level products are critical in developing custom reports that lighter versions of the software typically don't accommodate. These programs allow you to get details on a deeper level. The more sophisticated your business is, the more sophisticated your market research needs — and the more sophisticated your online survey software needs to be. Enterprise solutions aren't for companies with shallow pockets. The price tags on these powerful solutions start around $15,000 a year.

CreateSurvey

```
www.createsurvey.com
```

CreateSurvey describes itself as an online survey management system. That's a fancy way to say you can use the software to create multi-page surveys or quick polls. You can add in custom graphics, build your own layout, embed your survey onto your Web site, or even print it out and take it to the streets. What's interesting about this software is that it lets you migrate questionnaires from other formats. So if you've been doing your surveys on paper, CreateSurvey (see Figure 4-21) makes it easy for you to migrate the questions to its software. The Professional version is $949 a year.

KeySurvey

```
www.keysurvey.com
```

KeySurvey (see Figure 4-22) allows you to create, manage, deploy, and change surveys onthefly. KeySurvey is an enterprise level tool that gives you advanced bells and whistles, including the ability to automate the online data collection process or customize your respondent's individual online survey experiences by using different logic transitions. You can even launch personalized e-mail invitations and reminders to improve response rates. Of course, like most other online survey software programs, you can see the survey results coming in live and build custom reports at will. The company doesn't list its prices online.

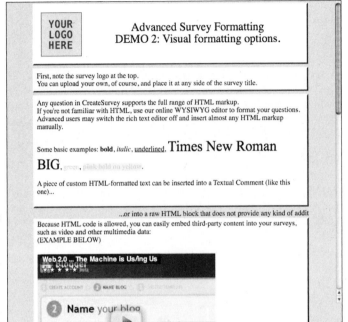

Figure 4-21:
A sample
survey
created
using Create
Survey.

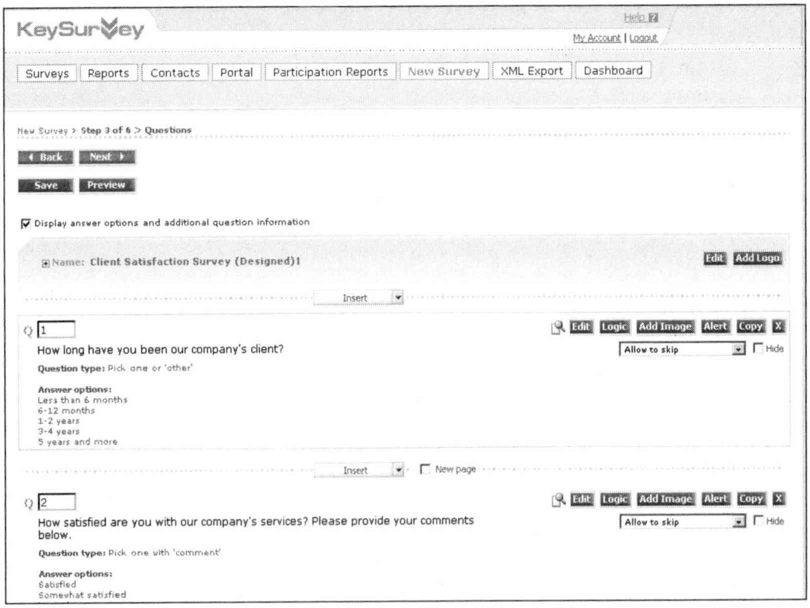

Figure 4-22:
Editing a
survey with
KeySurvey.

QuestionPro

www.questionpro.com

The QuestionPro Enterprise Edition (see Figure 4-23) is suitable for organizations that want a single flexible platform for conducting online surveys and analyzing data. The Enterprise Edition is designed to benefit a range of users within an organization. There's a user-friendly interface from which you can conduct complex online research. This version is ideal for organizations that need surveying capabilities for 5 to 50 or more users, to consolidate enterprise feedback on one platform, or integrate survey data with other enterprise systems.

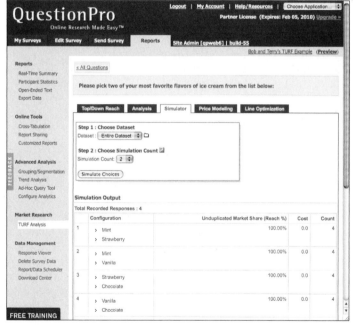

Figure 4-23: Running a market simulation report using Question Pro.

Qualtrics

www.qualtrics.com

Qualtrics (see Figure 4-24) bills itself as the easiest and most sophisticated survey software in the world. We can't validate those claims, but this research suite is robust. It can create complex surveys that aren't complex to administer. Like most other online survey software tools, you can do a free trial run. You have to pay up if you want to tap into some of the advanced surveys and advanced data management tools. Qualtrics' enterprise functions let you do some pretty cool stuff without much knowledge, like build brandable sites; collaborate with colleagues on survey functions; share panels, messages, and reports; and more.

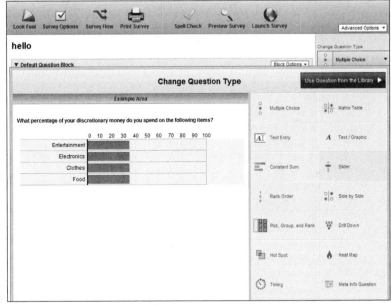

Figure 4-24:
Editing
a survey
question
in the
Qualtrics
editor.

Vovici

www.vovici.com

Vovici Enterprise Edition is for heavy hitters only. The company describes its service as an "enterprise feedback management (EFM) platform that provides control over feedback activities." That's a fancy way to say that it helps you keep your finger on the pulse of customer feedback. If you want the most advanced features available in online survey software and you have the budget, this solution can carry you a long way down the road to sophisticated online survey design and analysis. You can create the most complex surveys you can imagine with this software. Some of the advanced features include point-and-click control of survey branding, detailed quota management, advanced panel management, and detailed reporting and analysis.

ZipSurvey

www.zipsurvey.com

ZipSurvey (see Figure 4-25) is a hosted online survey software application. This isn't your average online survey software. It was created by psychologists for the unique needs of HR consultants and market researchers, but it's also a strong tool for anyone else who's interested in conducting online surveys. ZipSurvey uses a point-and-click interface to let you build a survey, secure e-mail tools that let you invite respondents to participate, and real-time analysis tools. If you need some help building your survey or analyzing the results, the folks at ZipSurvey will not only hold your hand, but they'll offer consulting — for a price. The ZipSurvey-Gold and ZipSurvey-Platinum options give you the chance to work with a Ph.D. to design, launch, analyze, and report on your survey. They'll also help you create the all-important action plan based on the results. Of course, this is a costly option. Prices range from free to $2,499 a month.

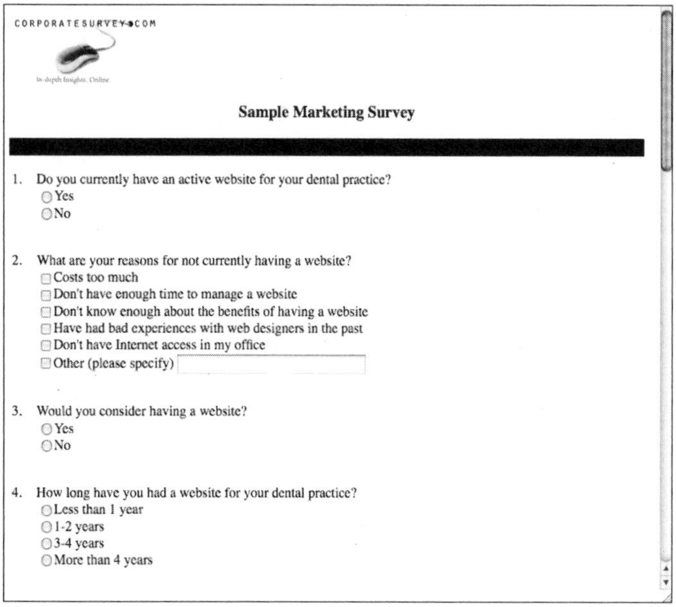

Figure 4-25:
A corporate survey built using ZipSurvey.

Zoomerang

www.zoomerang.com

Zoomerang (see Figure 4-26) offers a Premium Level (also known as enter-prise level) online survey software tool for multi-user survey sharing and collaboration. At this level, you can sort and analyze open-ended responses in seconds, calculate means and standard deviations, and compare subsets of response data. A unique differentiator with Zoomerang software is the ability enable cell phone users to take your survey — this is the wave of the future. Some of Zoomerang's newest features include the ability to import surveys from Word or text documents and to export survey questionnaires to Word or PDF documents. You can even share your results with a social bookmarking toolbar if you're the social media type. Zoomerang's Premium Level runs $599 a year.

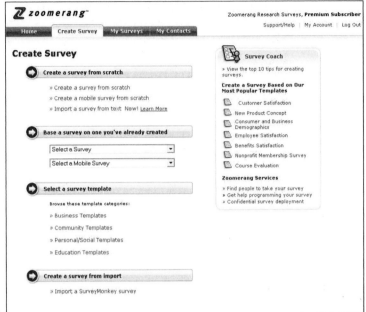

Figure 4-26:
Creating
a new
survey in
Zoomerang.

Part II
Building Compelling Surveys

The 5th Wave   By Rich Tennant

DataSuk
Service & Support

"Please answer the following survey questions about our company's performance with either, 'Excellent', 'Good', 'Fair', or 'I'm Really Incapable of Appreciating Someone Else's Hard Work.'"

In this part . . .

It's time to build some compelling surveys. In this part, we arm you with detailed information that will help you determine your survey objectives. We also show you how to tap into the power of survey templates and build question libraries that will potentially save you hours (and hours and hours) of time now and in the future. You even discover the ingredients of must-answer surveys so you can all but guarantee your respondents offer up the insights you crave.

One of the most important aspects of building compelling surveys is developing questions that get responses. We discuss what types of questions you could ask, the most common question types, and how to know which ones to use — and which ones not to use. We also shine a bright light on question development pitfalls so you don't stumble into the dark hole of obscure surveys.

When you're ready to launch your first online survey, you'll find a step-by-step guide in this part that holds your hand through issues like adding new questions, playing up respondent privacy, forcing responses, randomizing order answers, and other need-to-know online survey techniques. We even show you how to test your survey before you distribute it to the masses.

And when you're ready to advance to more complex online survey development, we won't leave you hanging. This part spells out complicated — yet powerful — strategies for mastering matrix extractions, advanced branching, custom survey functions, and multiple user surveys. These advanced techniques will take your marketing research to the next level!

Chapter 5

Preparing to Build Your Survey

....

....

Survey building is a snap when you use online survey software. Online survey software vendors have developed user-friendly software that makes it possible to build questionnaires that reach people you might not have access to any other way. You don't need any special skills — if you're comfortable surfing the Web and using a word processor, you're qualified — but you do need to plan your survey in advance. That's what this chapter is all about.

Everything rises and falls on objectives in the online survey world. If you don't determine your objectives at the beginning of the journey, you won't know if you've reached your destination when you get there. What's more, when you get to the end of the survey road, your results might be completely, utterly useless if they don't meet with your market research goals.

Determining your survey objectives is, however, just the beginning. Another aspect of survey building is including the right ingredients. Those might differ from survey to survey, depending on your objectives and the type of survey you're conducting. But again, online survey software makes the actual building relatively simple. You can use template libraries and question libraries. You can use a variety of colors and images to enhance your questionnaire. You can do all sorts of things quickly and easily with online survey software that you can't do with paper-based or telephone surveys.

In this chapter, you discover how to determine your survey objectives, how to tap into the question and template libraries to streamline your survey-building efforts, how to use the language of color to your advantage, and when to add images, graphics, and motion. So get ready to strategize, because it's time to make your online survey blueprint.

Identifying Your Survey Objectives

Before you begin building your online survey — or even sharpening your tools — you need to know something about your organization and your respondents. Before you ever put pen to paper (or in this case finger to keyboard) you need to consider who your audience is, what your organizational goals are, and what the specific goal of your online survey is.

You need to be sure an online survey is the best method of gathering the information you need. Sometimes a focus group or some other form of market research is a better choice. It's tempting to rely on the online survey for everything because online surveys are easier and less time-consuming to conduct than focus groups, telephone interviews, in-person interviews, and other forms of market research. (Turn to Chapter 1 for a more in-depth look at some other types of surveys you might want to consider.) The time it takes you to conduct your survey shouldn't be the only deciding factor — reaching your objective must be the force behind your choice!

Your survey objective could be to

- ✔ Improve customer satisfaction or customer loyalty

- ✔ Boost the attendance of your events by determining what potential attendees might want or what past attendees found most valuable

- ✔ Improve retail store traffic with a Web site–useability survey that reveals where customers are getting confused

- ✔ Or some other noble goal

For more on how to avoid making mistakes in this area, see Chapter 17.

After you have determined that an online survey is the right medium for your market research, you need to develop clear, concise questions. You can ask various types of questions, but not every question type is made of the right material. To understand the types of questions you can ask — and when you should use them — see Chapter 6. You also need to understand the basic survey options in order to build the vehicle that will drive you toward the insights you need.

A certain excitement comes with starting a new online survey. You can almost smell the valuable insights awaiting you. As you explore this cost-effective tool for finding out more about your customers, clients, employees, and partners, you probably still have a few questions rolling around in your mind about the best way to approach an online survey project. You can find the answers to them in this section.

Are browsers busting your online survey?

Nobody likes to deal with techie issues — unless you're a techie — but with online survey software, you need to consider some issues if you want to avoid *survey abandonment* (when a person who began taking your survey decides not to finish it). Because participants depend on a Web browser to navigate your survey, you need to do some testing to make sure that your online survey not only displays well on various types of browsers but that it also works on different browsers.

As with Web design, you should test your survey on the most popular Web browsers (Internet Explorer, Firefox, Chrome, and Safari). But remember that several versions of each browser are available to consumers, and those with older machines might be using very old versions. The general rule of thumb is to test the most current browser version as well as the previous version (that is, Internet Explorer 8 and Internet Explorer 7). If possible, test your online survey on as many browsers as you can to see how it works and looks. Try and anticipate any potential issues. This way, you can ask your respondents at the beginning to use a browser that displays the online survey in the best possible manner.

The first step to any successful online survey is to determine the objectives of your study. The second task is to phrase the objectives as questions or measurements. If you can't develop questions that lead to measurements, you're better off looking at other ways to gather data such as focus groups or measurements. Online surveys tend to focus in on more quantitative data collection.

Here are some steps to help you prepare your online questionnaire:

1. **Review the basic objectives of the study.** What are you trying to discover? What actions do you want to take as a result of the survey? The answers to these questions help you make sure online surveys are right for you.

2. **Visualize the relevant information you'd like to have.** What will the output report look like? What charts and graphs will be prepared? What information do you need to be assured that action is warranted?

3. **Rank each topic in Steps 1 and 2 according to the value of the topic.** List the most important topics first. Revisit Steps 1 and 2 of this list to make sure the objectives, topics, and information you need are appropriate.

You can't solve the problem if you ask the wrong questions. Taking the time to make sure you understand what you need to discover, how you'll organize the data, and what actions you'll take when you receive the responses is a vital starting point.

4. **How easy or difficult is it for the respondent to provide information on each topic?** If it's difficult, do you have another way to obtain the information by asking another question?

This is probably the most important step. Online surveys have to be precise, clear, and concise. Due to the fickle nature of the Web, if your questions are too complicated or difficult to understand you'll have a high drop-out (individuals that quit the survey before completing it) rate.

5. **Create an unbiased sequence for the questions.** Make sure the questions you ask first in the survey don't bias the results of the questions that come later. Sometimes providing too much information, or disclosing the purpose of the study, can create bias. For example, if you disclose in the beginning of the survey that you're collecting results on behalf of a restaurant chain, respondents who may have had a poor experience with the restaurant might not bother to respond.

It's always wise to add some introductory text before you start firing off survey questions. Your introduction should explain the project and what the respondent is required to do. Being the professional that you are, you also want to include a "Thank You" at the end of the survey and offer up information about how the respondent can find the results when they're published.

6. **Determine what type of question is best suited to yield the type of answer you're looking for and then provide enough information to meet your analysis requirements.** There are many choices for question types — probably more than you ever imagined — and a fine line to walk as you make the decision on which type(s) to use. To find out more about the various question types and when they're appropriate, check out Chapter 6.

Break or branch — you decide

If you're working on a complex survey, you might wind up with a survey design that's rather intimidating for your respondents — unless you use page breaks or branching. Here's how these nifty tools work. Page breaks let you avoid having a huge scrolling survey, and you can introduce them as often as you see fit. However, there is one caveat with page breaks of which you should be aware: Don't use too much of a good thing.

If you use so many page breaks that you end up with one question per page, it increases the amount of time it takes you to complete a survey.

That also increases the chance for survey drop-outs. Branching is the second strategy for breaking up complex surveys. This tool makes your surveys smart. You've probably seen surveys that offer directions such as, "If you answered no to Question 1, then proceed to Question 4." Directions like that cause respondents to get frustrated, thus increasing the drop-out rate. Using branching automatically routes the respondent to the correct questions based on their responses to previous questions — without making them figure out which question to proceed to.

Generally, tougher analysis requirements lead to more a complicated questionnaire design. However, a couple of tools are available to make life easier: *page breaks* (a break in the survey that sends you to the next page) and *branching* (a feature that lets you jump to a specified question based on responses to previous questions; also called *skip logic*). In essence, branching serves up different sets of questions to different people.

7. **Write the questions.** What's a survey without questions? It's no survey at all. As you write your questions, keep in mind that you might need to write several questions for each topic and then select the best one. You might also be better off dividing the survey into multiple sections.

8. **Sequence the questions so that they're unbiased.** As already noted in Step 5 — but it's worth repeating — sometimes providing too much information (or disclosing purpose of the study) can create bias.

9. **Repeat all the preceding steps to find any major holes in your survey.** Are the questions really answered? Have someone review it for you.

10. **Time the length of the survey.** A survey should take less than five minutes. At three to four questions per minute, you're limited to about 15 questions. Keep in mind that one open-ended text question counts for three multiple choice questions. ***Note:*** Most online software tools record the time it takes for the respondents to answer questions.

11. **Pretest the survey.** Ask 20 or more people to take the survey and offer feedback . . . detailed feedback.

You can create a quick "feedback survey" on your survey. Develop a few open-ended questions about your survey. What were the recipients unsure about? Did they have questions? Did they have trouble understanding what you wanted? Did they take a point of view not covered in your answers or question? E-mail the project survey to your test group as well as the feedback survey.

12. **Revise, revise, revise.** Revise your online questionnaire incorporating the feedback that you received.

13. **Send the survey.** Congratulations! It's time to build your survey. For more on how to actually build your online survey, check out Chapter 7.

Getting to Know the Template Library

Most online survey software vendors offer template libraries. Survey templates are a shortcut to help you get started building your survey. If you're familiar with templates for Microsoft Word or for Web sites, you'll feel right at home.

Using QuestionPro as our example, you can find templates based on publicly available information and best practices that will save you a lot of time in its handy-dandy online library. Here's how:

1. **Go to the QuestionPro Web site and log in.**

   Log in to your QuestionPro account using your username and password.

2. **Click the Create a New Survey button just below the group of tabs across the top. Choose Copy a Survey Template in the resulting window and click Continue.**

3. **Browse through the available templates (see Figure 5-1), find one that most closely matches your survey project, and select it by clicking the radio button and clicking Continue.**

Figure 5-1:
Taking
advantage
of survey
templates.

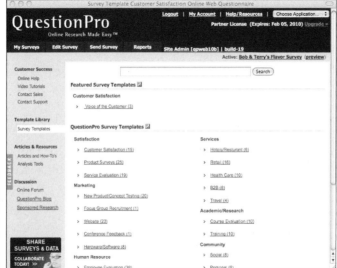

4. **Choose a layout that suits your fancy from the drop-down list and click Finish.**

Understanding the Question Library

It would be nice if you could refer to a library chock-full of survey questions that had a guarantee of being answered by survey recipients. Well, no one has come up with that feature yet, but many online survey software vendors do offer a question library that makes things much easier for people who plan to continue using online surveys as part of their market research.

The *question library* lets you create a template library of questions that you can reuse again and again. Some questions can inevitably be reused in other surveys in different formats and locations. The question library saves you time by letting you save those questions for future use.

Here's how to build a question library, again using QuestionPro as our example:

1. **Go to the QuestionPro Web site and log in.**

   Log in to your QuestionPro account with your username and password.

2. **Choose your survey.**

   Click the Edit link next to the survey you're like to select. You'll be taken to the Edit Survey screen.

3. **Scroll down in your survey to the question you want to copy.**

4. **Click the Copy link, choose Copy Question To Library in the resulting window, and then click the Copy Question button (see Figure 5-2).**

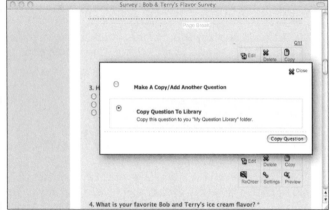

Figure 5-2:
An example of adding a question to your question library.

When it comes time to tap into your treasure trove of questions, it's easy to pull from the question library to add questions to a new survey. Here's the process using QuestionPro:

1. **Choose your survey.**

   Click the Edit link next to survey you want to select. You'll be taken to the Edit Survey screen.

2. **Find the point in your survey where you'd like to add the new library question and click the Add New Question link.**

3. **In the resulting window, choose My Question Library from the drop-down box in the section titled Library/Survey (see Figure 5-3), and then click Next.**

   You now see a list of the questions from your library that you can add to your survey.

   You can also directly add the questions from another survey by selecting the appropriate survey.

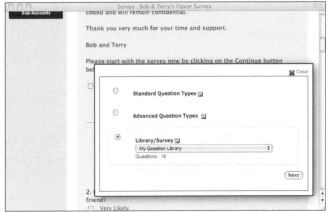

Figure 5-3:
An example
of adding a
question to
your survey
from the
question
library.

4. **From the list of library questions, check the box next to one or more questions you'd like to add and click the Copy Questions button.**

   This will add the questions to your survey.

5. **Choose the question you want to pull from the question library and click the Add This Question button.**

   You can select multiple questions and add them at once by holding down the Control (Ctrl) key as you click the questions you want to add.

Beware of getting too carried away with using questions from a question library. Because using a question library is an easy way to create a survey, people sometimes forget to edit the questions they're adding in to ensure the questions fit the focus of the new survey. If you don't pay attention, you'll end up with a survey that contains questions that have nothing to do with the topic of the survey.

If you want to edit the questions you've stowed away in the question library, feel free. All you have to do go to the My Surveys tab as you normally would and then click the My Question Library link. You'll be taken to the familiar Edit Survey screen where you can edit these questions as you normally would.

Offering Survey Instructions

You can accomplish plenty of work in a word-processing document before you actually begin building your online survey. One step is to write your online survey instructions. How to complete your online survey might seem obvious to you — after all, you're the one who wrote it — but it might not be obvious to others. Don't take even the smallest chance that your would-be respondents might close the browser before they ever get started on your online survey. Offer clear instructions.

Your survey instructions should be brief and give an overview of how to navigate the survey rather than getting granular about specific questions. (If individual questions in your survey need specific instructions, you can add them in when those questions are presented.) The goal of online survey instructions is to reiterate how long the survey should take, address what to do when respondents aren't sure they know the answer, whether or not they can go back and change their answers, the deadline for completing the survey, and how to cash in on any incentives you might offer for participating in the survey (see Figure 5-4).

Always offer a contact e-mail address on the instructions page. If you haven't answered all the would-be participants' questions, they might choose to contact you for more details. By the same token, they might want a hard copy instead. It's up to you if you'd like to provide it, but you should make it as easy as possible for participants to contact you with any concerns that might cause them not to complete your online survey.

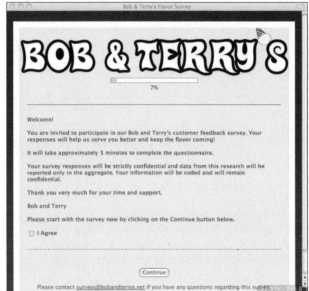

Figure 5-4: A sample survey's instructions.

Picking Questionnaire Colors

If music calms the savage beast, do colors encourage people to finish or abandon surveys? There's every reason to believe that colors can make an impact on survey response ratios. Online survey software applications typically offer you the ability to choose colors for screens and text. But before you do, read the following sections.

There's a psychology to color. (See the section "Understanding the Language of Colors," later in this chapter.) In other words, colors evoke different moods and responses in people. Although colors can dress up an otherwise bland black-and-white survey, using too much color or using the wrong colors might leave you red-faced and black-eyed.

Using colors appropriately

There are some general guidelines when it comes to using colors in online surveys. The first guideline says colors can be helpful when used appropriately. The correct use of color can reinforce your product brand, help guide people through the online survey more easily, and subconsciously encourage the respondent to continue to the end.

That said, you can also damage your efforts to gain respondent insights if you use color the wrong way. If your colors make it difficult to read the survey, you're well on your way to *survey abandonment* (when a person who began taking your survey decides not to finish it). If the colors are too distracting, they might impede the flow of the survey. And if you use the wrong colors with the wrong audiences, you might even send subconscious signals you wish you hadn't. You find out more about that in the later section about understanding the language of color.

 If you've ever purchased clothing online, you know all too well that colors don't always appear on your computer screen the same way they appear on the actual clothing when you look in the mirror. Different computer screens are configured with different color densities, so be careful about using colors that are too dull or too bright. And check the colors you're thinking about using on several different monitors to see whether the color's appearance is consistent before launching your survey.

Figuring out font and text size

Font and text size are important considerations as you're preparing to build your online survey. Like colors, some online survey software applications don't give you a choice. But if you have a choice, you should select wisely. Two basic types of fonts exist: serif and sans-serif. *Serif* is like a Times New Roman font; it has short lines at the ends, tops, and bottoms of the characters. *Sans-serif* fonts are blunted and straight-edged. Of course, there are many different types of fonts within those categories. Ultimately, you want to choose a font that's easy to read on the screen. Times New Roman (serif) and Arial (sans-serif) are both good choices and are widely used on the Web. As far as text size, a 12-point type is a good starting point. If your survey targets kids or senior citizens, you might consider bumping up the text size to 14- or even 16-point for maximum readability. Be sure to test your online survey and ask the test group about the font and text size to determine whether you've settled on a user-friendly combination.

Keeping your brand name in mind

Ideally, the colors you choose need to connect the product's usage to its audience. If you're conducting an online survey about power tools and adult males are your audience, you wouldn't want to use lavenders and pinks. So when you choose colors for your online survey backgrounds, keep branding in mind.

For example, if you go to a hardware store today and walk down the power tools aisle, you'll discover that all the major companies have claimed their own branding color. Milwaukee Tool is red. DeWALT is yellow. Black & Decker is deep blue-green. If you consider the colors of your product or brand and use them correctly, you've just enhanced your online survey.

Understanding the Language of Color

Colors have psychological impact on people. Indeed, color is actually an entire language in and of itself that speaks volumes to the consumer's subconscious. Understanding what those colors communicate is vital to choosing the right colors to accent your online survey. In fact, understanding the deeper meanings of colors can help you choose the most appropriate combinations.

Investigating the color gamut

You might be surprised to hear the true meaning of colors. Your subconscious mind probably already speaks the language well, but if you've never taken a moment to consider what colors are saying, now is the time. Here's how the color palate communicates to your mind:

Adding graphics to your online survey

The most sophisticated online survey software offers the ability to add graphics, images, charts, motion, sound, and links. But just because you have the ability to jazz up your survey doesn't mean you should. If these features don't add to the objective of your survey and they don't make it easier for participants to respond to your questions — in other words, if they don't add value — then don't use them. Using graphics for the sake of using graphics is a distraction at best and a cause for survey abandonment at worst. In some cases, using graphics, motion, sound, and the like might even jam up your respondent's browser and leave them unable to complete the survey. That said, used appropriately, these tools can help you put your questions in context, get insights into questions about the appearance of a new product, or otherwise offer information you can't offer any other way.

- **Black:** Black typically communicates authority and power. Black is a good choice for typefaces because it contrasts nicely against most light backgrounds.

- **Red:** Red is a color of high emotion. Studies show it stimulates shoppers and appetite. That's why red cars are known for their sex appeal. Red is a hot color that signifies low price.

- **Blue:** The opposite of red, blue is a cool color that communicates elegance and quality. Blue is the most popular color in the world. It crosses cultures and nationality.

- **Green:** This color is rarely used in retail settings except lawn and garden or food establishments. Green symbolizes health and nature. Green is eternally associated with the environment, nature, and things that are good for you.

- **Yellow:** Yellow is another attention-grabber and should be used only as a background. Yellow typefaces are difficult to read.

- **Purple:** This color signifies royalty, luxury, and wealth.

- **Brown:** Brown is a good choice for industrial applications because it's earthy and signifies reliability and genuineness. UPS has done well with its drab brown brand.

Some colors have been marketed in certain ways and have become engrained in the customer's mind to mean certain things. The key to color marketing is to tap into what human beings are already prewired to accept.

Settling on color shades and combinations

Different shades of these colors can produce varied meanings, so we recommend that you stick with basics and keeping color combinations simple until you master the language. The idea is to connect with the audience and use color to facilitate online survey responses. As with typefaces, color consistency is important, so choose your colors wisely and stick to the same set of colors throughout your survey. Just as you would use a good headline or a catch phrase, you need to use colors that connect in people's minds in a positive way. Color is an endless subject of study, but you can use it to enhance your online surveys.

The international language of color

Just as verbal languages are different in various parts of the world, so is the color of language. In the United States, blue can communicate freedom. It's also a calming color. Whether you live in the U.S. or in Africa, certain colors play the same role in nature. Then there are cultural applications.

In the U.S., people go to funerals wearing black. In China, they wear white because it is the color of death and mourning. In Europe, green has political ties to the Green Party and the Green Movement. In America, green often has connections with recycling and being environmentally friendly.

Chapter 6

Developing Questions that Get Responses

. . . .

. . . .

Developing questions that get responses — that's the overarching goal of survey development. After all, if your questions are so confusing that people can't understand them, you won't get many insights. By the same token, if your questions are full of industry jargon, you might get incorrect insights. And if your questions are misleading, you might get skewed insights.

Developing online survey questions is half art, half science. It's a true right-brain-left-brain activity. Your questions need to be logical and easy to understand, and they must use proper grammar. That's the left brain. But you also need to be creative enough in your question-asking endeavors that you keep your respondents engaged and unlock the valuable attitudes, beliefs, and opinions you need to make decisions for your organization. That's the right brain.

You might be surprised to discover how many different types of questions you can ask. However, you have to become familiar with an entirely new language in order to understand your options. Sure, you might be familiar with multiple-choice questions. But there are many more sophisticated types of queries that can uncover insights you couldn't get any other way. From dichotomous questions to rank order scaling and from constant sum questions to staple scales and beyond, the possibilities aren't endless, but they certainly are numerous.

In this chapter, you also discover there's a right away and a wrong way to develop questions. There are plenty of mistakes you can make on the road to developing survey questions, but hang tight — we're about to guide you in the right direction so your questions evoke the best responses from your respondents.

Tying Questions to Survey Objectives

Before you ever develop your first online survey question, consider this golden rule: Every single question you develop should tie back to your survey objectives. After you develop your questions — and even while you're in the midst of the development process — keep your survey objectives at the top of your mind. Your survey objectives might be finding weak spots in your customer service department, gauging opinions on a new product or service, or any number of other possibilities. The point is that you're trying to make decisions, and you need some guidance from people who have insights you can't get any other way.

Before you even think about launching your online survey, read each question and ask yourself whether the information you'll obtain from the answer relates directly back to your survey goals. If you discover that the answer is a nice-to-know but not a must-have, remove the question. The idea is to keep the survey as short as possible while gathering all the information you need to reach your objective.

The importance of contingency questions

Before we get into the myriad of other question types, it's important to discuss contingency questions. Also known as *filter questions* or *screeners, contingency questions* (see Figure 6-1) help you determine whether a respondent is qualified or experienced enough to offer the insights you need in your online survey. That's because this type of question relates directly to your survey objectives.

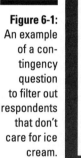

Figure 6-1:
An example of a contingency question to filter out respondents that don't care for ice cream.

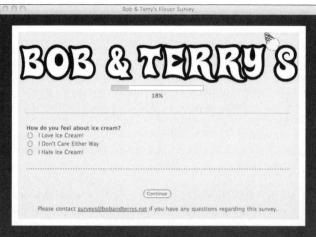

If you're trying to gain insights into gourmet pet food, you might ask: "Have you ever purchased gourmet pet food?" If the answer is no, you can offer a "thank you" and wait for responses to your gourmet pet food survey from someone who is more familiar with the products. You might also want to know the frequency of the purchases. If the respondent rarely buys gourmet pet food, her responses might not be weighted as heavily as if she purchases it every week.

Contingency questions aren't always aimed at eliminating respondents from your survey altogether. Sometimes these questions just signal the online survey software to skip a specific section of questions because they're not relevant to that participant. For example, if your gourmet pet food survey deals with cats and dogs, but your participant only has a dog, a negative response to a contingency question that asks, "Do you have a cat?" would allow the participant to jump ahead to the next set of questions.

Are you getting valid answers?

Seeing your online survey responses begin to roll in is exciting. We don't want to rain on your parade, but we should mention an important caveat of survey answers before you head outside to do some cartwheels: validity. *Validity* is whether the survey measures what it intends to measure. Authors have written entire books on the topic of survey reliability and validity — that's how important the topic is. If your survey questions aren't tied to your survey objectives, your questionnaire won't pass the validity test.

Here's an example: If you want to know about a respondent's social networking use, it wouldn't make sense to ask how many social networks he belongs to. Belonging to a social network is not a valid indicator of social network usage. Many people join numerous social networks and never participate in the conversation. By the same token, many join only one social network and engage with the community throughout the day. Validity in this case would be to ask directly about the amount of time the respondent spends using social networks.

Of course, some people might not offer valid answers. That's a danger with any type of survey. Online surveys have the advantage of complete anonymity in the sense that there is no in-person or even over-the-phone interviewer. If respondents feel uncomfortable sharing, are embarrassed, are trying to be politically correct, or don't remember the specific details related to a question, they might not give valid answers.

You can reduce this possibility in your online survey by reminding participants throughout the survey that the answers are confidential and anonymous. You can indicate that the behavior or attitude you're querying about isn't uncommon in order to take the respondent's guard down. For example, "Research indicates 50 percent of retail workers have turned their back on shoplifting. Have you ever looked the other way when you suspected a shoplifter at work?"

If you're trying to get more accurate answers, you can also attach a time-frame to the question, such as "How many times in the past week have you used a social network?" And always give participants a way out. Not everyone has an opinion or wants to share an opinion on certain topics. You can do this buy asking, "Do you have an opinion about social networking?" or by offering a multiple-choice question with a "no opinion" option.

Knowing the Types of Questions You Can Ask

So you've decided that you need a better understanding of the characteristics of the people who visit your Web site, buy your product, or of some other business-related question. By developing a focused and effective questionnaire, you can more efficiently and accurately pinpoint the information that helps you make more informed decisions.

Developing a questionnaire is as much an art as it is a science. And just as an artist has a variety of colors to choose from in the palette, you have a variety of question formats with which to build an accurate picture of your customers and clients and the issues that are important to them.

Dichotomous questions

The *dichotomous question* is one that offers the readers two options, usually opposites. It's generally a yes-or-no question, such as "Have you ever purchased a product or service from our Web site?" The respondent simply answers "yes" or "no." Dichotomous questions might also be true/false statements or ask about gender (male/female).

If you want information only from product users, you might want to ask this type of question to *screen out* (filter) those who haven't purchased your products or services. Researchers use screening questions to make sure that only those people they're interested in participate in the survey.

You might also want to use yes-or-no questions to separate people or branch into groups of those who have purchased and those who have not yet purchased your products or services (see Figure 6-2). After the groups are separated, you can ask different questions of each group. For example, you might want to ask the have-purchased group members how satisfied they are with your products and services, and you might want to ask the have-not-purchased group members what the primary reasons are for not purchasing. In essence, your questionnaire branches to become two different sets of questions. To find out more about branching, see Chapter 7.

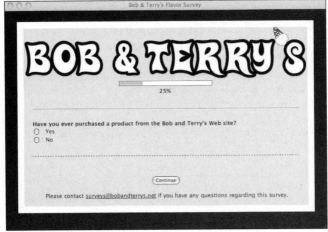

Figure 6-2:
An example
of a dichoto-
mous
question.

Multiple-choice questions

Everyone is familiar with multiple-choice questions. These consist of three
or more mutually exclusive categories. Multiple-choice questions can ask for
single or multiple answers. For example, you can ask the respondent how
she heard about your company and offer her seven options. You could then
instruct her to choose one answer, three answers, or as many answers as
you've included in the list of possible choices. Here's an example:

How did you first hear about our Web site?

> Television
>
> Radio
>
> Newspaper
>
> Magazine
>
> Word-of-mouth
>
> Internet
>
> Other (Please specify) _____

For this type of question, it's important to consider including an "other"
category because there might be other options or answers (in this example,
avenues by which the person first heard about your site) that you might have
overlooked. The takeaway here is that the "other" category gives respondents
a chance to offer their own view if you didn't include a response they could
agree with or one that's accurate.

Understanding closed-end questions

Like dichotomous questions, multiple-choice questions, ratings, and ranking questions are sometimes referred to as *closed-end questions*. One of the beauties of this question type is that you can ask a large number of questions in a short amount of time. Closed-end questions also allow you to assess understanding or attitudes and measure knowledge or ability.

Closed-end questions have three key advantages. First, they make it easy for the respondent to answer — the choices are all laid out. Second, they make for a quicker survey because they require less reflection than open-ended questions. Third, they make it easy to analyze the data and offer summaries to your team. For example, "50 percent of respondents said they liked vanilla ice cream the best."

Like anything else in life, closed-end questions have some disadvantages. For starters, closed-end questions limit the response options. Sometimes things aren't always black and white. In those cases, a yes-or-no question might limit the response. By the same token, multiple-choice questions can't always offer every possible option. That's why the "other" option with a blank for the respondents to offer an additional response is helpful. Closed-end questions also lack detail and depth as they have the potential to overlook options that one might not expect. For example, let's say you asked a question about favorite flavors of ice cream but you didn't include options for rocky road or mint chip because you weren't aware of the flavors.

Multiple-choice questions should offer responses that are mutually exclusive. *Mutually exclusive responses* are those for which the respondent can't choose more than one answer. Sometimes you might want to allow your respondents to choose more than one option from the list. In that case, signal them to select all that apply so they know it's okay to choose more than one.

Rank order scaling questions

Rank order scaling questions allow a certain set of brands or products to be ranked based on a specific attribute or characteristic. These are sometimes called *ordinal scale questions*. For example, you might know Toyota, Honda, Mazda, and Ford are the top four brands of cars most likely to be purchased by consumers. You can choose to request that the options be ranked based on a particular attribute, such as reliability or resale value.

You can allow or disallow ties in the ranks. If you allow ties, several options will have the same scores. If you don't want to allow ties, be sure to tell the respondent that no two items can share the same ranking. Here's an example:

Based on what you've seen, heard, and experienced, please rank the following brands according to their reliability. Place a 1 next to the brand that is most reliable, a 2 next to the brand that is second-most reliable, and so on. Remember, no two brands can have the same ranking.

_____ Honda

_____ Toyota

_____ Mazda

_____ Ford

Ranking questions are valuable in online surveys because they help uncover the attitudes and allow respondents to choose from various options. The respondent can express his or her opinion about the importance of the choices you offer so you can fine-tune your promotion, product, service, or program to accommodate consumer preferences.

The downside of ranking questions is that they're more difficult for respondents to answer. They also limit the number of possible responses to what you've listed, thereby potentially skewing the answer. In the preceding example, the respondents might think a BMW is the most reliable but are forced to choose from a list of brands about which they aren't familiar or don't think are reliable at all.

Rating scale questions

A *rating scale question* requires a person to rate a product or brand along a well-defined, evenly spaced continuum. Rating scales are often used to measure the direction and intensity of attitudes. Here's an example of a comparative rating scale question:

Which of the following categories best describes your last experience purchasing a product or service on our Web site? Would you say that your experience was:

Very pleasant

Somewhat pleasant

Neither pleasant nor unpleasant

Somewhat unpleasant

Very unpleasant

Be sure to provide a neutral position among your potential responses, as well as the same number of positive and negative responses. If your scale is tipped in favor of a positive or negative response, it will skew your online survey. Typically, you want an odd number of choices in the rating scale with the neutral in the center.

The semantic differential scale

The semantic differential scale asks a respondent to rate a product, brand, or company based on a seven-point rating scale that has two bipolar adjectives at each end. Confused? Here's an example:

Would you say our Web site is:

(7) Very attractive

(6)

(5)

(4)

(3)

(2)

(1) Very unattractive

Unlike the rating scale, the semantic differential scale doesn't have a neutral or middle selection. A person must choose, to a certain extent, one or the other adjective.

Staple scale questions

The *staple scale* — a questioning method that sets out to determine the degree of an attitude, opinion, or behavior — asks a respondent to rate a brand, product, or service according to a certain characteristic on a scale from +5 to –5, indicating how well the characteristic describes the product or service (see Figure 6-3). These are sometimes called *interval scale questions*. Here's an example:

When thinking about Data Mining Technologies, Inc. (DMT), do you believe that the word *innovative* aptly describes or poorly describes the company? On a scale of +5 to –5, with +5 being a very good description of DMT and –5 being a poor description of DMT, how do you rank DMT according to the word *innovative?*

+5

+4

+3

+2

+1

0

−1

−2

−3

−4

−5

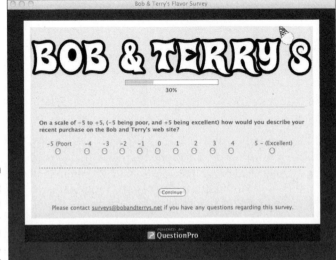

Figure 6-3:
An example
of a ques-
tion with a
staple scale.

Digging into consumer behaviors

Sometimes you need to gather information about consumer behaviors before you launch into the survey. In some cases, the answers to those questions might disqualify a respondent. In other cases, the answer might allow the respondent to skip ahead in the survey to a more relevant section or prompt an open-ended question to allow the consumer to explain more in-depth.

For example, if you're conducting an online survey about TV-viewing behaviors, it's helpful to know how frequently the respondent watches television. If the answer is, "I don't watch television," you might ask an open-ended question such as "Why don't you watch television?" just to understand the behavior. The answer might provide key insights related to your study. By the same token, you might want to distinguish between those who watch TV one or two hours a week and those who watch for six or seven hours a week to identify trends among heavy TV watchers compared with infrequent TV watchers.

The pros and cons of scale questions

Scale questions have a strong advantage: They offer greater accuracy and precision than yes-or-no and true-or-false questions. They're also relatively easy for the respondent to run through quickly. Perhaps the only downside to scaled questions is that they're more difficult to write. You need to know a good deal about the topic at hand to develop this type of question.

The constant sum question

A *constant sum question* permits collection of ratio data, meaning that the data is able to express the relative value or importance of the options (as in option A is twice as important as option B). You can use this type of question when you're relatively sure of the reasons for purchase, or you want input on a limited number of reasons you feel are important. These are also called *ratio scale questions.*

A question, for example, might ask the respondent to divide 100 points between a set of options to show the value or importance he places on each option. The respondent would distribute the 100 points giving the more important reasons a greater number of points. The computer would prompt the respondent if his total didn't equal exactly 100 points. Here's how it looks in living color:

> When thinking about the reasons you purchased our TargetFind data-mining software, please rate the following reasons according to their relative importance:

Seamless integration with other software	_____
User friendliness of software	_____
Ability to manipulate algorithms	_____
Level of pre- and post-purchase service	_____
Level of value for the price	_____
Convenience of purchase/quick delivery	_____
Total	100 points

The open-ended question

Also called an *essay* or *short-answer question,* the *open-ended question* seeks to explore the qualitative, in-depth aspects of a particular topic or issue. It gives a person the chance to respond in detail. Online surveyors use open-ended questions (see Figure 6-4) to discover relevant issues they might not have thought to ask specific questions about and to obtain a fuller set of responses than a multiple-choice or other question type would allow.

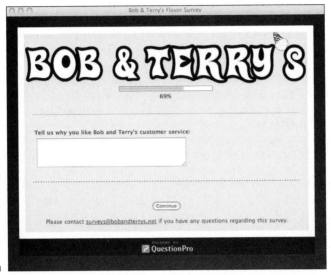

Bob & Terry's Flavor Survey

BOB & TERRY'S

69%

Tell us why you like Bob and Terry's customer service:

Continue

Please contact surveys@bobandterrys.net if you have any questions regarding this survey.

QuestionPro

Figure 6-4:
An example
of a basic,
open-ended
question.

For example, if the respondent indicates that she didn't find what she was looking for, you might ask "What products of services were you looking for that were not found on our Web site?" The answer might turn up products you never would have thought of. Of course, just because one person suggests something, that doesn't make it a trend. But if a large percentage of the respondents to an open-ended question hit on the same issue, it's worth exploring.

Open-ended questions have their pros and cons. Open-ended questions can help you identify issues that are timely and relevant in the eyes of your respondents, offer new perspectives on a topic, clarify a respondent's position on a question, and provide a level of detail you can't get with other question types.

However, there's a downside. Open-ended questions require more time to complete. They also press the respondent to think harder and communicate those thoughts logically. Open-ended questions might also yield a big goose egg. Respondents might offer incomplete or irrelevant answers. Answers to open-ended questions also take longer to analyze because there's no numeric value to associate with them. You have to read the answers one-by-one and spot the trends. Although open-ended questions are important, don't overuse them.

It's best to include at least one open-ended question because it conveys to your respondent that you're really listening — giving them warm fuzzies. The most effective surveys include no more than one or two open-ended questions. If you ask any more than that, you'll be spending all your free time sifting through piles of text, looking for trends. For information on how to analyze open-ended questions most effectively, see Chapter 13.

The demographic question

Demographic questions are an important part of your questionnaire because they're used to identify characteristics such as age, gender, income, race, geographic place of residence, number of children, and so forth. Perhaps most of your customers come from the northeast, are between the ages of 50 and 65, and have incomes between $50,000 and $75,000. That's important to know, don't you think?

Here are some examples of demographic questions:

- ✔ Are you male or female?
- ✔ Which age group do you fall in?
- ✔ What is the highest level of education completed?
- ✔ What is your marital status?
- ✔ What religion are you?
- ✔ What is your occupation?
- ✔ Do you work full-time or part-time?
- ✔ Which range best describes your annual income?
- ✔ What is your race or ethnicity?

It's best to offer a range of multiple-choice options rather than a fill-in-the-blank line on issues of income and age. Ethnicity or religion might require space where respondents can type in their answer because there are so many possible options. You might want to list the most common choices and then an "other" choice in those categories.

It probably isn't necessary to ask all those questions in every survey. Just ask what you need to know and nothing more. (**Hint:** It should tie back to your survey objectives.) The point is that demographic data helps you paint a more accurate picture of the group of individuals you're trying to understand. And by better understanding the type of people who use or are likely to use your product, you can allocate promotional resources to reach these people in a more cost-effective manner.

You can also find psychographic or lifestyle questions in the template files. These questions go a step beyond your typical demographic data to provide an in-depth psychological profile and look at activities, interests, and opinions of respondents.

Don't front-load your online survey with demographic questions. You might scare off otherwise willing participants by bogging them down with too many questions before they even get into the meat of the survey. Instead, offer a section at the end of the survey where you can gather this type of information.

You should use demographic questions at the beginning of a survey only when you need to filter respondents based on some characteristic, such as age or income.

Understanding When to Ask Which Type of Question

You can ask many different types of questions — probably more than you even considered when you set out to develop your questionnaire. So how do you know when to ask what question? It depends on what you're trying to measure. Survey questions typically attempt to measure one of four categories: behavior, attributes, attitudes, and beliefs.

For example, if you're conducting an online survey that evaluates nursing home services, you need to know which of those four categories you want to measure. If you want to measure behavior, you should ask whether the respondent has any family members currently in a nursing home. If you want to measure attributes, you can ask whether there is enough or not enough staff to handle the needs of those family members. If you want to measure attitudes, you might offer a ranking scale that ranks the service. And if you want to measure beliefs, you might offer a rating scale.

For all the different question types, you'll run into some more often than others in the world of online surveys. These are single- and multiple-select questions, open-ended text, comment box, and matrix table. Understanding these four basic types will take you a long way down the path of a successfully answered survey.

✔ **Single- and multiple-choice questions:** This is a set of question types that allows respondents to choose from a predefined set of answers.

✔ **Open-ended text:** If you aren't sure what in the world your respondents will say, you can rely on the open-ended the question to let them express themselves freely.

✔ **Comment box:** Comment boxes are customary to online surveys. This is essentially an open-ended text box with multiple lines to allow the respondent to, well, comment.

✔ **Matrix table:** No, not the movie. You use the matrix table question type when you want your respondent to rate a list of dimensions against a list of attributes. (Figure 6-5 shows a sample matrix table question.) For example, it's common to ask someone how important timeliness is in relation to his or her satisfaction with ordering a meal at a fast food restaurant.

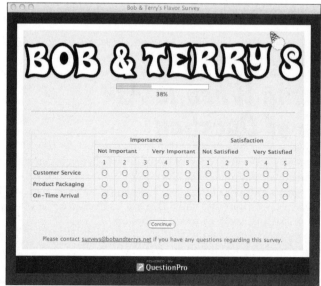

Figure 6-5:
An example
of a matrix
table
question.

Avoiding Question Development Mistakes

Developing questions that people will answer is an art. Like all art, writing strong questions demands plenty of work, patience, and feedback from others. But beware! There are plenty of pitfalls on the road to developing winning questions. You have to be careful about so-called loaded questions, misplaced questions, confusing questions, and other potential problems that can cause your survey to be a big flop. These are the most common problems you'll face as you set out to develop your questionnaire.

Loaded and leading questions

The slightest change in a question's phrasing can produce vastly different results. "Could," "should," and "might" might sound almost the same to you, but interchanging these words can produce a 20 percent difference in agreement to a question. Strong words that represent control or action, (such as *prohibit*) produce similar results; for example, "Do you believe that congress should prohibit insurance companies from raising rates?" Sometimes wording is clearly biased; for example, "You wouldn't want to go to Rudolpho's Restaurant for the company's annual party, would you?"

Misplaced questions

Questions placed out of order or out of context should be avoided like the plague. The second question in Figure 6-6, "What is your favorite ice cream flavor," is irrelevant if the respondent chooses "I don't care either way" or "I hate ice cream" — this just confuses and frustrates the respondent even more. To keep free of this disease, use a funnel approach. Here's how it works: Put broad and general questions at the beginning of the questionnaire as a warm-up. Then add in more specific questions, followed by more generally easy to answer questions like demographics. Misplaced questions are more than just a mistake — they could be a fatal flaw.

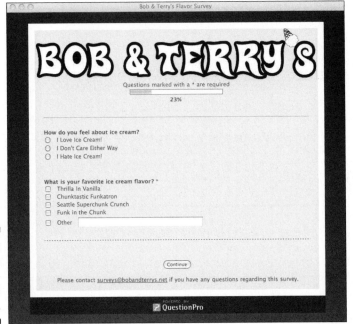

Figure 6-6:
An example of a misplaced question.

Mutually nonexclusive response categories

Multiple-choice response categories should be mutually exclusive so that the respondents can make clear choices. Nonexclusive answers (see Figure 6-7) frustrate the respondent and make interpretation difficult at best. Figure 6-7 should be two separate questions, "Do you think we should sell new flavors of ice cream?" and then, "Do you think we should upgrade the retail uniforms?" You might wind up with inaccurate answers if you fall into this trap.

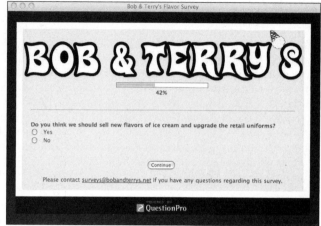

Figure 6-7:
An
example of
nonexclusive
answers.

Nonspecific questions

"Do you like orange juice?" might seem like a clear question to you, but it's not specific enough to offer much information. There are many different aspects of orange juice to like or not to like, such as taste, texture, nutritional content, Vitamin C, the current price, concentrate, fresh squeezed . . . The lesson here? Be specific about what you want to know. This question development mistake might leave your answer basket empty.

Confusing or unfamiliar words

Words like caloric content, bits, bytes, mbs, and other industry-specific jargon and acronyms are confusing. Make sure your audience understands your language level, terminology, and, above all, what you're asking. If you make this question development mistake, you might end up frustrating your consumers, leading to survey abandonment. Or you might get inaccurate answers that throw off your entire analysis — without even knowing it.

Nondirected questions giving respondents excessive latitude

"What suggestions do you have for improving tomato juice?" The surveyor hopes to get information about taste, but the respondent might offer suggestions about texture, the type of can or bottle, mixing juices, or something related to the juice's use as a mixer or in recipes. To avoid this question development mistake, be more specific. For example, "What suggestions do you have for improving the taste of tomato juice?"

Forcing answers

In some cases, the respondents might not want to — or might not be able to — ante up the information requested. Privacy is an important issue to most people. Questions about income, occupation, finances, family life, personal hygiene, and beliefs (personal, political, religious) can be too intrusive, and the respondent might reject them. If you force the answers, you might unknowingly force respondents to drop out of your survey.

Nonexhaustive listings

Do you have all of the options covered? Nonexhaustive listings might leave some of your respondents feeling left out in the cold. If you're unsure, conduct a pretest using the "Other (please specify)" option (see Figure 6-8). Then revise the question, making sure that you cover at least 90 percent of the respondent answers.

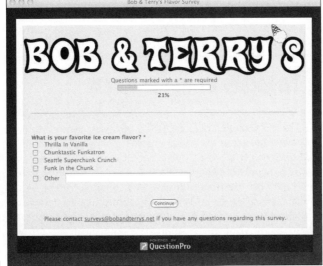

Figure 6-8: An example of giving the respondent an "other" option.

Unbalanced listings

Unbalanced scales might be appropriate for some situations and biased in others. The balanced scale is more appropriate when, for example, measuring alcohol consumption patterns. You might use a quantity scale that makes the heavy drinker appear in the middle of the scale. The extreme opposite ends of the scale, in this case, would reflect no consumption and a nearly impossible amount to consume. An unbalanced listing would be appropriate for a hospital, however, because people expect all hospitals to offer good care. In that instance, you might use a scale of excellent, very good, good, and fair — people do not expect poor care.

Double-barreled questions

"What is the fastest and most convenient Internet service for you?" That's what they call a double-barreled question. Because the fastest might not also be the most convenient, you should ask two questions instead of one. The danger of making this question development mistake is confusing the respondent and getting the answer to part of the question — and you don't know which part.

Keeping questions independent

When you use dichotomous questions, make sure answers are independent. For example, the question "Do you think of basketball players as being independent agents or as employees of their team?" Some people believe that they're both. You should therefore use two separate questions here instead of one dichotomous question.

To know or not to know

Although this chapter deals primarily with question development, sometimes the selection of answers you provide can have an impact on the survey. The "don't know" response is a good example. There are two schools of thought on whether to use "don't know" as a possible response option. On the one hand, some argue that if you don't offer the "don't know" option, you might cause respondents to skip the question because they have no opinion. In that case, you have no way of knowing whether they accidentally skipped the question, whether they skipped it because they didn't want to answer it, or whether they skipped it because their answer was "I don't know."

On the other hand, some argue that offering a "don't know" option is a cop-out for some participants. Imagine getting survey for which half of the responses were "don't know." You either didn't qualify your respondents or they were in too big a hurry to think about how they really felt. The balance here is to use "don't know" when there's a genuine chance that the respondents might not know, such as on questions that relate to product knowledge. For example, a respondent might not know how much horsepower his engine has, but he should know the make and model, the color, how long he's had the vehicle, and so on. Matters of opinion or common knowledge questions shouldn't offer a "don't know" choice in the list of response options.

Long questions

Multiple-choice questions are the shortest and easiest to answer. Open ended questions are the longest and most complex to answer. When you increase the length of questions and surveys, you decrease the chance of receiving a completed response.

Longer surveys see higher survey abandonment rates. *Survey abandonment* is when a person who began taking your online survey decides not to finish it. It could be that their computer crashed or that they were called into a meeting, but survey abandonment is frequently caused by surveys that never seem to end. It's tempting to throw a few additional questions in at the end of the survey since you have a captive audience, but if your questions aren't related to your survey objective you might confuse the participants by suddenly taking a right turn.

Questions on future intentions

Yogi Berra once said that making predictions is difficult, especially when they're about the future. Predictions are rarely accurate more than a few weeks (or in some case months) ahead. It's a major mistake to ask too many questions about future intentions unless, of course, your online survey is truly focused on predicting future behaviors. Even still, the accuracy is questionable because things and people change.

Chapter 7

Building a Compelling Survey

*Y*ou wouldn't build a skyscraper — or even remodel your kitchen — without first gathering the tools and materials you need to do the job right. You'd either waste a lot of time running to Home Depot every day to get something you forgot you needed or you'd build something that would fall apart faster than you put it together.

The same is true of online surveys. Building an online survey that elicits insights to help drive revenue growth, enlist new members, measure employee perceptions, or measure some other organizational goal depends on having the right tools and materials on hand. Your tools are found in online survey software. The materials are the questions themselves.

Of course, you also need to know how to use the tools to actually build the building, or in our case, actually build the online survey. That's where this book, and specifically this chapter, comes in. It offers you a blueprint, if you will, for building a compelling online survey from start to finish without leaving out a single detail in between. That's important because research shows that poor survey design has a direct impact on response rates.

In this chapter, you explore how to use the tools you need to build an effective online survey, how to dive in deeper with some advanced options, and how to delete test data so that it doesn't skew your results. So put on your hard hat and roll up your sleeves — it's time to start building!

Understanding Basic Survey Operations

Building a survey doesn't require a construction license, an architecture degree, or even past experience with online software. The online survey tools are relatively easy to use, even for the beginner. That said, you need to become familiar with your online survey software long before you sit down to actually launch a survey. You'll need to skate a small learning curve before the big day comes.

In a nutshell, the four basic survey operations are add, edit, copy, and delete. These should all be familiar concepts to you if you use other types of software. If not, don't worry — these simple commands are easy to master. With a trial run or two, you'll be well on your way to executing response-generating surveys with your online survey software.

We're going to use QuestionPro as our guinea pig for this chapter. If you've been following along from the beginning of the book, you've already set up an account back in Chapter 3.

Adding a new survey

Maybe you're creating a survey for the first time, or maybe you need a quick reminder on how to add a new survey to your account. If you're ready to get your hands dirty with online survey building, follow these simple steps to create a new survey:

1. **Log in to your QuestionPro account by entering your username and password.**

2. **Click the first tab you see when your account opens — My Surveys.**

3. **Click the Create New Survey box.**

   The Survey Creation Wizard opens.

4. **Select New Survey (From Scratch), click the Next button, enter a descriptive name for the new survey in the text field, and then click the Next button.**

   Make sure to enter a survey name that's logical and easy to remember.

5. **Select a survey theme from the available drop-downs, click the Next button and then click the Finish button.**

6. **On the Edit Survey screen (you'll see the tab at the top has changed to Edit Survey in the upper-left), click the Add a Question to This Survey button.**

7. **Select the question type you want from the available list.**

   You can find out more about question types in Chapter 6.

8. **Enter your question and answers in the appropriate fields (see Figure 7-1).**

   Using multiple choice as an example, you tell the Survey Creation Wizard how many answers you need before entering the question-and-answer text — meaning that if you want to provide three answer choices, you indicate that first before indicating the question-and-answer text. The wizard then shows you what you have entered.

   If needed, click Start Over and change the text or specifications for the question.

Figure 7-1:
Adding a
question to
your survey.

9. **When you're satisfied with the question, click Save Question and the question appears back in the builder (see Figure 7-2).**

10. **Now you're ready to continue by adding your next questions — just repeat Steps 6–9 until you've completed adding questions to your survey.**

With online survey software, it's okay to forge ahead to the end of the questionnaire if you aren't quite sure how you want to phrase certain questions in the middle. You can always come back later and edit your survey after you're done with your first round of survey building. In fact, most survey software tools give you an option to go back and edit as many times as you want. How else could you create the perfect survey?

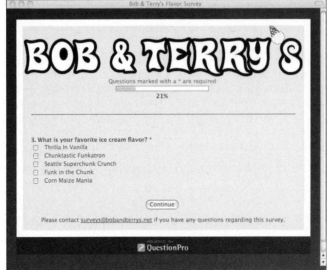

Figure 7-2:
Your
finished
question on
ice cream
flavors.

Edit your survey

Maybe you forgot to ask an important question. Perhaps you made a mistake and need to correct it — a typo, a badly phrased question, or something similar. Don't panic. You can edit your survey for any reason before you send it. It's simple. Here's how to edit a survey in QuestionPro:

1. **Log in to your QuestionPro account by entering your username and password.**

2. **Click the first tab you see when your account opens — My Surveys.**

   A list of all your surveys appears.

3. **Click the Edit link that corresponds to the survey you want to change.**

   This will bring you back to the Edit Survey screen.

4. **Edit questions by clicking the Edit link to the right of each question to make changes to each question in your survey.**

5. **Save changes by clicking the Save Question button (see Figure 7-3) before exiting, or your labor will be in vain.**

The Welcome screen

Everyone likes a warm welcome. Survey takers are no different. That's why many online survey software programs let you put in a Welcome screen, as shown in the following figure. Use the words you use on your Welcome screen strategically because this could be a make or break point in your survey. If you get off on the wrong foot with your would-be respondents before they even start walking through your survey, they might just walk out the virtual door and back to their busy lives.

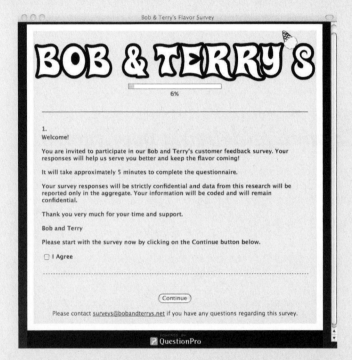

Your Welcome screen should be inviting. It should offer up the title and purpose of the survey, perhaps offer reasons why the participants were selected if applicable, quickly spell out privacy protections, give an estimate of how long the survey will last, and give clear instructions on how to collect any incentives or prizes you offered. Here's the catch: You need to do it all in a few sentences. If you start off with a long letter, you might scare off your would-be respondents. Oh, and don't forget to offer a link that they can click to begin taking the survey and an e-mail address in case they need help or run into technical issues you need to know about.

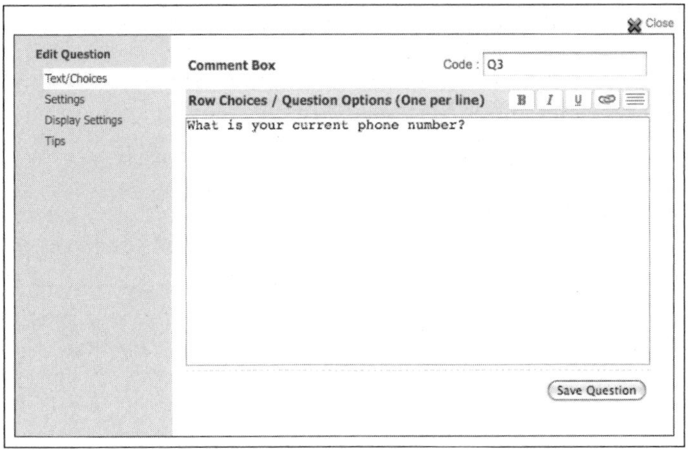

Figure 7-3:
Editing a
question in
your survey.

Copying or deleting your survey

If you're intending to create surveys in multiple languages (you find out more about multilingual surveys in Chapter 8), you'll want to make a copy of your survey for translation. By the same token, if you want to copy your survey to use as a template for a similar survey intended for a different audience, online survey software makes it possible.

Maybe you want to delete a survey altogether because it was merely a practice session or you were using it as a training tool to teach someone else on your team about the virtues of online survey software. Perhaps you decided the online survey was off-base (perhaps your goals changed) and it's easier to start over than to try to do a complete reconstruction.

Copying or deleting an online survey is easy with user-friendly software tools. Here's how to copy or delete a survey using QuestionPro:

1. **Log in to your QuestionPro account by entering your username and password.**

2. **Click the first tab you see when your account opens — My Surveys.**

   A list of all your surveys appears.

3. **Choose the survey you want to copy or delete by clicking the name of the survey.**

4. **Toward the right side of your screen, you'll see several links: Copy, Edit, and Delete. Follow these guides:**

   a. If you want to copy the survey, click the Copy icon and voila — an identical copy of the original survey with all the questions and formatting is created for you.

If you decide to make a digital carbon copy of your online survey, use some wisdom. Create a new name for your copy so that you don't get confused. If you're merely using the copy as a jumping-off point for another, similar online survey and you don't distinguish between the original and the copy, you could wind up causing yourself plenty of extra work.

b. *If you want to delete your survey, click the Delete icon and it disappears from your survey list when you refresh your browser.*

Most online survey software warns you before you delete your survey for all eternity (see Figure 7-4). If you somehow make a mistake and delete your survey by accident, you can typically count on the software to offer the option to "undelete" the survey. It's sort of like the Undo command in Microsoft Word. In QuestionPro, this is called the Recycle Bin (located in the lower-left navigation bar on the My Surveys screen).

c. *If you want to edit your survey, see the previous section in this chapter.*

Figure 7-4:
Deleting your survey and starting over.

Adding a New Question

Now that you have the big picture, it's time to drill down into the nitty-gritty, hands-on aspects of actually inputting your insight-driving questions into the online survey software program. Here's a blow-by-blow description for adding new questions to one of your existing surveys, again using QuestionPro software as an example:

1. **Log in to your QuestionPro account by entering your username and password.**

2. **Choose the survey you want to edit by clicking the name of the survey (you'll then be taken to the Edit Survey screen).**

3. **On the Edit Survey screen, click the Add New Question link.**

   This takes you to the Question Wizard. From the Question Wizard, you'll see a drop-down menu that offers options for the various types of questions you can ask.

4. **Select the question type of your choice and click the Next button.**

5. **Enter the question and answer text on the next screen that appears (see Figure 7-5).**

   You can use the formatting links provided to apply HTML formatting to the question text. This is also where you enter the answer options (one per line).

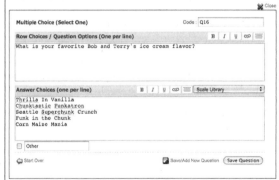

Figure 7-5: Adding question text.

Most survey tools provide the option to assign question codes to each question for your internal reference. These codes can be useful for identifying questions as you're working on your survey. Likewise, you can select various question-numbering options for your convenience.

As you're setting up your question-and-answer options, you'll need to press Enter to indicate the end of one answer option and the beginning of a new one.

If you want to let your respondents choose "other" as a response to your question, select the Other check box. You can also enter your custom text for this option. You can even set up the dimensions for the Text Input box here.

Did you get a last-minute inspiration? Having second thoughts about a particular question or its answer options? Never fear, most tools offer an Edit option so that you can go back and change things.

Check boxes versus radio buttons

Before you go any further, you need to understand the differences between check boxes and radio buttons. It's easy enough to get them confused if you've never heard the lingo, but after you catch on, you'll never forget it.

Also known as *multi-select-based questions,* *check box questions* let users choose more than one option for the same question. You'd want to use this question type to let people "select all that apply." That's different from *single-select questions;* these questions use *radio buttons* that allow respondents to choose

one — and only one — option for a given question. So you might have ten options but want the respondent to make a decision on just one.

If you want a radio button instead of check boxes in your multiple-choice question, you have to be purposeful about it. You need to tell the system that you intend the respondent to select more than one item. If more than one answer choice is allowed, the browser displays check boxes rather than radio buttons. Radio buttons are displayed for single-answer questions only.

6. **If you thought you were finished but you just remembered you forgot a critical question, simply click the Save/Add New Question button and add as many more questions as you want.**

7. **When you're satisfied that you've asked everything you might want to know in this particular survey, click the Save Question button to seal the deal and close the window.**

8. **You can optionally click the Preview button next to your newly added question to view your beautiful new question (see Figure 7-6).**

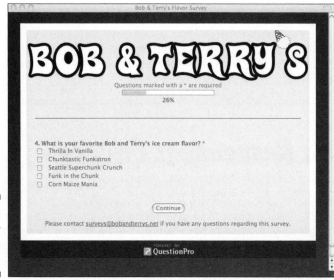

Figure 7-6:
Your newly added question.

The pros and cons of drop-down menus

A *drop-down menu* is a menu of options that appears below the item when the user clicks it. The question is when to use a drop-down menu instead of a list of options with a radio button that participants can click. Here's how it works: The respondent clicks the drop-down menu and the choices are displayed (see the following figure).

The respondent then scrolls to the item he feels best answers the question and clicks that option. Use drop-down menus with caution. If the default answer appears in the text box instead of a "choose your answer" instruction, the respondent might not realize he has a choice or he might think he's already answered the question.

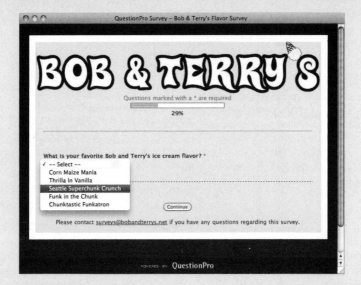

However, you can find value in drop-down menus. Sometimes, your list of possible responses is so long that it would add too much length to the online survey. If your response list would bleed into another page, a drop-down menu is your only logical choice. A good

example is a question about which country someone lives in, or even which state. The list of possibilities is too long to fit on a single screen. Drop-down menus work best. Just be sure that the respondent understands how to use them.

Reinforcing Respondent Privacy

Privacy is a major issue on the Internet today. Advocacy groups are fighting for stricter guidelines, and consumers are growing more protective of how they share their information, and with whom they share it. That's why you need to play up respondent privacy in your online survey. Be sure to take the opportunity in your invitation, at the beginning of your online survey, and at its conclusion (see Figure 7-7) to assure your respondents that the information they share is confidential and that you won't share their e-mail address or other personal data with anyone.

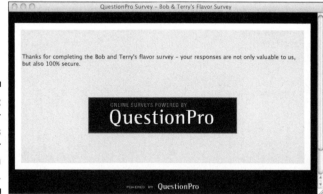

Figure 7-7:
Assure your respondents that their information is safe.

Forcing a Response

Nobody likes to be forced to give an answer to a question — it reminds us of when we were kids and someone broke the window and mom forced us to fess up about who did it. But if you absolutely must have an answer to your question, you can set up your online survey software to force a response. A *forced response* is when the respondent is required to answer your thought-provoking question before he or she can move on to the next question. If you decide to force the issue, here's how to do it using QuestionPro:

1. **Log in to your QuestionPro account by entering your username and password.**

2. **Click the first tab you see when your account opens — My Surveys.**

   A list of all your surveys appears.

3. **Select the survey that contains the question for which you would like to force a response.**

4. **Find the question you want to force a response to and click Settings.**

5. **Select the Enable Validation (Require Response) check box (see Figure 7-8) and click the Save Settings button.**

Select this option

Reordering Questions

There might come a time when you create a survey today and decide tomorrow, right on the brink of launch, that you really need to change the order of the questions to get the best possible responses.

Maybe you're in danger of biasing the survey with your question order. Maybe your first questions are too lengthy or complicated, and you might be in jeopardy of intimidating your participants. Or, maybe you've just decided on a more logical question hierarchy. No matter the reason, good online survey software makes it easy. Here's how to reorder questions using QuestionPro:

1. **Log in to your QuestionPro account by entering your username and password.**

2. **Click the first tab you see when your account opens — My Surveys.**

   A list of all your surveys appears.

3. **Click the Edit Survey link for the survey in which you would like to reorder the questions.**

4. **Find the question you want to reorder and click the Reorder link next to it.**

5. **Move the question to come earlier or later in the survey by clicking the up or down arrow to change its position (see Figure 7-9).**

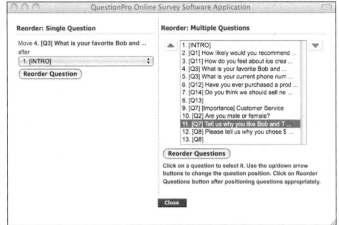

Figure 7-9:
Changing
the order of
a question
in a survey.

6. **When you've placed the question in the desired location in the question list, click the Reorder Questions button to move your questions.**

Survey abandonment typically happens early on in the survey. If you can get your survey respondents past the halfway mark, they're more likely to press on to the end of the questionnaire — especially if you've offered an incentive — because they've already invested so much time in the process. Make the early questions quick and easy to answer, in formats they're most comfortable with, like *dichotomous questions* (generally a yes-or-no question or a male/female question) or multiple-choice questions.

Randomizing the Order of Answer Options

Randomizing the order of answer options in a survey can be a strategic decision. In some cases, it makes sense to randomize the answers of a survey to eliminate any chance of bias from your respondent (see Figures 7-10 and 7-11). Enterprise-level online survey software makes randomizing the order of answer options in your survey as easy as a few clicks with your mouse and a few strokes on your keyboard.

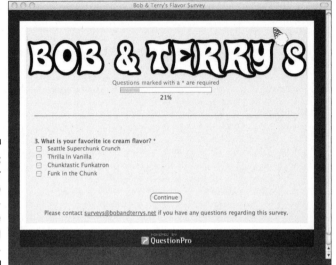

Figure 7-10: Answer options to a question before randomizing them.

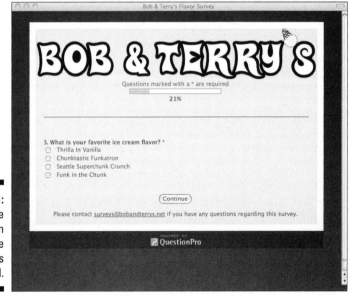

Figure 7-11: The same question with the answers randomized.

Here's how to tap into the power of randomizing the order of answer options using QuestionPro:

1. **Log in to your QuestionPro account by entering your username and password.**

2. **Click the first tab you see when your account opens — My Surveys.**

   A list of all your surveys appears.

3. **Click the Edit Survey link for the survey in which you would like to randomize the order of answer options.**

4. **Find the question you want to randomize the answer options for and click the Edit link next to it.**

5. **Select the Randomize Answer Options option.**

6. **Be sure to click the Save Question button after you're done.**

Making Multilingual Surveys

Do your potential respondents speak languages you've only dreamed you could understand? Are your respondents buying your products in countries you've only dreamed you could visit one day? Whether your respondents speak English, Spanish, French, German — even Chinese and Japanese — or some other language, enterprise-level online survey software offers you the ability to reach them in their own tongue. Here's how to create and execute a multilingual survey using QuestionPro:

1. **Create the survey.**

   First things first: Create the survey in English or the main language you're working with. (See Chapter 3 for more on creating a survey.)

2. **Click the Edit Survey tab in the upper-left to switch to the Edit Survey screen.**

3. **Enable the default language by choosing Display Options in the upper-left navigation bar and then, under the section labeled Language, choosing the default language for your survey from the drop-down list.**

   This will be the initial language for the survey.

4. **Begin configuring the survey for different languages by clicking the Add/Edit Language Versions link.**

5. **In the resulting dialog box, choose the language you'd like to offer to your respondents and click the Add Language Version button.**

   Repeat this step for each language you'd like to add. When you're done, click the Update button and then close the window.

6. **Open the language editor.**

   Click the Add/Edit Questions link in the upper-left to edit the questions in your survey, and then click the Edit button to the right of a question to open the question editor. Now click the Language Version link on the lower-left of the question editor dialog box.

7. **Provide language translations.**

   The drop-down in the upper-right corner will be populated with each language that you added in Step 5. Select the first language, then proceed to fill in each field with the corresponding translated text. Once you're done, click Save Question. Repeat this step for each language you've added from Step 5 and then close the window when you're complete.

8. **Now simply repeat Steps 6 and 7 for each question in your survey.**

When you use multilingual surveys, you can do your data analysis individually for each of the languages. For example, if you want to see how all your Spanish-speaking respondents feel about the taste of ice cream, you can filter out only these results in your reports. You can easily do an analysis of all the results regardless of the language chosen by the respondent — the results are stored in aggregate by default. Simply run the Real Time Summary report (or any report) as you normally would.

Using Question Separators

Question separators (see Figure 7-12) do just what it sounds like they do. (Don't you love it when technology is appropriately named?) *Question separators* break up the survey into multiple pages for a better look and feel. When you add a question to the survey, separators are usually added by default. If you want to remove the question separator, you'll have to take the required steps to do so, but don't worry, it only takes a minute.

Using QuestionPro, you'll notice that after each question, you see a Remove Separator toggle link. To remove the separator, just click this link. The question separator is removed and the link changes to Add Separator, just in case you change your mind and want to reenter the separator.

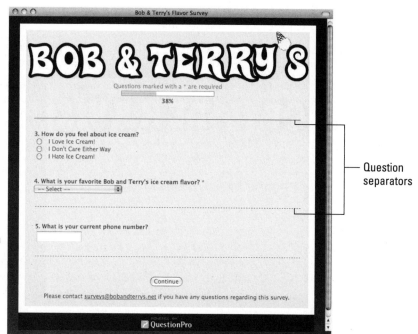

Question separators

Figure 7-12:
Grouping
questions
with a
separator.

If you're wondering why you'd want to remove the separators, here's one good reason: to group certain questions in the survey together. If you want to remove all the question separators at once, just edit your global options in the Edit Survey section (choose Remove Separators from the Options menu).

The value of progress bars

Everybody likes to feel they're making progress toward a given goal. The same holds true with online surveys. Letting your participants know how far they've progressed in your online survey can help reduce survey abandonment rates. That's because if a respondent is three-quarters of the way through your questionnaire, he sees a light at the end of the tunnel. He's most likely to take a few minutes to wrap up the survey before going home for the day or before watching his favorite TV show at night. The progress bar (see the following figure) can backfire if your survey is too long, though. If your respondent has already spent 15 minutes taking your survey and hasn't even hit the halfway mark, there's a strong chance he'll ditch out before wasting any more time.

(continued)

(continued)

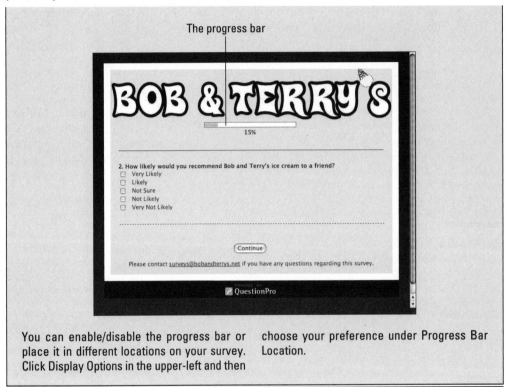

You can enable/disable the progress bar or place it in different locations on your survey. Click Display Options in the upper-left and then choose your preference under Progress Bar Location.

Finalizing Your Survey before You Launch It

Entering your questions into the online survey software doesn't mark the end of your journey. Believe it or not, you're still at the starting line, revving up your engine for a race to marketing research insights. You have a few more steps to complete before you can actually begin your race and eventually cross the finish line — where you'll pick up your prize in the form of online survey results.

Before you launch your well-planned, objective-focused online survey and get the results you're so eagerly expecting, you need to be absolutely sure that your survey isn't going to be derailed and leave your marketing research in flames. You do this by previewing your survey, testing your survey, and finally, deleting your test data.

Previewing your survey

Congratulations. If you're reading this, it means you've built a survey. You've entered all your questions. You've navigated multiple-choice options. You've accessed the question library. Maybe you've even reordered some questions and randomized some answer options. Before you show anyone else your marketing research masterpiece, do yourself a favor: Preview your survey.

As you preview your survey, be careful to slowly move page by page to check for spelling errors, questions that aren't ordered appropriately, and any branching that's been enabled.

Here's how to preview your survey in QuestionPro:

1. **Log in to your QuestionPro account by entering your username and password.**

2. **Click the first tab you see when your account opens — My Surveys.**

   A list of all your surveys appears.

3. **Click the Edit Survey link for the survey you would like to review.**

4. **Click the Preview button at the top of the screen.**

5. **Review your survey.**

   Page through your survey to discover any errors.

6. **Edit your changes.**

   If you've found any issues, go back and edit your survey.

Testing your survey

Testing your survey is vital to a successful launch. If you have any issues with your question development, survey-building skills, or survey length, now is the time to find out. Online survey software companies let you send your survey to a test group before you launch it to your target audience so that you can make any adjustments or improvements.

A best practice is to send your survey to people in your own organization first to work out the initial kinks and bugs. You might find that a link is broken or that a question doesn't offer all the possible answers. These are issues that you should address internally before anyone else sees the survey.

If you want to be doubly careful, test the survey with friends and family who have a more objective view about the topic at hand. You and your team might be too close to the survey at this point to notice subtle issues like question bias or industry jargon. After you get the nod from your test group, you're ready to distribute your survey to the masses. For more on how to distribute your survey, read Chapter 9.

Here's how to send out a test survey using QuestionPro:

1. **Log in to your QuestionPro account by entering your username and password.**

2. **Click the first tab you see when your account opens — My Surveys.**

   A list of all your surveys appears.

3. **Select the survey you would like to send to your test group for review.**

4. **Click the Send Survey tab.**

   This screen allows you to send out an e-mail invitation to your test group. The e-mail invitation is an important part of your testing process. Click the Send Email button.

   You can find customizable features for sending e-mail invitations under the Send Email Invitation link. For this example, we'll use the quick e-mail invitation.

5. **Enter the e-mail addresses for the members of your test group and click the Send button.**

   Enter one e-mail address per line in the To box, as shown in Figure 7-13.

   You can choose to receive an e-mail that contains a copy of the responses from your test group as they come in. This can give you faster feedback. If any issues arise, you can identify them in the response. Of course, the responses are irrelevant for your market research, but they could signal question bias or confusion.

6. **Distribute your survey to your test group by clicking the Distribute My Survey button.**

   Your survey is immediately distributed to your test group.

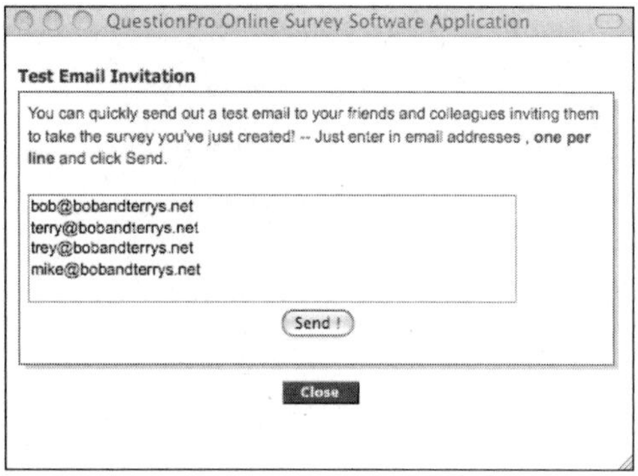

Figure 7-13:
An example
of sending a
test invite to
colleagues.

> QuestionPro Online Survey Software Application
>
> **Test Email Invitation**
>
> You can quickly send out a test email to your friends and colleagues inviting them
> to take the survey you've just created! -- Just enter in email addresses , one per
> line and click Send.
>
> bob@bobandterrys.net
> terry@bobandterrys.net
> trey@bobandterrys.net
> mike@bobandterrys.net
>
> (Send ↑)
>
> Close

Be sure to consult with the test group to get feedback on the ease of use, colors, language, and other aspects of your online survey. This is more than a test of the technology — it's also a test of the actual flow of the online questionnaire.

Deleting test data

There comes a time in every survey's evolution when you need to delete the test data you've collected during test trials. If you forget to clear out all the test data from the database before starting to collect "real" data, your results will be skewed. So tie a string around your finger or put an alert in that smartphone you carry everywhere. Here's how to delete the test data using QuestionPro:

1. **Log in to your QuestionPro account by entering your username and password.**

2. **Click the first tab you see when your account opens — My Surveys.**

   A list of all your surveys appears.

3. **Select the survey you would like to delete the test data for.**

4. **Click the Reports tab.**

   On the Reports tab, you'll see a subsection called Data Management in the lower-left corner.

5. **Click the Delete Survey Data link in the Data Management section.**

6. **Click the Clear Responses button.**

A dialog box opens asking you to verify that you want to clear the results (see Figure 7-14). Click the OK button and you'll have a clean slate. This prevents your results from being skewed when you send your online survey to your target audience.

Figure 7-14:
Deleting
previous
responses in
QuestionPro.

Chapter 8

Exploring Different Survey Types

· ·

· ·

An online survey is an online survey is an online survey. Not quite. Although they share common characteristics, each online survey you conduct is at least slightly different from — if not totally dissimilar to — others.

Sure, every online survey has questions, but some might rely more heavily on complex question types — and in-depth analysis formulas — than others. Yes, every online survey is seeking answers from a target audience, but some might also have broader implications for your brand image. Yes, all online surveys aim to drive actionable information, but some surveys might focus on customer satisfaction while others delve into employee perceptions.

The point is that you find any number of different online survey types you could launch, each with its own nuances. Certain types of online surveys could bring tremendous value to your organization — and you either never thought of them or didn't even know they existed.

At the same time, you have some strategy issues to consider — such as the frequency of your surveys, planning question types for specialty surveys, and exploring classic concepts in market research — that translate well to online survey software. So, if you want to find out more about complex survey functions, you've come to the right chapter.

By the end of this chapter, you'll graduate from novice to guru. You'll understand how to take advantage of lesser-used survey types that can save you time, save you money, and give you a competitive advantage. If you apply what you discover in this chapter, you'll know more about your customers and your employees, and you'll understand how your market strategies could potentially pan out better than you might have ever dreamed possible.

Calling On Customer Satisfaction Surveys

What are your customers saying to you? Sure, you might get a glimpse into the psyche of your customers through the calls they make and the e-mails they send to your customer service department. But, in most cases, the people who take the time to call are angry and upset about some aspect of your service. Although it's helpful to know when customers have an immediate complaint so that you can resolve the problem and restore the relationship, waiting for your customers to contact you with their concerns is a reactive approach — rather than a proactive approach — that won't take you very far down the road to building stronger customer relationships. A proactive approach to building stronger customer relationships is the utilization of customer satisfaction surveys (see Figure 8-1).

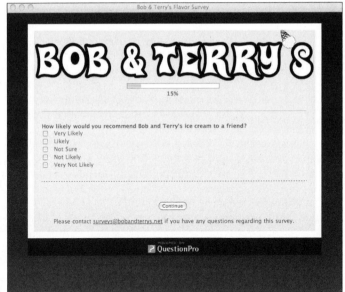

Figure 8-1:
A common customer satisfaction survey question.

Savvy organizations reach out to customers through customer satisfaction surveys designed to uncover their strengths and weaknesses. When you understand your organization's strengths and weaknesses, you can shine public light on your strengths (for example, "Our customers rate us number one for delivery speed"). Just as important, you can shine a private light on your weaknesses with your leadership, roll up your sleeves, and begin working to fix the underlying issues that are causing customer dissatisfaction.

Customer satisfaction survey timing is everything

You've heard it said before: Timing is everything. Yes, it's a cliché, but some clichés are clichés because they're just plain true. When it comes to online surveys that measure customer satisfaction, this cliché fits like the proverbial glove. Timing is vital. You want to send your online surveys to customers as close as possible to the transaction or interaction you have with them.

If you've ever called your bank's customer service number, for example, you've probably been asked more than once to stay on the phone to complete an automated customer satisfaction survey after you finish speaking to the customer service representatives. The bank is trying to get your opinion while your experience is still fresh in your mind. You might also have been alerted to a chance for a ten percent discount on your next purchase at your favorite online retailer if you use the code on the back of your receipt to complete an online survey. It's the same logic. The bank wants to get your insights while the experience is still top of mind. If you distribute your online survey several weeks after a transaction, you might get some overall insights into how the customer feels about your organization, but the details of that transaction might be dim in their memory. That means the online survey results might not be as accurate as they could be.

A closing thought: While *transactional surveys* (surveys that measure the customer's satisfaction in relation to a particular transaction) need to be conducted as quickly after the customer experience as possible, *relationship surveys* (surveys that measure the satisfaction of customers who have an ongoing relationship with your organization) don't mandate such urgency. Transactional surveys measure the pulse of your organization on any given day. Relationship surveys measure the overall health of your brand. If you're merely sending a survey about the general customer perceptions around your brand, you could do this as an annual survey.

The generally accepted rule of thumb with marketing is this: Acquiring new customers is ten times more difficult and expensive than retaining existing ones. This is one of the fundamental driving forces behind the widespread adoption and interest in customer relationship management (CRM) software and related customer retention strategies; customer satisfaction surveys are a customer retention strategy.

Frederick Reicheld of Bain & Company put it this way: "A five percent increase in customer retention rates increases profits by 25 to 95 percent." Satisfied customers not only stay with your organization, but they also refer others to your brand. But dissatisfied customers might tell their friends about their bad experience, and they tell their friends, and so on. It pays to dive into customer satisfaction surveys head first.

Measuring customer perceptions

As with any other survey, successfully measuring customer satisfaction begins with defining your specific objectives. Customer satisfaction is a broad topic in the sense that it can look somewhat different from industry to industry. Customer satisfaction in the fast-food industry, for example, might measure how satisfied a customer is with the taste of the food, the accuracy of the order, or how long she had to wait to get her double cheeseburger, curly fries, and diet root beer.

By contrast, customer satisfaction in the automobile industry might measure aspects such as long-term performance of the car, the layout of the interior features, or the perceived value. For a nonprofit company, customer satisfaction might relate to the organization's ability to reach its stated goals efficiently. And for an e-commerce site, customer satisfaction could be measured by characteristics such as product selection, prices, and order fulfillment. The list goes on and on.

Regardless of what industry you're in, keep this in mind: An effective customer satisfaction survey program should focus on measuring customer perceptions about how well your organization delivers on the critical success factors and dimensions of the business. Broadly speaking, these usually include factors like service promptness, staff responsiveness, and understanding the customer's problem.

Reasons you should conduct customer satisfaction surveys

The Robert Francis Group, a business advisory to IT executives, has done its own research into conducting customer satisfaction surveys. The result: A baker's dozen of reasons why you absolutely must get onboard with customer satisfaction surveys:

1. Demonstrate commitment to listening to customers.

2. Enhance profits.

3. Gain feedback from customers about products, services, and/or support, outside of what customers provide the salesforce.

4. Improve customer satisfaction and retention.

5. Improve quality of service.

6. Increase market share.

7. Increase repeat business.

8. Learn where the company stands in comparison with its competitors.

9. Measure and compensate the sales organization.

10. Obtain information on product developments, priorities, and requirements.

11. Obtain input on new products or services.

12. Provide a way for unhappy customers to vent.

13. Target resources on issues of concern to customers.

Don't fool yourself: A customer satisfaction survey that doesn't gather customer perceptions is no customer satisfaction survey at all. It's a waste of your time — and your customers' time, too. Take the time to plan and design an online customer satisfaction survey that drives insights into how you can improve your products and services.

Deciding on survey frequency

You need to be sure that your customers are satisfied, but you don't want to chase them down with a questionnaire every time they have contact with your company. People are busy, and your efforts to find out whether they're satisfied could lead to an ironic twist — annoying your customers. Deciding how often to conduct an online survey demands a dash of wisdom and a sprinkle of strategy. The baseline is the frequency of customer contact. If your customers visit your shop for maintenance services every six months and you only survey them once a year, you're missing an opportunity to root out any dissatisfaction. You should send them a survey twice a year. If your customers visit your shop every month to purchase supplies, however, the same logic doesn't apply. Sending your customers a survey every month would be overkill, but sending them a questionnaire every quarter shows them you care.

Like any other online survey type, three tips can take you a long way down the road to customer satisfaction insights: Keep it simple, keep it short, and keep your promises. You don't need to ask more than a handful of questions in a customer satisfaction survey. Limit your queries to specific products or customer service in general or the overall company itself so that you don't end up with a five-page survey. You don't want to annoy your customers in your efforts to better serve them, do you? Also, if you promise to improve your customer service in response to the survey, make sure that you follow up and let your participants know what changes you're making so that you don't look like a time-wasting hypocrite.

Understanding the underlying benefits

In a research study by Rice University Professor Dr. Paul Dholakia and Dr. Vicki Morwitz, published in *Harvard Business Review,* an experiment concluded that the simple act of asking customers how a company was performing proved to be a great customer retention strategy. The study was conducted over the course of a year. Researchers sent one set of customers a satisfaction and opinion survey. The other customer group was not surveyed. After a year, twice the number of people from the surveyed group renewed their loyalty toward the company.

The research study offered a couple of interesting rationales based on consumer psychology behind this phenomenon. The research study found that customer satisfaction surveys do the following:

- ✔ **Reinforce positive feelings:** Customer satisfaction surveys reinforce positive feelings about your brand. This stems from part of the human psychology that wants to "appreciate" a product or service that the customer already likes. The survey feedback loop is merely a tool to express this. The survey is a vehicle to "interact" with the company and reinforces the customer's commitment to the company.

- ✔ **Increase awareness of products and services:** Surveys can be considered vehicles of communication — both inbound as well as outbound. Most people consider surveys as a data-collection exercise, but customer satisfaction surveys can also serve as a medium for disseminating information.

It's important to note this caveat: In most countries, including the United States, "selling under the guise of research" is illegal. However, we all know that information is disseminated while collecting information. Additional disclaimers can be added to the survey to make users aware of this fact. For example, you can include a statement such as "We will be collecting your opinion and informing you about products and services that have come online in the last year."

- ✔ **Cause people to form opinions:** The very process of asking people their opinion can cause them to form an opinion about something they might otherwise never have considered. This is a very subtle and powerful argument for conducting online surveys that's similar to the philosophy behind the "product placement" strategy used to market products in movies and television shows. A good example of extensive and exclusive use of product placement is found in the blockbuster movie *The Italian Job* (the vehicle of choice was the MINI Cooper).

Although sending online surveys to your customer base can have this "product placement" effect, proceed with caution. Overuse of this strategy could backfire. This effect should be seen as a side benefit rather than a motivation for conducting online surveys, or you could meet with customer criticism.

Building real-time relationships

Online surveys are a critical tool in the customer relationship dialog. One of the most attractive aspects of online surveys is the ability to carry *bidirectional information,* a two-way information exchange that benefits both sides.

The research conducted by Dholakia and Morwitz (see the previous section) shows that customer satisfaction surveys not only deliver information that is critical for your business but also enhance and build upon the established relationship you have with your customers.

The case for user satisfaction surveys

If your organization serves businesses, your ultimate customer might not be the business itself. It might be the actual users of your products and services. In other words, if you conduct a customer satisfaction survey with a corporate buyer who deals with your company, that buyer might be pleased with the sales process, the price, the speed of fulfillment, and so on. But what about the employees at the company who actually use your products and services on a daily basis? Business-to-business organizations should consider drilling down to the next level: user satisfaction surveys. After all, if the users complain to the corporate buyer, the corporate buyer might eventually look for another source. Your customer satisfaction surveys won't give you a clue that a problem exists, and by the time you figure out that the users are unhappy, you could lose the client.

Recent advances in technology have made it incredibly easy to conduct real-time surveys and opinion polls. Online tools make it easy to frame questions and answers and create surveys on the Web. Distributing surveys via e-mail, Web site links, or even integration with online CRM tools such as Salesforce.com have made online surveying a quick-win solution for building real-time relationships with your customers.

Planning your customer satisfaction questions

Understanding what makes a satisfied customer helps you build better customer relationships. Of course, understanding what makes a satisfied customer depends on asking the right questions. You should include three key questions in any customer satisfaction survey (see Figure 8-2). How you ultimately word them might be different, but the heart of the questions is the same:

- **How satisfied are you with XYZ product?** Put this question early in your survey to avoid the participant being influenced by other, more detailed questions about specific products and services.

- **How likely are you to purchase another XYZ product in X time frame?** When appropriate, include a time frame. If you're asking about cereal purchases, you would ask about the intent to purchase at the customer's next visit. If you're asking about a vehicle, the time frame isn't as important. You might ask, "How likely would you be to buy another Honda when you need a new car?"

- **How likely are you to recommend XYZ product to friends or colleagues?** This is a question that demands a scaled answer, such as "likely, very likely, somewhat likely," and so on. To tally results, you need to set forth common answer types.

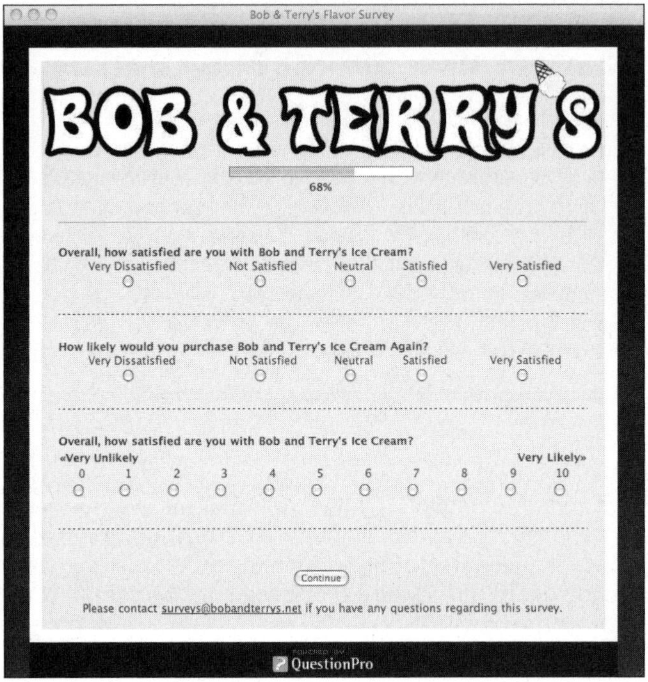

Figure 8-2:
A typical
customer
satisfaction
survey.

These are the so-called staples of customer satisfaction and therefore a good place to begin, but these questions don't drill down into the whys behind the whats. This is where your planning comes in to determine the specific questions and question types to use in your customer satisfaction survey.

Beyond the staples of customer satisfaction surveys, you also need to ask questions that offer insights into specific products and services. Armed with this information, you can brag where you have bragging rights and race to heal your Achilles heel. Here are some of the types of questions you should ask:

✔ **Rate importance:** Ask your customers to rate the importance of your products and services based on characteristics like customer service, product packaging, and timeliness of delivery (see Figure 8-3).

✔ **Rate satisfaction:** Ask your customers to rate their satisfaction with the products and services based on characteristics like timeliness of delivery, customer service, and merchandise options.

✔ **Allow comments:** Allow your customers to express themselves more directly with a comment box.

Be sure to ask a few customer profile questions at the end of the survey, especially if it's important for you to know whether your respondents are male or female, their demographic, their geographic location, or some aspect of product usage, such as frequency, business or pleasure, and so on. You might find out that males and females, for example, have much different perceptions of your products and services. As a result, you need to work harder to please a certain group or make adjustments to your product line or service strategy.

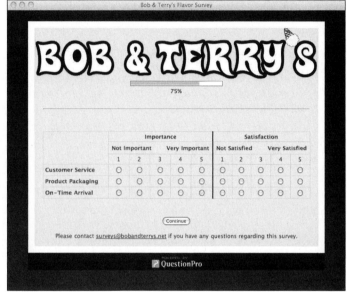

Figure 8-3:
A side-by-
side matrix
question
that
measures
importance
and satis-
faction.

Don't let the suspense kill you. If you want to know how to analyze the results of your customer satisfaction survey, skip ahead to Chapter 13.

Measuring performance attributes

The American Marketing Association (AMA) has taken a keen interest in customer satisfaction surveys — so much so that the organization developed the *AMA Handbook for Customer Satisfaction*. The handbook calls out the performance attributes that most companies should consider measuring. For example, you find product attributes such as value-price relationship, product quality, product benefits, product features, product design, product reliability and consistency, and range of products or services offered by your organization. You also find attributes related to service, such as guarantees or quality, delivery, complaint handling, and problem resolution. Finally, you find attributes related to specific transactions, such as courtesy, communication, ease or convenience of acquisition, company reputation, and company competence. Keep in mind that just because you can measure all of these attributes doesn't mean that you should attempt to measure them all in a single survey. Maintain your focus on the task at hand, such a product design or delivery, and save your other questions for future customer satisfaction surveys.

Conducting a customer satisfaction survey

Conducting a customer satisfaction survey is simple with online survey software. Review the following steps using QuestionPro as an example:

1. **Log in to your QuestionPro account by entering your username and password.**

2. **Click the first tab you see when your account opens — My Surveys.**

3. **If you've already created a survey and want to add new questions to it, select it from your list of surveys in the My Surveys section and then proceed to Step 4.**

   If you're starting a survey from scratch, click the Create New Survey button to open the Create New Survey dialog box.

4. **Enter a descriptive name for the new survey in the text field.**

   Be sure to enter a name that is logical and easy to remember.

   Be sure not to skip over the online survey instructions screen. Without clear instructions, you could be sending your respondents on a frustrating journey. If you need a strategy for how to develop this copy, read Chapter 5.

5. **Select the question type you want from the available list.**

   You discover more about question types in Chapter 6.

6. **Enter your question in the field.**

   Using the multiple-choice example, you would enter the question-and-answer text. For example, if you have five choices, you enter your five choices, one per line (See Figure 8-4).

7. **When you're satisfied, click Save Question and the question appears back in the builder.**

   Now you're ready to continue by adding your next questions.

8. **Repeat Steps 5–7 until you've completed creating or adding to your survey.**

   Don't worry, you can always go back later and make changes.

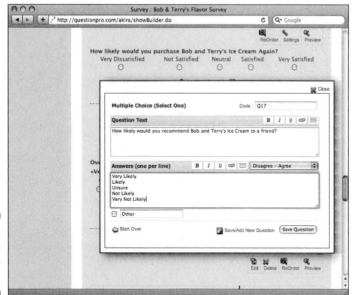

Figure 8-4:
Adding a
question to
your survey.

Measuring Customer Loyalty

Most businesses are faced with a fairly straightforward question today: How do I measure success? Obviously, looking at the balance sheet every month can give you some insights into how your organization is performing. But why wait until the numbers tell you how loyal your customers are — or aren't — when you can be proactive with customer loyalty surveys that tell you far more than your balance sheets ever could?

Customer satisfaction and loyalty go hand in hand with the well-being and long-term growth of your organization. In other words, the success of your company depends on how satisfied and loyal your customers are. If you aren't conducting customer loyalty surveys (or at least including customer loyalty questions in your surveys; see Figure 8-5), you're missing golden opportunities to respond to your customer needs right now. That's because loyal customers lower acquisition costs and increase profitability.

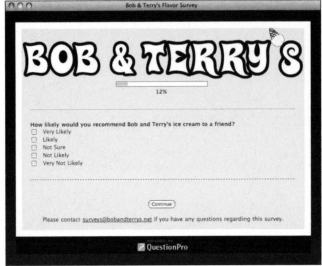

Figure 8-5:
A typical
customer
loyalty
question for
a survey.

Rating your customers' loyalty

Customer loyalty surveys are perhaps the simplest to deploy and analyze. That's because you only need to ask the one magic question and then have your participants rate their answer on a scale of 0 to 10.

Be sure to explain to your survey participants that a rating of 0 means that they aren't at all loyal to your company. Given the chance, participants who give a 0 rating can and will forget about your brand name and rush to a competitor. A participant who gives a loyalty rating of 0 signals that he isn't at all happy with your products and services and might be a good candidate for a customer satisfaction survey so that you can find out where you went wrong — and hopefully win him back. On this same scale, a rating of 10 means that the customer is as loyal as your mother. You'd have to really screw up — and screw up repeatedly — to push this customer away.

Categorizing loyalty scores

After you've collected your customer loyalty responses, you can categorize them into three different segments:

- ✔ **High scores:** Scores of 9–10 are outstanding. These customers are your *promoters* and *idea merchants* — they're very satisfied and will trumpet your product or service any chance they get.

- ✔ **Middle scores:** Scores of 7–8 signal room for improvement. These customers are *passively satisfied* — they might be loyal to a degree, but a

better price or a new competitor might just as easily woo them away if
you aren't careful.

- ✔ **Low scores:** Scores of 0–6 mean you're heading for a disaster just off-
shore. These customers are the *detractors* — they're fairly unsatisfied with
you, and they'll most likely leave you for a competing product or service.

Analyzing loyalty scores

Analyzing loyalty scores is fairly simple. If 60–70 percent of your customer
base scores between 9 and 10 on the rating scale (in other words, very happy
with your product or service), congratulations. Your brand is benefiting from a
word-of-mouth sales force that's beating the streets for you 24/7/365. Your customers are generally happy with your product offering and are willing to put
their reputation on the line for you by recommending your product or service.
By contrast, if 60–70 percent of your customer base scores between 0 and 6 (in
other words, they're unhappy with your product or service), you need to call
an emergency meeting. Your company could soon go out of business, leaving
you to conduct market research on what went wrong as you look for a new job.

The Net Growth/Satisfaction score is another important customer loyalty measurement. You can determine this score by taking the percentage of promoters
(high scores) minus the percentage of detractors (low scores). The result is a
net indication of how many customers are effectively growing your company.

Customer loyalty or customer satisfaction?

You might be wondering why a customer loyalty survey is necessary when a customer
satisfaction survey already asks how likely the
customer is to purchase your product or service again. The answer lies in the statistical
phenomenon call *sample bias* — data that's
skewed because the selection of a sample is
not representative of the target population.

Most traditional customer satisfaction surveys
tend to be long and cumbersome and demand
a lot of time and attention from your customers. This leads to a very low response rate. This
low response rate, in turn, does not accurately
represent your customer base. For example,
customers who are unhappy are not likely to go
through a long customer satisfaction survey.
The other challenge with traditional satisfaction

surveys is that they're much more difficult to
analyze and might produce ambiguous results.
Customer satisfaction surveys have their place,
but management might be more inclined to rush
to action if they see customer loyalty survey
results that are, well, in the toilet.

Customer loyalty surveys skirt these issues.
Think about it: If your customers get an e-mail
with a single question embedded, the response
rate to such a quick-to-complete survey will
be much higher. The higher response rate can
eliminate the sample bias, and you have the
relevant data that you need. You can conduct
longer customer loyalty surveys with a select
group of customers and ask questions, but
oftentimes less is more if you're looking for the
most accurate measure.

Customer loyalty surveys in action

Customer loyalty surveys are so vital to your organization that a couple of mini–case studies are in order. QuestionPro, for example, believes in practicing what they preach, so every time a user clicks the Logout button to exit the online survey software, QuestionPro serves up a single question to the user. Sometimes it's a question about features. Other times it's a question about general customer satisfaction. Still other times, it's a comment box. These questions come from a pool of predefined questions so that the user doesn't always get hit with repetitive queries.

The result: QuestionPro consistently sees that the response rate on the question "Would you recommend this service to a friend or colleague?" is higher than that for any other questions. QuestionPro puts this information into action in two distinct ways:

- ✔ First, the company uses the data to continuously monitor its customer satisfaction score. Any dips and spikes can be generally correlated to marketing events or changes in customer service training.

- ✔ Second, it helps the company set goals for the support and marketing staff. For example, if scores are down, the company not only needs to set goals to raise the score but also perhaps needs to hold training sessions with customer service staff or launch new marketing promotions.

Reichheld's customer satisfaction research study (published in the *Harvard Business Review*) looked at Enterprise Rent-A-Car's use of customer loyalty surveys. Every month, Enterprise asks its customers just two simple questions: "What was the quality of your service?" and "What is the likelihood that you will rent from Enterprise again?" With simple questions, Enterprise is able to gather and publish results in real time, giving its U.S. branches quick feedback on how they are performing while also offering an opportunity to learn from the best practices of better-performing branches.

Reichheld put it succinctly in his article: "The path to sustainable, profitable growth begins with creating more promoters and fewer detractors and making the net-promoter number transparent throughout your organization. This number is the one number you need to grow. It is that simple and that profound."

This quote underscores a basic concept: Online survey software tools not only make it easy to implement customer satisfaction and customer loyalty surveys, but they also assist you in proactively measuring the success of your relationship with your customers. A project that used to demand three to six months and a staff of technology experts to complete can now be accomplished in a single day. Companies that take advantage of online survey software can advance their goals and have a distinct advantage over the competition.

Feeling competitive? Many companies have adopted the net-promoter score as a standard benchmark for customer loyalty. As a result, it's a great way for you to compare how you're doing with the rest of your industry.

Conducting online shopping cart abandonment surveys

In the world of e-commerce, sometimes customer satisfaction surveys aren't possible — especially when your would-be customers abandon their shopping cart before you seal the deal. *Shopping cart abandonment* is when a visitor leaves your site in the midst of a transaction.

Your Web Analytics software can tell you in no uncertain terms your *shopping cart abandonment rate,* which is the rate at which visitors exit a Web site during the shopping-cart process before completing the sale. (For a good study on Web Analytics, pick up Wiley's *Web Analytics For Dummies,* by Pedro Sostre and Jennifer LeClaire.) But your Web Analytics software can't tell you why visitors abandoned the shopping cart. The good news is that online surveys can.

 Understanding why people abandon shopping carts and registration pages gives you the opportunity to make improvements to your site. Maybe you had too many steps in the checkout process or the registration form was too long. You can't optimize if you don't realize what the issue is. You can program your online survey software to pop up with a question when customers leave your site (see Figure 8-6) so that you can get the information you need to avoid the same scenario with other customers.

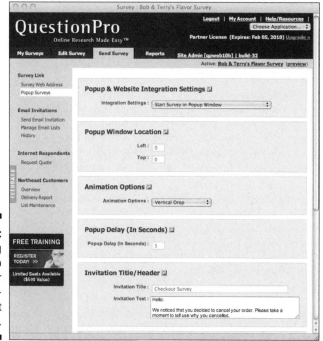

Figure 8-6: Configuring a pop-up window for an abandonment survey.

Conducting Employee Exit Interviews

Employee exit interviews. Nobody likes to conduct them, but employee exit interviews hold valuable information that you need to make your organization a better place to work. Employee exit interviews cover everything from benefits and working conditions to opportunities for career advancement and the quality and quantity of the workload (see Figure 8-7) to relationships with coworkers and supervisors.

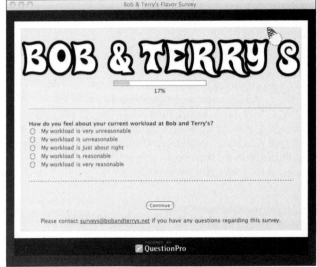

Figure 8-7:
An employee feedback question.

Employee exit interviews might offer insights that help you recruit new employees and retain the ones you have. Employee exit interviews can even help your organization avoid costly lawsuits by documenting the real reasons for the stated departure. An employee who first told you he was leaving for family reasons and later files a discrimination claim will have a harder time proving his case in court if you can provide a signed exit interview.

An employee exit interview has several elements and is commonly divided into three broad sections: reasons for joining the company, the reasons for leaving, and an analysis of employee exit trends among various departments in the company. Within these sections, the survey deals with questions about the job itself, the supervisor, the department, management, compensation and benefits, and open comments.

Getting a quick pulse on the employee

The employee exit survey's introduction and initial multiple-choice questions give you a quick pulse on why employees joined your company in the first place and why they decided to leave. These sets of questions can help you answer questions like these:

- ✔ What is the most important reason people choose to work in the company?
- ✔ What are the top three reasons employees are leaving the company?
- ✔ How do the reasons vary with the various departments within the organization? For example, do employees in the IT department leave because of salary issues more than other departments?

Rating job attributes

The next series of questions allow the employee to rate the different attributes, such as the job itself or the management. A five-point scale is typically the most appropriate way to measure job attributes. These sets of questions can help you identify potential problem areas within your organization that are causing people to leave.

If an employee ranks a particular item low — perhaps he strongly disagrees with a statement such as "My workload is reasonable" — you can signal your online survey software to automatically present the exiting employee with an open-ended text question. This allows the employee to express himself directly and gives your Human Resources department an opportunity to discover problem areas in the organization and decide how to address persistent problems. The employee might even offer suggestions about what can be done to improve the situation. If it's a valuable employee, HR might be able to work through the issue and retain the employee by taking his or her suggestions.

Closing survey gaps

In the third and final section of the employee exit interview, you can ask additional open-ended questions to capture data that might not have been covered in the other areas of the survey. This section should be monitored for gaps in the survey itself.

Do your employees have an attitude?

The most successful businesses are constantly keeping a close eye on their employees' attitudes. *Employee attitude surveys* offer a series of multiple-choice items grouped along one or more dimensions of the organization. Employee attitude surveys can be used to solicit employee opinions on a variety of topics such as the company's success in communicating its mission to employees, or local issues such as the quality of the working environment. With online survey software, you can create an employee attitude survey to track your employees' attitudes toward your company and trend them over time. If something changes — for better or worse — you can investigate the potential root causes and make improvements where necessary.

If a large percentage of people have comments about a particular issue, it should be added to the rating attribute section of the survey so that you can capture that data qualitatively and measure it analytically. For example, if a large percentage of people have comments or issues with working excessive hours, it usually makes sense to add that as an item in the job attributes section of the interview.

An employee exit interview might not be necessary if you take the steps to make sure that your employees are happy right where they are. Thankfully, you can conduct other survey types among your employees, such as employee satisfaction surveys (see Figure 8-8), job evaluations, training evaluations, company evaluations, and employee attitude surveys.

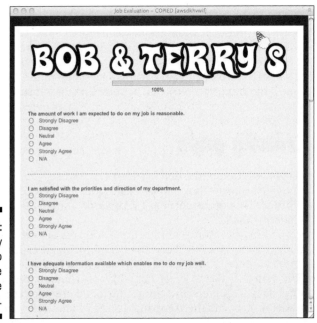

Figure 8-8:
A survey used to measure the pulse of the employees.

Conducting Market Research 2.0

The concept of Web 2.0 — the second, more interactive generation of the World Wide Web — has ushered in Web-based software that allows everyday Joes to perform complex tasks. Web 2.0 has impacted the world through social media, but it's also impacting the market research world through sophisticated tools often referred to as Research 2.0. Research 2.0 goes beyond the qualitative approach to market research with its structured questions and answers.

One example is Ipsos Mori. The group has done some cutting-edge experiments with its Opinionator Web site. The site lets users offer their opinions as statements, and others rate and comment on them. Meanwhile, Nielsen BuzzMetrics launched BlogPulse, an automated trend-discovery system for blogs. BlogPulse applies machine-learning and natural-language processing techniques to discover trends in the highly dynamic world of blogs.

Online survey software offers its own versions of advanced research capabilities. Instead of social media aspects, though, it offers sophisticated statistical models that provide insights into not just what people think, but how people behave. Indeed, some online survey software tools give the ability to predict what might happen if your organization does X, Y, or Z. One example is the Total Unduplicated Reach and Frequency (TURF) analysis tool.

Understanding the TURF Analysis

TURF is a statistical model that can be used to answer questions such as "Where should we place ads to reach the widest possible audience?" and "What kind of market share will we gain if we add a new model to our product line?"

The TURF analysis isn't completely new. It was originally developed to analyze media campaigns. But it has since been expanded so that market researchers can apply it to product, line, and distribution analysis. With some enterprise-level online survey software products, any multiple-choice answer can be analyzed using TURF, and you can discover the optimal configurations for maximizing *reach,* the proportion of your target audience that chooses a particular option.

Maximizing reach with TURF

TURF analysis is a very powerful technique that estimates market potential for a particular product or service. We'll use an example of an ice cream company that only has the resources to create one combination of two different flavors of ice cream. The company has to figure out which two flavors will satisfy the greatest quantity of its customers. But thousands of different ice cream flavor combinations exist — how can the company decide which two to produce?

The simple solution is to run an online survey, asking respondents for their favorite ice cream flavors. After the surveys are completed, most companies would pick the two flavors with the highest frequency in the survey data and start mixing up ice cream. However, this approach doesn't always lead to the most customers. Why? Consider Figure 8-9, which shows data from respondents who are asked, "Choose two of your favorite ice cream flavors from the list below."

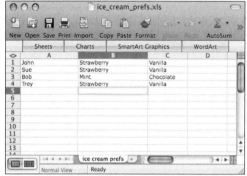

Figure 8-9: Example result set from an ice cream preference survey.

If you apply a simple frequency analysis (see Figure 8-10) to this data set (essentially choosing the two ice cream flavors that were most popular), you'll see that vanilla and strawberry were chosen most often. You might think that because these are the most selected, these must be the customers' favorite ice cream flavors.

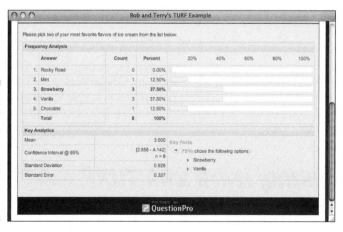

Figure 8-10: A frequency analysis using the real-time summary report in QuestionPro.

However, a simple TURF analysis can make you think twice about vanilla and strawberry. Look at the data in Figures 8-9 and 8-10 again. Per our frequency analysis, we would make John, Sue, and Trey quite happy (they chose vanilla and strawberry). Bob, on the other hand, would be bummed: We decided not to produce a product with either chocolate or mint — two of his favorite flavors. Our *reach* would be 75 percent of the population, or three people (John, Sue, and Trey). Now 75 percent might not be bad for some things in life, but when it comes to customer satisfaction, we want 100 percent. How do we get it? Keep reading.

Eliminating duplicate choices

The goal of TURF analysis, in the case of the example in the preceding section, attempts to answer this question: What two combinations of flavors would satisfy the largest number of customers? This is what is known as maximizing your *reach*. Taking a look back at Figure 8-9, you can see that choosing to produce any of these ice cream flavor combinations would give us a 100 percent reach: mint and strawberry, mint and vanilla, strawberry and chocolate, or vanilla and chocolate. In other words, choosing to produce any of these combinations would satisfy the desires of John, Sue, Trey, and even Bob. TURF analysis lets you dig deeper into your data and satisfy more customers.

Simulating configurations

Thankfully, most online survey packages offer a TURF simulator tool that can test every combination of answers with just a click of a mouse button. Using our previous ice cream example, you can use a TURF simulator to find the optimal choices that give you the maximum unduplicated reach. The tool runs through every possible configuration of choices at a time and gives you a sorted order of reach percent.

Review the following steps using QuestionPro as an example:

1. **Log in to your QuestionPro account by entering your username and password.**
2. **Click the first tab you see when your account opens — My Surveys.**
3. **Click the Reports link next to the survey you'd like to analyze with the TURF simulator.**
4. **Click the TURF Analysis link in the left navigation bar.**

5. **Click the Run Analysis link next to the question you'd like to analyze.**

   This loads the data set.

6. **Click the Simulator tab.**

   This takes you to the TURF simulator.

7. **Choose the simulation count.**

   Here you pick the number of combinations you'd like to test. In our ice cream example, we're looking for a combination of two flavors of ice cream, so we choose 2 from the Simulation Count drop-down menu.

8. **Click the Simulate Choices button.**

   This provides you with a report with every combination of ice cream flavor, sorted by reach percentage (see Figure 8-11).

   Using the TURF simulator, you see that a simple frequency analysis can lead you astray. Think about using TURF the next time you analyze your data — you might find a few needles in the haystack.

Figure 8-11:
Running the
TURF
simulator.

Part III

Distributing Your Survey to Target Audiences

The 5th Wave   By Rich Tennant

"Look-what if we just increase the size of the charts?"

In this part . . .

In this part, we show you how to prepare to launch your online survey by selecting your target audience, considering how you'll track responses, and pondering online survey publishing methods. We also help you steer clear of spam complaints — an absolute must in an age where violating spam laws can land you in a heap of trouble. We help you avoid these woes by spelling out your compliance options and showing you how to use spam compliance tools.

With the planning behind you, it's finally time to send your survey to the masses. You discover how to create an effective survey e-mail invitation, upload your e-mail addresses, and gently nudge your survey respondents (just in case they don't rush to your online survey site to offer up their all-important opinions). We also guide you through what's appropriate and how to demonstrate your best Web etiquette once your respondents have so graciously spent their valuable time to complete the survey.

Finally, we show you how to administrate the back end of your survey for ultimate flexibility. You discover how to prevent certain users from taking your survey, manually add in paper-based responses from hybrid surveys, tinker with time zones, and even print hard copies of your survey to share at your next market research meeting.

Chapter 9

Preparing to Launch Your Online Survey

*B*efore you send your survey to the masses, you have a few more decisions to make. Do you want to act like the Orwellian Big Brother and track your respondents back to their e-mail address for the possibility of future marketing opportunities? Or would you rather allow your respondents to have complete anonymity? Most online survey software applications give you the choice.

You also need to decide whether you want to publish your survey with a link or as a pop-up, or just send it through an e-mail invitation — or perhaps all three to maximize your response rates. Your decision on how to publish your survey will depend, in part, on whether you want to track your respondents or let them keep the brown bag of anonymity over their heads.

In this chapter, you discover how to select your target audience, set up your survey to track respondents or leave them anonymous, and publish your survey as a link or a pop-up. As you become more familiar with the world of online surveys, you might discover that different approaches work better for different surveys, and you can develop a list of internal best practices based on experiences with your target respondents. (For more information on best practices, read Chapter 18.)

Selecting Your Target Audience

You wouldn't ask a six-year-old girl which arthritis medicine works the best for her. Likewise, you wouldn't ask a 66-year-old man which pacifier comforts him the most. In other words, your questions should be appropriate to your target audience in content, tone, and sophistication. You can't reach out to audience members and compel them to respond without knowing who you're trying to reach and compel. Knowing your target audience, then, is vital to online surveying success.

It might sound simple to select a target audience. After all, you should know your organization's target, right? True, but different surveys seek different information. For example, is your target audience people who have been using your goods and services since you launched them? Or are the target folks those who have recently started using your goods and services? Is your target some subsection of users, such as women in Ohio or Hispanics or people who make more than $40,000? The better you define your target for a specific survey, the more accurate your results will ultimately be.

Here are a few suggestions for narrowing your target audience:

- ✔ By age, race, sex, or some other demographic
- ✔ By geographical location
- ✔ By recreational interests
- ✔ By problems they need to solve or challenges they face
- ✔ By specific behavior patterns (such as how often they do business with your company or how often they buy the product in question from any company)

These are just a few of the potential qualifiers that can help you get the precise answers you need from exactly the types of people you want to take your survey.

Recruiting Your Target Audience

If you know who your target audience is, you've cleared one hurdle to successful online surveys. But identifying your target audience is one thing — recruiting the audience members to take the survey is another. As you prepare to launch your online survey, consider how you'll gain access to your target audience.

You could send out a postcard to your mailing list, but this adds costs to your online survey and might contradict the reasoning behind using a Web-based tool to begin with. And what if you send out a postcard announcing your online survey to your target audience but your targets aren't very active online? The answer: They might not be comfortable with using online software tools and won't participate in the survey. In such cases, you might be better off choosing a different type of market research. For a comparison of various forms of surveys you can conduct, see Chapter 1.

In the world of online surveys, the three most common tools for recruiting people to complete your questionnaire are

- E-mail invitations
- Links to the survey on your Web site
- A pop-up window on your Web site that compels people to click through to the survey

Utilizing Online Panels to Obtain Your Target Audience

As you look at options for recruiting your target audience, you have to make a decision. At this important fork in the road, you need to figure out whether you're better served by building your own *online panel* or list of respondents or engaging an outsourced panel provider.

You can't always rely on the quality of survey respondents from external vendors. Sometimes it makes strategic sense to build out your own panel of respondents for market research studies.

When to consider building an online panel

In cases where you're dealing with a niche market, it makes sense to invest the time and effort in building out your own online panel of respondents.

Thanks to advances in technology and a competitive marketplace, the job of building out a panel is relatively easy. Just as companies have already figured out a way to provide a point-and-click interface to develop an online survey, you can also build out an online panel by using Web-based software. Within minutes, you can start collecting people who are interested in taking surveys.

Building out your own panel does take time — you'll need to set up the panel, manage the users, and most importantly, invite your customers to the panel. Finding respondents to join your panel can sometimes be challenging — if your business just started, for example. Another option is to simply engage an outsourced panel provider (which is essentially renting a panel).These panel providers are always recruiting people who are willing to take surveys for rewards or payment. When its time to launch your survey initiative, the providers will distribute your survey to their panel of survey takers on your behalf.

Our experience has shown another welcomed side effect to developing your own panel: Executives tend to trust the data generated by self-recruited panels much more than outsourced panels. The general perception is that self-recruited panels represent your customer base more accurately than outsourced panels.

Encouraging analytical decision making

One of the goals of a panel-based research initiative is to encourage analytical business decision making. An online panel not only encourages members within your organization to rely on research practices, but it also enables you to deliver forward-thinking solutions to complement your marketing initiatives.

Speaking from personal experience, some of the most innovative ideas that we've developed have actually been initiated by our customers. A panel-based research initiative enables the free flow of information back and forth on an ad hoc basis. This, coupled with the ability to project data into the future, gives your organization a significant advantage over your competitors.

Configuring your survey for panel integration

If you've decided to purchase a sample of respondents from a reputable panel company, you need to configure your survey to redirect to the company's servers upon completion so it can track the respondent. Most online survey providers can program this for you or will offer you a way to set this up yourself with a few simple mouse clicks. To enable this tracking in QuestionPro, follow these steps:

1. **Log in to your QuestionPro account by entering your username and password.**

2. **The very first tab you see when your account opens is called My Surveys. Click it.**

3. **Click the Edit link for the survey you want to configure for panel integration.**

4. **From the left navigation menu, click Finish Options.**

5. **From the drop-down list provided, choose the panel company's name, as shown in Figure 9-1.**

   You're presented with a survey URL link that you need to forward to your sample provider.

6. **E-mail the link to the sample provider so it will know the URL to use for your study.**

FEEDBACK

Figure 9-1:
Configuring
your survey
for sample
providers.

Using E-Mail to Recruit Survey Respondents

If you don't want to wait for people to stumble onto your survey (or if you want to make sure you're covering all your bases), you can choose to send an e-mail invitation to people and ask them to complete your survey. Of course, you need a list of e-mail addresses in order to do that. If you do have a strong internal mailing list, you're in good shape.

You can also rent e-mail lists, but there are plenty of dubious dealers out there, and the CAN-SPAM Act is always lurking in the background waiting to penalize people who break the law. If you don't rent a reputable list, you might end up being labeled a spammer or getting in trouble with the federal government. For more about spam laws, check out Chapter 10.

You can use e-mail as the vehicle to recruit survey respondents in three basic ways: attaching the survey to the e-mail, embedding the survey into the body of the e-mail, or including a link in the e-mail to the survey. Each option has pros and cons.

Your online survey e-mail invitation needs to be enticing in order to convince folks to click through to your survey. To find out more about how to write a compelling e-mail invitation, turn to Chapter 16. You can also find lots of tips there for increasing your response rates.

Attaching the survey to the e-mail

This method avoids your respondents having to link to your online survey. The recipient would open the attachment, download the survey, complete it, and send it back to you as an attachment. But this method is rife with downsides. For starters, people don't like e-mail attachments coming from people they don't know well because there are so many scammers, spammers, and hackers out there using e-mail as a way to distribute viruses. In addition, many respondents may feel uncomfortable knowing that their e-mail address is directly linked to their response — losing any hope of being anonymous. Finally, there is significant room for human error with this process (forgetting to attach the file to the e-mail, for example).

If you use this option, you stand a good chance that few recipients will respond to your survey. This is also a cumbersome method for all parties involved, and even if the recipients send a response it could get lost in cyberspace.

Embedding the survey in the e-mail

Embedding the survey in the body of the e-mail is one solution for eliminating the cumbersome steps of attaching the survey to the e-mail itself. This appears to be an easy route to getting answers because the respondents can click Reply, answer the questions right in the body of the e-mail, and send it back to you. But if they don't have time to finish the entire survey in one sitting (or their e-mail program or computer crashes), they might lose the work they've done so far and might be too frustrated or too busy to try again.

Embedding the survey in the e-mail might be an okay approach for short surveys, but even still, someone from your organization has to analyze the answers, and that's difficult to do without entering them into a database that can crunch the numbers. This approach also kills any hope of complete anonymity because you can see where the responses came from.

E-mailing a link to the survey

If you're using online survey software, sending a link to your survey in the body of the e-mail (see Figure 9-2) is the best practice. It solves all the issues of the other options. With a link, the respondents are guaranteed anonymity, don't have to worry about losing their answers mid-way through the survey if their computer crashes (most online survey software programs save your answers and let you go back and finish later), and the threat of e-mail viruses is lessened for those who have opted in to your surveys.

Bob and Terry's Customer Feedback Survey — Inbox
Delete Junk Reply Reply All Forward Print To Do
From: Bob and Terry <info@bobandterrys.net>
Subject: Bob and Terry's Customer Feedback Survey
Date: August 26, 2009 9:29:10 AM PDT
To: Robert McCord Hoehn
BOB & TERRY'S
Hello Rob:
Here and Bob and Terry's, we take great pride in our customer service. As a valued customer, we'd like to ask for 10 minutes of your time to take our short survey so we can continue to serve you better: click here to start survey
Thanks!
Bob and Terry
Powered By: QuestionPro
Privacy | Security
Surveys | Email Marketing | Web Polls
Survey Analytics | 3518 Fremont Ave N #596 | | Seattle | WA | 98103 | USA
Unsubscribe | Report Abuse
Link to the survey

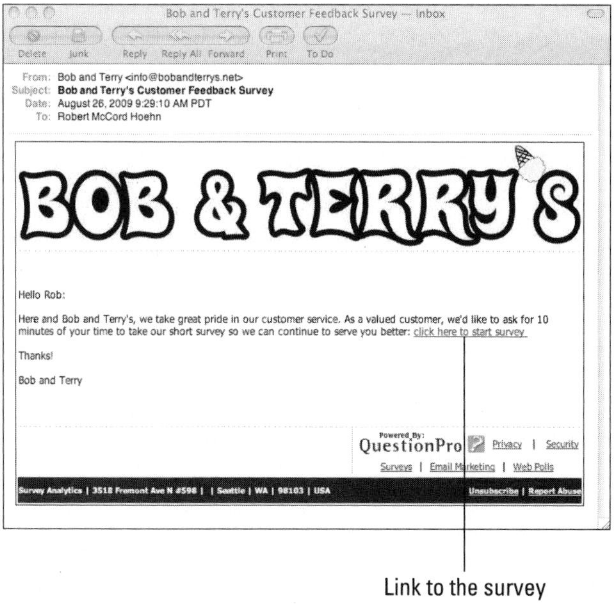

Figure 9-2: Using an e-mail invitation to link to your survey.

Publishing Your Survey as a Link on Your Web Site

If you've decided you don't want to track your respondents, you have the option of publishing your survey as a link on your Web site. All you have to do is use your e-mail program to create an e-mail list with all the addresses of the people to whom you want to send the survey. Then, copy and paste the link into an e-mail inviting respondents to complete the survey.

If you publish your survey as a link on your Web site, you can also use banner ads to advertise (and link to) your survey on as many sites as you'd like. Although the creation of banner ads is beyond the scope of this book, using them allows you to drill down to your specific target audiences. For example, if you need sports fans, you can advertise your survey on sites that draw that kind of traffic.

Publishing your survey as a link on your Web site means that you'll be collecting "anonymous" responses. In other words, you won't know any identifying information about the respondent, such as name or e-mail address, unless you actually ask for this information as a question in your survey.

Creating a link is simple. Here's how to do it using QuestionPro:

1. **Log in to your QuestionPro account by entering your username and password.**

2. **The very first tab you see when your account opens is called My Surveys.** Click it.

3. **From your list of surveys, select the survey you want to publish with a link.**

4. **Click the link for the Send Survey option.**

5. **On the Linking to Your Survey page (see Figure 9-3), enter the survey Web address (URL) and then copy the HTML that includes the link to your survey.**

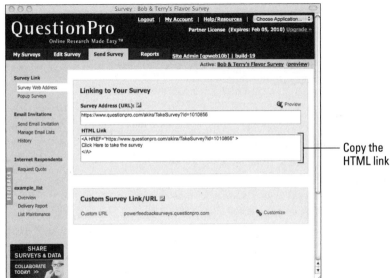

Figure 9-3: Entering the survey URL and HTML link to your survey.

6. **Paste the HTML link into your Web page.**

   Edit the Web page where you're like to publish the link, pasting the HTML link into the Web page.

7. **Check your site to make sure the link is working.**

   Go to your Web site and check the page where you placed the HTML link to make sure everything is working. If something went wrong, repeat this process and try again. It might be you forgot to save the edits to your Web page.

Publishing your survey as a link on your Web site can be convenient, and the advantages of this method are many:

✔ You don't need an e-mail list, nor do you have to send out your survey to recipients. (However, you can use this as a supplement to your e-mail invitations.)

✔ If you're linking to your survey by using banner ads, you can target niches that might be interested in your survey, like sports fans or dog lovers, by publishing the banner on relevant sites.

✔ The power to respond or not respond is in the hands of the site visitors — you aren't intruding on them in any way, but merely offering an opportunity to share their opinion.

The disadvantages of publishing your survey as a link are also many:

✔ People might not click on your link (or banner) — if your link (or banner design) isn't compelling they might be turned off by it, and if it's not positioned strategically on the site they might not see it.

✔ If you're linking to your survey by using banner ads, Web sites don't have to allow you to publish your banner, and even if they do the cost might be prohibitive.

✔ It might take you longer to get enough responses to constitute a full sample because it's a more passive approach to recruiting.

Publishing Your Survey as a Pop-Up on Your Web Site

Have you ever seen those pop-up survey invites while you're browsing the Web? Pop-ups can be an effective way to get the attention of folks browsing your site. That's why reputable online survey software providers offer *JavaScript code* — a scripting language most often used for client-side Web development — that you can use to set up pop-up surveys on your site. Here's how to publish your survey as a pop-up by using QuestionPro:

1. **Log in to your QuestionPro account by entering your username and password.**

2. **The very first tab you see when your account opens is called My Surveys. Click it.**

3. **From your list of surveys, select the survey you want to publish as a pop-up.**

4. **Click the link for the Send Survey option.**

5. **Click the Pop-Up Surveys option in the left navigation menu to publish your survey as a pop-up.**

6. **Configure the pop-up invitation (see Figure 9-4), skip count, and pop-up delay, and then save the pop-up settings.**

7. **Copy the HTML code at the bottom of the page and then paste it into your Web page.**

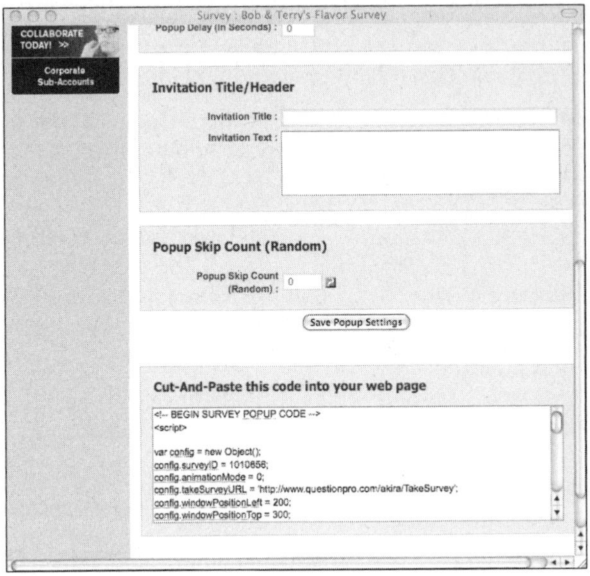

Figure 9-4:
Configuring
your survey
as a pop-up
on a Web
page.

8. **Check your Web page.**

When you visit your Web page, your survey pops up on this page (depending on your settings as defined in the preceding steps).

 Some people set their browsers to block pop-ups automatically so they aren't interrupted by while they're surfing the Internet. Even if the potential respondent has a pop-up blocker, most of the larger online survey software vendors have the ability to get around it.

There are advantages to publishing your online survey as a pop-up on your Web page. A pop-up ad definitely draws attention to itself because it pops up out of nowhere while you're surfing the Web. Pop-ups also offer anonymity to the respondents who complete your survey. Pop-ups push the envelope by causing users to have to either click through and take the survey or close the pop-up window. Either way, the viewer makes a conscious decision — and you don't have to worry about your e-mail invitation going into the junk folder or being reported as spam.

The potential downsides of publishing your online survey as a pop-up on your Web page are related to credibility. If your pop-up invitation is associated with a reputable Web site your would-be respondent visits often, it carries authority. But if your pop-up invitation is associated with a Web site people don't know or trust as much and they happen to stumble upon it during their Web surfing, you might not win them over. You might even annoy them with your attempts to gather their opinion.

One time only, please!

Before you launch your online survey, you need to consider how you can avoid the same person responding to your survey more than once. Repeat survey-takers skew the results, even if they answer differently each time they take the survey. When one person takes the survey two or more times, you no longer have a squeaky-clean representation of your target audience. When 100 people take the survey two or more times, you might as well throw out the results and start over because you've allowed your survey to become biased. Here's the challenge: If you offer anonymity to your respondents, it's more difficult to know whether they take the survey more than once. One way to get around this conundrum is to assign a unique identifier or password to each respondent. Another way is to review the IP addresses associated with each response, because every computer has its own unique IP address. This is a time-consuming process, though, and if you don't have the tech skills to do it, it's not a practical measure.

If you plan to use a pop-up ad to recruit participants for your online survey, offering incentives is a best practice. A pop-up ad is one of the most intrusive forms of inviting people to take your survey.

Keeping Track of Individual Respondents

When it comes to tracking your survey respondents, you have two options: You can track individual responses and co-relate them back to the respondent's e-mail address or you can collect anonymous responses. Your decision should be based on whether you need to track your respondent's every move.

If you want to publish a survey link on your Web site, send an invitation to your survey through your own e-mail tool, or print a generic link on a postcard that you'll mail to your respondents, then collecting anonymous responses is fine and good.

Keep in mind that if you choose anonymous tracking, you won't be able to send out *e-mail reminders*. An e-mail reminder is a resend of your survey invitation to people who have not yet completed the survey.

If you decide to link individual responses to e-mail addresses, you have to send out what's called a *Respondent Tracking URL,* a URL in your e-mail survey invitation that allows you to track the activities of your respondents. This is a unique URL to the survey that is created for each respondent. When the respondent clicks on the link, your survey software is able to identify the respondent via this unique URL. On the other hand, if you don't want to co-relate e-mail addresses with the individual responses, then you'll use the *Anonymous Survey URL* — a URL in your e-mail invitation that allows the respondents to remain anonymous — instead. You have to choose to include one or the other URL.

Again, if you want to send out reminders, you have no choice but to use the Respondent Tracking URL. That's because most survey software tools need to keep track of each individual respondent to know whether he or she has already completed the survey. Also, keep in mind that if you want to delete e-mail addresses from a particular group or if you want to delete an entire e-mail group after you've distributed the survey e-mail invitation. With some tools, this will mean you'll lose respondent tracking because the system will no longer have any way to correlate back to a particular respondent.

Here's an example of Respondent Tracking in action using QuestionPro:

1. **Log in to your QuestionPro account by entering your username and password.**

2. **The very first tab you see when your account opens is called My Surveys. Click it.**

3. **Click the link for the Send Survey option.**

4. **Click the link for the Send Email Invitation option.**

5. **Under the Send Email Invitation in the left navigation menu, click the Edit Email Invitation link.**

6. **Choose your option for tracking respondents.**

   In the edit mode, you can select one of the two options from the Insert Survey Link drop-down list above the large text area (shown in Figure 9-5):

   • If you want to track respondents and link their e-mail address with the response, simply select the Track Respondents option.

   • To collect responses anonymously, select the Keep Respondents Anonymous option.

Select your tracking option here

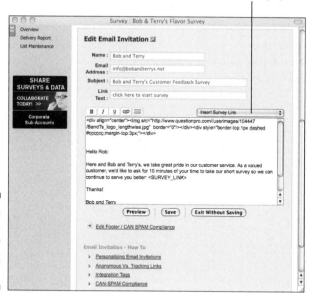

Figure 9-5:
Indicating
whether or
not to track
respondents.

Chapter 10

Steering Clear of Spam Complaints

S pam. Nobody likes it. Some people hate it. And if your online survey invitations get classified as *spam* (unsolicited e-mail), it could mark the end of a beautiful relationship — or at least a missed opportunity — between you and your would-be respondents. To be sure, there's not much chance of a happy ending for e-mails mistaken for spam. They typically either end up in a junk folder, perhaps never to be opened, or cause recipients to file complaints about your company.

If you're wondering what the big deal is about spam, just look at the cost of unsolicited e-mail to individuals and companies. Think about it for a minute. At the time of this writing, spam levels globally are at a two-year high of approximately 90 percent, according to MessageLabs. That means one in every 1.2 e-mails is spam. In some countries, that ratio is even greater.

Here's the problem: Spam costs are skyrocketing. Worldwide, spam costs e-mail users an estimated $130 billion, according to Ferris Research. That's $42 billion in the United States alone.

Now consider that these figures represent a 30 percent increase over 2007 — and that the 2007 figures represent a 100 percent increase over 2005 — and you can see the exponential growth of the unsolicited e-mail beast. The time it takes people to delete spam and look for *spam false positives* (legitimate messages mistakenly marked as spam) is the largest cost associated with unsolicited e-mail.

Spam is more than just a time-wasting, costly nuisance. It's also a threat to your personal identity. Web-based *malware* (software designed to infiltrate or damage a computer system without the owner's knowledge) authors are using spam as a vehicle to send harmful programs such as spyware and adware. Spammers also distribute e-mail–borne viruses and links to malicious Web sites. *Phishing scams* (attempts to acquire sensitive personal or corporate information) are also linked to spam.

In this chapter, we dive deep into the issue of spam as it relates to your online surveys. Specifically, you find out how to avoid spam complaints, review spam compliance options, and steer clear of your welcoming respondent's junk folder. Make no mistake about it: Spam issues are critical to the success of your online survey campaign, so get your highlighter out and make some notes.

Avoiding Spam Complaints

Forgetting to say "thank you" is one thing. Being considered a spammer is quite another. The first spamming instance can get you classified as rude. The second can get you classified as illegal. Don't worry, though, because reputable online survey software vendors take measured steps to make sure that you don't wind up on the *blacklist* (a list of e-mail addresses that are blocked from sending e-mail) of an Internet service provider. By following your online software vendor's antispam methods, you can keep people from thinking you're sending them spam when all you're really trying to do is get their valued opinion.

You find three benchmarks for determining whether your online survey e-mails — and other e-mails you might send for commercial purposes — are classified as spam:

- ✔ **Legal standards:** Outlined in the CAN-SPAM Act of 2003.
- ✔ **Professional standards:** Defined by both consumer advocates and the e-mail marketing industry.
- ✔ **Consumer preferences:** Might be completely different from the laws and professional standards.

Your goal is to keep your online survey e-mail invitations and follow-up messages legal, professional, and preferable. If you can hit all three chords, your e-mail will be music to your recipients' ears. If your recipients think you're spamming them, it's all too easy with Web-based e-mail programs to click the Report Spam button and report your messages as unsolicited e-mail (see Figure 10-1). It's also easy for Webmasters to block your message at the server level.

Check out recommendations from the Email Sender & Provider Coalition (ESPC; www.espcoalition.org) for an in-depth look at the evolving best practices on delivering e-mail and complying with spam laws. The group was formed to fight spam while protecting the delivery of legitimate e-mail. The ESPC is working on solutions to spam and deliverability concerns through a combination of legislative advocacy, technological developments, industry standards, and strategic public relations.

You're just a click away from being reported

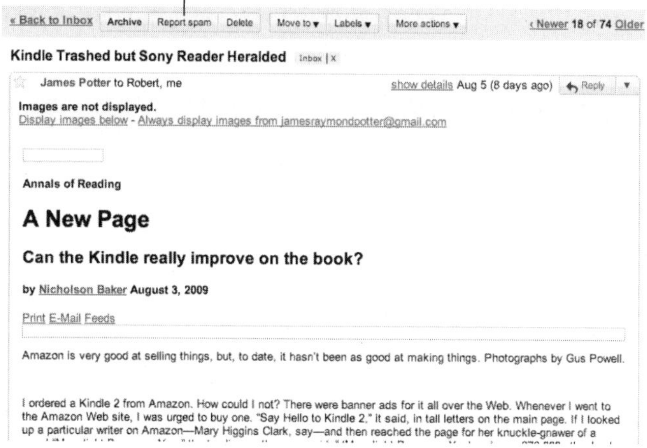

Figure 10-1:
Gmail
and other
Web-based
e-mail
programs
make it easy
to report
spam.

If you don't want your e-mails to get reported as spam, look at your online survey invitations and follow-ups through the eyes of the recipient. Consider consumer perspectives before you click the Send button so that your recipients are less likely to respond by clicking the Report Spam button or blacklist your company altogether. Here are three common reasons why recipients classify e-mail as spam:

✔ **I didn't ask for this.** Have you ever received e-mail from a company that automatically subscribed you to its e-mail list without asking? If you didn't ask for the e-mail, it's unsolicited. That's the very definition of spam. Don't automatically enroll customers to your list and start barraging them with e-mail — get their permission first. To find out how to get permission the legal way, see the section "Collecting e-mail addresses the legal way," later in this chapter.

✔ **I don't know the source.** With so many e-mails flooding inboxes today, recipients want to be able to quickly identify the source of the message. If they can't tell where the e-mail came from — or if the subject line looks spammy (see the section "Avoiding Spam Filters," later in this chapter) — your e-mail might be classified as spam.

✔ **I don't want frequent e-mails.** Consumers don't like to be bombarded with too many e-mail messages from the same company, even if they did opt in for the communications. If your messages are sent too frequently, are too long, or don't provide value, they might be classified as spam.

Handling survey e-mail invitations with care

Unless you've been living under a rock since the early 1990s, you know all too well what spam is. And you know you don't want to be classified with the pornography peddlers, the identity thieves, and the Viagra pushers that are running rampant on the Internet. If you mishandle your e-mail list, it can cause head- aches for your organization and even for your online survey software vendor's staff. If that's not enough to encourage you to distribute your online surveys with care, consider this: Improper handling of an e-mail list can cause a drop in your survey response rates as well as a dip in your study's credibility.

Understanding Spam Laws

Have you ever heard of the CAN-SPAM (Controlling the Assault of Non-Solicited Pornography and Marketing) Act of 2003? The law established requirements for organizations that send commercial e-mail. The law also spells out penalties for spammers — and companies whose products are advertised in spam — if they violate the law. Finally, the law gives consumers the right to ask e-mailers to stop spamming them.

The following sections aim to help you understand industry practices, but we're not attorneys. If you need to make decisions regarding legal compliance, consult with your legal counsel. In the meantime, you can visit www.ftc.gov/spam to help you determine whether your e-mails are in compliance.

Determining whether your e-mails are subject to CAN-SPAM

The CAN-SPAM Act of 2003 deals with commercial e-mail messages, not personal e-mails to friends or internal corporate e-mails. Based on the CAN-SPAM Act, here's the general takeaway:

- ✔ If you're sending out e-mail for the primary purpose of advertising or promoting a commercial product or service (including content on a Web site), you're liable to the CAN-SPAM Act.

- ✔ On the other hand, you're exempt from most provisions of the CAN-SPAM Act if you're sending a "transactional or relationship message" e-mail that facilitates an agreed-upon transaction or updates a customer in an existing business relationship so long as it doesn't contain false or misleading routing information.

If you use your personal e-mail account for business reasons, you could end up getting flagged as sending spam. If the recipient views your e-mail from your personal address as commercial in purpose, you could be in violation of CAN-SPAM, professional industry standards, or consumer preferences.

Collecting e-mail addresses the legal way

Much like everything else in life, there's a right way and a wrong way to do things. When it comes to collecting e-mail addresses to build your list, the right way complies with the CAN-SPAM Act.

The law deems certain e-mail address-collection practices illegal. The law also requires you to receive permission from subscribers before you send some types of content. You might have heard this dubbed *permission-based e-mail marketing* or *opt-in e-mail,* terms used to describe the practice of some-one deliberately choosing to receive e-mail from an organization. The CAN-SPAM authors call it *affirmative consent.*

You might have tapped into potentially illegal e-mail address-collection methods — or you could tap into illegal collection methods. That's because the lines aren't always clear to the inexperienced eye. To protect your organi-zation's interests, make sure that you always have permission to send e-mail to every individual on your list. You can avoid potential CAN-SPAM violations by implementing the following practices:

- ✔ **Never purchase an e-mail list from a company that lets you store the e-mail addresses as a data file.** E-mail addresses stored in a data file can be easily duplicated. You have no guarantee that members of this list have offered permission — or would give you permission — to e-mail them. It's likely that you'll either waste your money or breed enough spam complaints to give you indigestion.

  If you don't have a list of respondents to complete your survey — which is often the case when you're conducting market research — you might be better off purchasing a list from a sample provider than buying an e-mail list. Sample providers recruit people to take surveys 24 hours a day, 7 days a week, 365 days a year so that you don't have to. Here's the best part: All panelists have already opted in to receive survey invites, so you don't have to worry about the CAN-SPAM Act. Phew!

- ✔ **Never collect e-mail addresses from Web sites and online directo-ries.** Certain software programs can harvest e-mail addresses from the Internet. *Harvesting bots* (software that scans Web pages, postings on forums, and other sources to gather e-mail addresses) are popular. But sending e-mail to the lists they gather violates the CAN-SPAM Act because the recipient has not offered consent.

✔ **Always use e-mail address collection services with caution.** E-mail address collection services might rely on harvesting bots. That said, legitimate e-mail address-collection services do exist that have confirmed permission from every subscriber. These lists come at a premium and might or might not fit in with the budgeting needs of your online survey project.

✔ **Never borrow or trade e-mail lists with other businesses.** Trading e-mail lists with a complementary business partner might seem like a good idea, but it violates the affirmative consent mandate in the CAN-SPAM Act.

✔ **Always rent e-mail lists from a company with CAN-SPAM–compliant practices.** You might be surprised to find out that many — if not most — companies that rent e-mail lists aren't compliant with spam laws. Remember, permission-based lists always come at a premium.

Visit the Email Experience Council online at `www.emailexperience.org`. This is the e-mail marketing arm of the Direct Marketing Association. There you'll find the latest thinking, best practices, and strategies in e-mail and digital marketing.

Knowing what content is required in your e-mails

Even though you aren't selling anything — other than the promise of better products and services based on the insights you glean from the online survey responses — the CAN-SPAM Act nonetheless requires you to include certain, specific content in your commercial e-mails. Be sure to include the following points in your e-mails to avoid CAN-SPAM violations:

✔ **Offer a way for your subscribers to opt out — or unsubscribe — to your future e-mails.** The CAN-SPAM Act requires you to permanently remove anyone who unsubscribes from your e-mail list within ten days of the *opt-out* request, an option that allows people to ask you not to send them future e-mail messages (see Figure 10-2). What's more, you can't add that person back to your list without express permission.

✔ **Be sure that your e-mail includes your physical street address.** Even though we increasingly live in a digital world, the CAN-SPAM Act requires you to include your physical street address in every commercial e-mail communication. If you have more than one office, include the address to your headquarters, as shown in Figure 10-3.

If you have a home-based business and don't want to post your home address to the public, you have two options: Rent a post office box or use a virtual office provider. Both are considered legitimate street addresses.

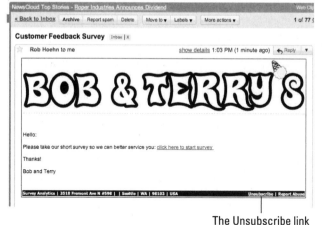

Figure 10-2:
An
Unsubscribe
link allows
recipients
to opt out of
e-mails.

The Unsubscribe link

Figure 10-3:
Always
include
your mailing
address in
the footer
of the
survey invite
e-mail.

Include your physical mailing address

✔ **Make sure that your e-mail header information clearly identifies your organization.** *E-mail headers* include the From line, Subject line, and your e-mail address. It's your responsibility — and it's to your benefit — to make sure that this information clearly represents your company.

If the recipient doesn't recognize the source of the e-mail, he could classify your message as spam and possibly launch a compliant. What's more, current CAN-SPAM laws prohibit you from misrepresenting your From address. Make sure to use a real, working e-mail address as your From address.

✔ **Make sure that your subject line isn't misleading.** Clever and compelling subject lines are encouraged. Subject lines that offer false promises or otherwise attempt to trick recipients into opening the e-mail violate the CAN-SPAM Act. Be clear that you're conducting an online survey with statements such as "Your opinion is valued" or "Annual Customer Service survey enclosed."

Avoiding Subject lines that look like spam

Avoiding Subject lines that look like spam can help your online survey invitations and follow-ups escape the trash folder. Browsing through your own junk folder can give you some important clues about the current spammer Subject line tactics so that you don't accidentally use similar keywords or techniques.

Subject lines that look like spam tend to use lots of exclamation points or question marks, along with symbols like dollar signs or asterisks. Other examples include using all capital letters — this is the equivalent of yelling in the digital world — or using the recipient's first name in the subject line. Another spammer trick is putting RE: or FW: in front of the Subject line in an attempt to trick the recipient into thinking the e-mail is a response to something they sent or a forwarded e-mail from a colleague. Blank subject lines also raise a red flag, as well as vague subject lines like "Check this out" or "Hi!"

✔ **Make sure that your e-mail complies with any applicable guidelines for sexually oriented material.** If your online survey invitation contains any reference to sexually oriented material — maybe you're conducting a survey about the use of pharmaceutical side effects — be sure that your e-mail Subject line complies with the CAN-SPAM Act supplementary guidelines. The Subject line should also clearly state that the content of the e-mail is adult in nature without being explicit in the way you describe the content. You can access the supplementary guidelines on the Federal Trade Commission (FTC) Web site at www.ftc.gov/spam.

If you want to find out more about how to enhance your e-mail professionalism, pick up a copy of *E-Mail Marketing For Dummies,* by John Arnold (published by Wiley) for best practices on how to go beyond CAN-SPAM compliance to impress your recipients with your e-mail etiquette.

Preventing Your E-Mails from Landing in the Spam Folder

It's one thing for would-be respondents to flag your online survey e-mail as spam. It's quite another to land in a potentially willing participant's spam folder (also called a junk folder) by mistake, forever lost among the hundreds of unwanted messages labeled as unsolicited by *spam filters,* a software program that examines incoming e-mail and sorts spam into a separate folder (see Figure 10-4). Of course, neither scenario is ideal, and even the most respectable e-mail marketers have struggled with this issue from time to time due to the sensitivity of spam filters.

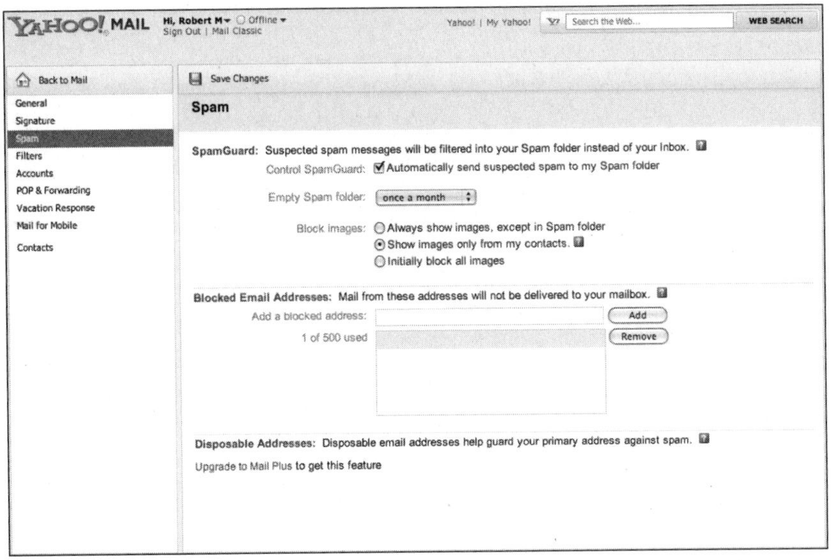

Figure 10-4:
People can
configure
spam
settings in
applications
like Yahoo!
Mail.

Your online survey vendor should have CAN-SPAM compliance tools that help you avoid the wrath of lawmakers. You'll find information on these tools in the section "Reviewing CAN-SPAM Compliance Tools," later in this chapter. But what can you do about getting mistaken as spam by technology bells and whistles in server software? There's no simple answer, but some guidelines can help you stop your online survey invitation from accidentally getting junked. These guidelines (covered in the following sections) address getting permission from recipients, keeping their permission, and managing unsubscribers. For a more in-depth study on avoiding the junk folder, read *E-Mail Marketing For Dummies,* by John Arnold.

Many online survey software vendors provide a Help file that details how to whitelist their e-mail servers. If you're sending e-mails within your own company, it's smart to send this information to the IT department so that they can configure the firewall appropriately.

Getting permission to send e-mails

Even though you aren't technically doing e-mail marketing, much of your success in getting online survey responses relies on following the e-mail marketing industry's best practices. When it comes to avoiding CAN-SPAM complaints and ending up in e-mail programs' junk folders, getting permission from your recipients can take you a long way down the road to delivered e-mail.

Staying off the blacklist

Also known as a *blocklist,* a *blacklist* is a database that contains the domain names and server addresses of suspected spammers. Internet service providers (ISPs) and other companies that monitor spam complaints maintain blacklists. Server addresses and domain names are added to blacklists based on the number of spam complaints consumers file against them. If you send e-mail that gets too many spam complaints, you might wind up on this list. Therefore, you need to follow the best practices outlined in this chapter to avoid spam complaints.

You can also request that your online survey e-mail recipients add you to a whitelist. In contrast to a blacklist, a *whitelist* is a list of e-mail addresses or IP addresses that are known, trusted, and/or explicitly permitted. Whitelisted e-mails do not land in the junk folder but are automatically passed through *e-mail firewalls* — software that's programmed to identify and block e-mails that appear untrustworthy — and spam filters despite subject lines, messages sizes, or other characteristics that typically flag e-mail as spam.

The bottom line is that you must get permission to send people e-mails from your corporation that aren't solicited. In other words, if the customer, member, or guest didn't initiate the correspondence (for example, she didn't complete a form to subscribe to your newsletter; see Figure 10-5), you need permission to get the e-conversation rolling. Even if you already have permission to e-mail your list, you need to read this section if you want to bolster your chances of keeping that permission.

Beware of cheap e-mail lists that claim to include your target audience. You can find lots of offers to blast your e-mail to millions for pennies on the dollar and CDs with clean lists for a few bucks. Remember: If it seems too good to be true, it probably is. You might not only waste your time, but you might also receive complaints if you use these lists.

Keeping permission to send e-mail

One of the most common ways to keep the permission of a recipient who has already chosen to opt in to your newsletter is by periodically sending him an e-mail asking for permission to continue sending them your newsletter. For example, you could send a recipient an e-mail stating "We'll be sending our monthly newsletter beginning next week. If you do not wish to receive the newsletter, click the Unsubscribe link below to remove yourself from our list."

But even with this general guidance, some best practices in the permission-based e-mail marketing world can help you build your list of loyal subscribers who become prime candidates to complete your online surveys:

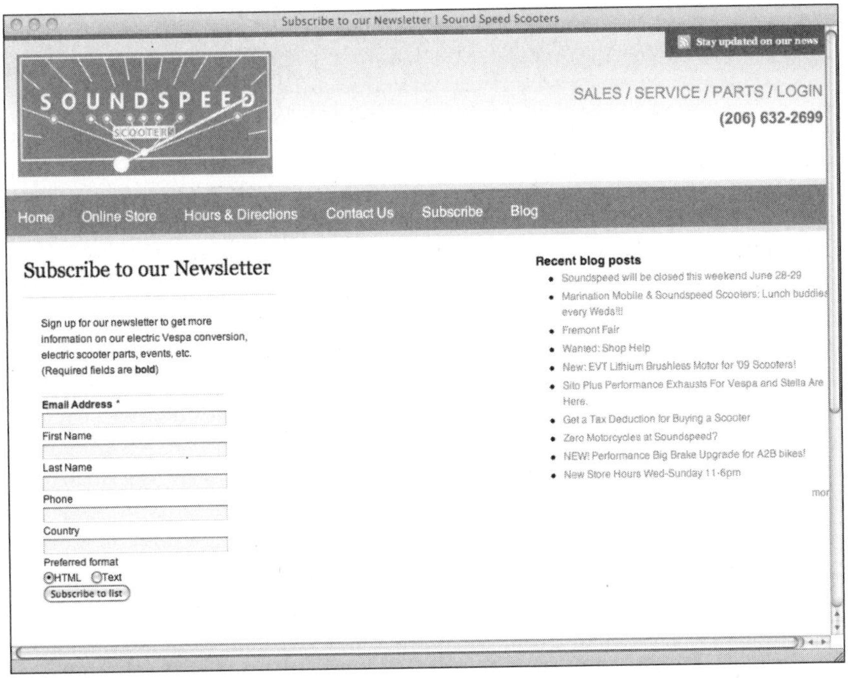

Figure 10-5:
Getting
permission
from a
customer
with a
typical
opt-in form.

✔ **Offer plenty of options:** When people subscribe to your e-mail list, give them a list of preferences, such as how often they'll receive e-mails, whether they want to receive information only, receive special promotions, receive newsletters, and so on, and in what format — text only or HTML — they want to read your e-mail.

✔ **Don't over–e-mail:** Don't e-mail your list more than four times to invite and/or remind subscribers to take your online survey. Even though you aren't selling anything, your recipients could begin to resent e-mails that are too frequent unless they've opted in for communications from your organization at such frequencies.

✔ **Post your privacy policy:** Much like you do on your company's Web site, your e-mail communications should always include a link to your privacy policy. Privacy policies help establish trust.

✔ **Stay current:** Keeping permission sometimes means keeping current contact information. If your subscribers change e-mail addresses and you don't know about it, you lose the contact. Be sure to offer a way for your subscribers to update their contact information and preferences.

✔ **Always offer an opt-out:** Don't presume anything. Just because someone signed up for your list a year ago, it doesn't mean that she won't want to unsubscribe tomorrow. That's why every e-mail you send needs to offer an Unsubscribe link. If you make it difficult for subscribers to opt out, they may end up resenting your organization.

You might want to create a "menu" of choices to allow a recipient to opt out of certain types of messages (such as sales messages) while continuing to receive informational messages. But you must include the option to end any commercial messages from the sender in that menu.

Managing e-mail unsubscribes

The nature of permission-based e-mail marketing means that you'll most certainly not get everyone's permission. If one of your recipients clicks the Unsubscribe Me link in your e-mail — or if he responds with Unsubscribe in the subject line — you're tasked with following through on the request or risking violation of CAN-SPAM laws. That means you have to manage your unsubscribers. By doing so, you are respecting their privacy, their choice, and the overall relationship.

If you're using e-mail marketing software or online survey software to send your invitations, surveys, and follow-ups, these programs should automatically remove unsubscribers from your list without any action on your part. However, if you're sending e-mails through Microsoft Outlook or some other e-mail software program, you'll have to put in measures to manage unsubscribers manually or risk having your ISP terminate your account or block all e-mail to its domain.

Manually managing your e-mail list can be time consuming, but if it's your only option, here's some practical advice for completing this all-important mission. The best place to start is by storing your subscriber data in a format that's easy to work with, typically a Microsoft Excel spreadsheet. When someone in your list unsubscribes, update your spreadsheet immediately. If the person unsubscribed by mistake, you can always manually insert her name back into the list when she notifies you — but until then, don't contact her again.

Practicing opt-in and opt-out best practices

If a person is added to a commercial e-mail list, that person must actively request not to be included or retained on the list in order not to receive future communications. According to the Email Sender & Provider Coalition (ESPC), relying on opt-out without a prior business relationship is tantamount to sending unsolicited commercial e-mail and is a violation of the ESPC Pledge.

Even with a prior business relationship, the best practice is to notify the person of the sender's intent to communicate with him or her at the point of address collection or in the first communication to the person, and then to upgrade permission to opt-in status, preferably confirmed as soon as possible. In this instance, following an opt-in request, an opt-in e-mail is subsequently sent to the person notifying him that some action is necessary before his e-mail address is added to the list. The person must respond or take other equivalent action to be considered "confirmed."

Avoiding Spam Filters

Spam filters are a nemesis to many legitimate e-mail marketers and online researchers looking to conduct surveys. Unfortunately, spam filters sometimes throw *false positives* and mistakenly mark your legitimate message as spam.

Some call this spam's casualty of war, and it's costing companies time and money. Although a move is afoot in the e-mail industry to reduce false positives, experts agree it's inevitable that some percentage of legitimate e-mail will not be delivered.

Spam filters judge your e-mail based on a list of criteria common to junk mail, including spammy phrases like "Buy now!" and the overuse of exclamation marks!!!!!!!! You have a few tried-and-true tips to consider as you craft your online survey invitation (and subsequent e-mails) that can help you avoid the junk folder:

- ✔ **Make sure that you rent a clean e-mail list.** If you decide to rent an e-mail list to expand your base of potential respondents, only rent clean e-mail lists from reputable e-mail list brokers. Check references, review the client list, read testimonials, and otherwise do your homework on the e-mail list vendor to be sure that it's CAN-SPAM-compliant.

- ✔ **Weed your internal lists often.** Your internal list should be updated regularly. Unsubscribe requests should be honored immediately, and e-mails that bounce should be weeded. What's more, your internal list needs to be scanned for duplicates. If individuals on your list receive the same e-mail four times in one day, they might unsubscribe or nominate you for the blacklist.

- ✔ **Send messages from a real person.** Don't send e-mails from `survey@ yourdomain.com`. Send them from the name of the person that is in charge of conducting the survey. And don't use symbols or numbers in the From field because this flags spam filters.

The spam index

A *spam index* is a measure of how likely your online survey e-mail invitations are to be classified as spam, and the index can be your best friend. That's because it can help you identify potential problems with your e-mail invitations before they end up in your recipient's junk folder or draw CAN-SPAM violations against your organization.

Each online survey software vendor has different policies, but reputable vendors typically offer a scale that marks e-mail lists as Good, Fair, Poor, or Restricted. A Good rating means that no major issues were found; Fair indicates some issues; Poor and Restricted indicate a list that's highly spam-suspect or unacceptable, and the vendor will not deliver e-mail through its system to your list.

✔ **Avoid spammy phrases in the Subject line.** Using words like "Buy now," "Free," or "Enter to win" can cause spam filters to classify your e-mail invitation as spam. Buzzwords or phrases like "While supplies last" also appear spammy. See Figure 10-6 for several examples of spammy phrases in Subject lines.

Figure 10-6: An example of spammy Subject lines.

✔ **Don't use large fonts or large images.** Large fonts signal that the sender might be trying to embed malicious content into the e-mail. The same is true of images. Don't send your invitation as a single image with all text included because many spam filters will automatically mark your messages as suspect.

✔ **Test your e-mail before you send it.** Send your e-mail to the personal addresses of company employees to see how their spam filters respond before distributing your online survey to the masses. If your e-mails aren't delivered to popular services like Gmail, Hotmail, Yahoo! Mail, and AOL, you might need to make adjustments.

Reviewing CAN-SPAM Compliance Tools

When it comes to online survey software, you have built-in compliance options. That's important because the Federal Trade Commission (FTC), the nation's consumer protection agency, is authorized to enforce the CAN-SPAM Act.

CAN-SPAM also gives the Department of Justice (DOJ) the authority to enforce its criminal sanctions. Other federal and state agencies can enforce the law against organizations under their jurisdiction, and companies that provide Internet access can sue violators.

Here's the bottom line: You don't want to violate this law. Reviewing compliance options in your online survey software can keep you on the safe side of e-mail surveys.

Enabling the CAN-SPAM compliance tool

Some requirements of the CAN-SPAM Act are in your hands. It's up to you to ensure that you aren't confusing people about the intent of the invitation or making untrue promises. Most survey software vendors include a tool or wizard to ensure that your e-mails are CAN-SPAM-compliant. When you enable QuestionPro's CAN-SPAM Compliance Tool, for example, you are covered in two key areas of the law. All e-mails you send out via QuestionPro's system automatically offer an Unsubscribe link and a postal mailing address. It's simple to enable the QuestionPro CAN-SPAM Compliance Tool. Just click My Account, click the CAN-SPAM Compliance check box, and then fill in the required information (see Figure 10-7).

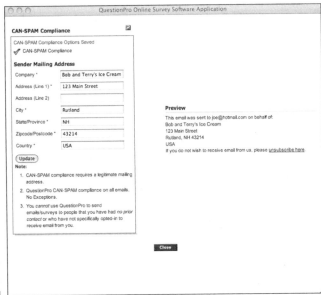

Figure 10-7:
The QuestionPro CAN-SPAM Compliance Tool.

Reporting spam abuse

Most reputable online survey software vendors send a Report Abuse link with every survey invitation e-mail or follow-up e-mail that you send to their platform. The recipients click the Report Abuse link to report the e-mail as spam. This is done to proactively measure and find out, in advance, when a large percentage of users report e-mails coming from you as being spam.

Online survey software vendors typically don't take any action as long as your abuse reporting rate is within 10 percent of the threshold rate.

In the case of QuestionPro, the threshold is calculated daily and is an average abuse reporting rate across all its clients. The threshold rate is not a fixed number but a moving average across all clients.

You can't disable the Report Abuse link. If you want to send out e-mail using an online survey software vendor's system, it's mandatory that you abide by CAN-SPAM laws. The vendors are at risk as well, and they include the Report Abuse link to protect themselves.

Chapter 11

Sending Your Survey to the Masses

*T*his is the moment you've been waiting for. You're confident in the power of online surveys to drum up the information you need to make decisions about your products and services. You've chosen your online survey software vendor. You've developed your questions and entered them into the system. Now, it's finally time to send your survey to the masses so that you can start gaining the insight you hoped for when you discovered online surveys in the first place.

It all starts with creating a *survey invitation* (the e-mail your respondent receives asking him to complete your survey). After all, you've worked too hard to leave it to chance that someone will stumble upon your survey during a visit to your Web site. You need to compel respondents to take your survey — and you do that with an e-mail invitation.

You also have a few technical matters to attend to at this stage in the online survey game (such as uploading the e-mail addresses of your respondents), but your online survey software makes it painless. When it comes to the cleanup issues to handle after the survey, like a heart-felt thank you, online survey software can help you address in a jiffy.

In this chapter, you find out how to build survey samples that give you the best chance of valid responses. You also discover how to send out your online survey. We show you how to create your invitation, upload your e-mail addresses, send out respondent reminders, and more.

Selecting an Online Survey Sample

So you have your survey perfectly dialed in on your online survey software. Everyone has given his or her two cents, and the boss has signed off on your questionnaire brilliance. You've even decided on the reports that you're going to build when the results come pouring in. Soon you'll be the data rock star of your organization, and you're considering the best way to ask for a raise. You just need one more all-important thing — respondents.

Amid the euphoria of having an effective, ready-to-go online survey, you overlooked the fact that you don't have any people — or at least not enough people — to take your survey. You need a *sample,* a group of people that fit a particular demographic who are willing to take your survey. And you need a sample because it's faster and cheaper to conduct a survey with a representative group of the overall population than it is to survey the entire population. Even if you're just surveying a handful of your employees in your 20-person company, you still need to make sure that your sample — the ones who participate — are representative of the entire employee base.

Understanding sampling error

Sampling isn't always a simple process. You have something called sampling error to contend with. The *sampling error* is the error that inevitably arises when you don't observe the entire population. You might have seen opinion polls heralded on your favorite cable news station that offer the results of an election or poll with a plus or minus two points. That plus or minus is the sampling error.

The sampling error gives you a clue as to how accurate your results really are. A low sampling error is cause for celebration because you can be reasonably sure that your results reflect the opinions of your entire target audience. A high sampling error, however, is cause for concern. The general rule of thumb is this: The smaller the sample, the greater the sampling error. Larger sample sizes tend to better reflect the overall population. If you survey 100 percent of the population, of course, you would have no sampling error. But then you wouldn't be sampling.

Who's to blame for poor results?

Gathering survey respondents who represent the target population is critical to your efforts to gain relevant insights that can drive your organization's goals forward. When something goes wrong — when you didn't get the response rate you hoped for or the insights you needed — you might be quick to point fingers at the *survey panel company* (the company that gave you the list of people willing to participate in surveys like yours) and their sampling techniques. But before you pick up stones and take aim at the panel company, do some soul-searching of your own. More times than not, you'll discover that issues existed with your questionnaire. That's right. The blame could fall right on your pretty little head.

Be open-minded for a moment and consider the facts: If respondents didn't take your survey, or bailed on you halfway through, or only completed every other question, your survey might have been too long. Your questions might also have been too difficult to understand. And it's also possible that the design of your survey layout was to blame. You might get away with blaming your survey panel company one time, but if your online surveys consistently see low response rates, you need to face the music. The problem is probably on your end of the computer, not the company's. For some great tips on increasing response rates, read Chapter 16.

Deciding on sample size

Even if you set out to survey the entire population of your organization, your membership, your customer base, or some other group, you can't guarantee that just because you send an online survey they'll complete it. Sure, you can implement all the best practices for e-mail invitations and boosting response rates, but you can't engage in arm-twisting tactics to get the insights you need. (Would you really want your respondents answering out of duress anyway?)

You need to decide how large a sample you need to get results that are accurate enough to act on. You need to consider these three key factors as you noodle your sample size:

- ✔ **How much sampling error can you stomach?** Your answer to this question probably depends on how vital the market research is to your bottom line. If you're merely conducting an opinion poll on how effective your commercials are at drawing people to the store, you can stomach more sampling error than you could if you were researching a major new product line.

- ✔ **How large is your population size?** If your target audience is one million consumers who buy blue widgets, you might have more wiggle room in your sampling error than if your target audience is made up of 5,000 people who buy blue widgets. When the targeted population size is larger, you might get away with less precision. When the targeted population size is small, you need laser precision.

Studies show there's not much difference in sampling error when you're talking about hundreds of thousands of people. In other words, your sampling error will probably be similar regardless of whether your target population has 100,000 people or 100 million people. That's why presidential polls, no matter which polling firm conducts them, typically have the same margin of error. It's with smaller sample sizes where researchers see higher sampling errors.

✔ **How diverse is your target population as it relates to your survey subject?** Are you conducting an international survey, a multilingual survey, or some other survey that cuts across cultures? Sampling error is critical. If your results are skewed toward one country, one culture, or one language, your sampling error skyrockets.

Getting the Skinny on Sampling Methods

Before you can gather a sample, you have to clearly define the target population. There's only one person who can tell you who your target population is — the person staring back at you in the mirror while you're brushing your teeth every morning. The guiding light in sampling is sticking with your survey objectives, so if your objective is to discover the apparel preferences of teenagers, you obviously wouldn't sample senior citizens. Your goal is to find a sample that paints a picture of the entire population with all its characteristics.

You need to understand two terms as you set out to gather a sample: probability samples and nonprobability samples. *Probability samples* give every member of the population a chance of being selected in the sample and involve random selection of that general population. *Nonprobability samples* do not give every person a chance to be selected and are nonrandom. The key difference you need to understand is that you can't calculate the sampling error with nonprobability samples because information about the sample and the population is sketchy. Within probability and nonprobability sampling, you have many different methods from which to choose as you endeavor to select a pool of participants that represents your target population. The following sections discuss the most common options for selecting a pool of participants.

Convenience sampling

Convenience sampling is a nonprobability method of sampling typically used to explore a new concept or idea. You would consider convenience sampling when you aren't ready to invest a large portion of your market research budget. You're still testing the waters to see how deep you want to dive. Convenience samples are selected because they're convenient and inexpensive.

Cluster sampling

Cluster sampling is a probability method of sampling in which natural segments or groups are clear within a target population. Here's how it works: The total population is broken out into clusters, and a sample of those clusters is surveyed. Members of individual clusters have similar traits, but each cluster has somewhat different characteristics, even though they're part of the same overall target population. Maybe you're conducting market research on ice cream and the target population is people who like ice cream, but clusters might be based on age, culture, or some other trait.

Judgment sampling

Judgment sampling is a nonprobability method that includes a sample based on your gut instincts. In essence, you select the sample based on your best judgment, which is based on your experience. If you aren't confident in your industry or in your surveying skills, avoid judgment samples. If the judgment sample doesn't really represent the population, your bad judgment call could cause skewed results.

Quota sampling

Quota sampling is a nonprobability method that combines stratified sampling and either judgment sampling or convenience sampling. With quota sampling, you have to first identify a statistical subpopulation and indicate how it reflects the overall population. After you've done this, you can turn to convenience or judgment sampling to select the necessary number of participants from each subpopulation. If that sounds confusing, just think of it this way: You have quotas for each subpopulation that you have to meet to get the insights you need.

Random sampling

Random sampling is a probability method in which each member of the population stands an equal chance of being chosen for survey participation. This is the purest form of sampling because there's an unpredictable element to it. Think of it this way: Your would-be participant names are in a big bowl. You mix up the bowl and pull out a name, mix up the bowl again and pull out another name, and so on. Everyone in the bowl stands an equal chance of being selected. This is akin to a random drawing in a raffle. This is the most time-consuming type of sampling — and the most expensive — that you can undertake, but it's also the most accurate because it offers a true sample of the target population.

Creating a random sample is quick and easy with Microsoft Excel software. (If you need to find out more about how to use this software, pick up a copy of Wiley Publishing's *Microsoft Excel 2010 For Dummies,* by Greg Harvey, Ph.D.) If you have an Excel spreadsheet that contains your 5,000 customers and you need to build a random sample of 900 to launch a customer satisfaction survey, you can do it by following these steps:

1. **Open the Excel spreadsheet that contains your 5,000 customers.**

2. **Add a new column in your Excel spreadsheet and call it something along the lines of** random_number.

3. **In the first cell below your heading row, type the command** =RAND() **and then press Enter.**

4. **Copy and paste the first cell into all the other cells for this column of 5,000 e-mails.**

5. **Click the Data tab in the Ribbon, and then click the Sort button in the Sort & Filter section.**

6. **In the Sort dialog box that appears, select** random_number **from the Sort By drop-down menu and then click the OK button.**

   Excel sorts the records by the random_number column.

7. **Take the first 900 e-mails displayed in your Excel rows and voila — you have a random sample of 900 participants out of your 5,000 customers!**

Snowball sampling

Snowball sampling is a nonprobability method of referral-based sampling you can use when the target population is extremely limited. For example, you don't find too many native Floridians between the ages of 65 and 75 who still live in Florida. It might cost you a small fortune to find the ones who are still around. That's when snowball sampling comes in handy. This method depends on your early survey participants offering referrals to others who match the same target audience. The downside is that you can drum up respondent bias in a hurry because you have no guarantee you'll get a strong sample of the overall target population.

Systematic sampling

Systematic sampling is a probability method of sampling where you choose participants at consistent intervals, such as every fourth person in a group. Some call this *Nth name selection* because you choose every Nth person. This is a pure form of random sampling that simplifies survey participant selection. If you have 1,000 people in your target population pool, you could simply select every Nth person and you'd have a representative sample without bias.

Using a Survey Panel Company

So you've decided not to rely solely on your e-mail list and Web site to attract survey respondents. Okay, then you need to know how to choose a *survey panel company,* a company that prerecruits groups of people who are willing to take surveys and provides you with the list for a price (because the panel company typically pays the would-be participants to take surveys).

As in any industry, you find good eggs and bad eggs out there. You can't risk your market research on rotten panels, or rotten panel companies. Understanding what legitimate survey panel companies can and can't do is essential to a successful experience. Reputable survey panel companies share some common characteristics. Before you sign on the dotted line — and sign your name on a check — consider the earmarks of reputable companies:

- ✔ **Contact information:** Reputable companies list contact information on their Web site. You can speak to a live person who can explain the process and answer your questions. Shabby outfits don't list anything more than an e-mail address, and if a problem arises, you can be sure that you won't get an answer.

- ✔ **The privacy factor:** A reputable company lists its terms and conditions on its Web site, as well as the privacy policy. The privacy policy is a vital issue when it comes to online surveys. Protecting the privacy of your respondents is critical to maintaining goodwill with your brand, so you should only work with panel companies that take privacy seriously. They should also assure you that your market research is secure and private.

- ✔ **Incentives:** Reputable panel companies might offer perks for your respondents, such as sweepstakes entries, raffles, or gift certificates. This is not an unusual practice — after all, you're paying for the names. The panel company is just sweetening the pot so that you can get higher response rates and use the company again. It's smart business. However, if the incentives seem too extravagant, that should signal you that something is awry.

- ✔ **Affiliated credentials:** You should always look for affiliated credentials. Not every company is part of the Better Business Bureau, but those types of organizations do add credibility. In the online survey industry, a good sign is membership in the Council of American Survey Research Organizations (CASRO). CASRO membership companies annually reaffirm their commitment to the CASRO Code of Standards and Ethics for Survey Research. For more on CASRO, visit its Web site at www.casro.org.

After you've chosen a survey panel company for your project, the next step is to invite respondents to take your survey. Generally, the panel company handles this for you — your only job is to give the company the link to your completed survey.

Some survey software vendors, such as Zoomerang, offer their own panel of respondents. In this case, little configuration is required when purchasing a sample. Other survey software vendors, such as QuestionPro, provide a simple configuration step that automatically links your survey to your chosen survey sample company. To configure your QuestionPro survey to work with a survey sample company, follow these steps:

1. **Log in to your QuestionPro account by entering your username and password.**

2. **Click the first tab you see when your account opens — My Surveys. Then select the survey you want to work with.**

3. **Click the Edit Survey tab.**

4. **In the navigation bar at the left, click the Finish Options link in the Survey Control section.**

5. **From the Select Finish Option drop-down menu, choose your survey sample company from the list (see Figure 11-1) and then click the Save Changes button.**

   QuestionPro gives you a special link to your survey that's formatted specifically for the survey sample company you selected in Step 5; this is the link you e-mail to them.

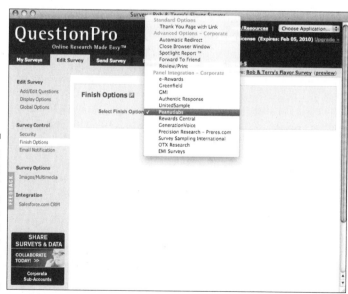

Figure 11-1:
Configuring your QuestionPro survey to work with a survey sample company.

Planning Your Launch Date

After you've conducted your sample, it's time to plan the launch of your online survey. If you plan a pool party in the middle of a hurricane, you probably won't get too many RSVPs. In other words, timing is everything. This theory also holds true in the online survey world. If you launch your online survey at the wrong time, your response rates are going to reflect the faux pas.

Here's a helpful analogy: Think about planning the launch date of your survey in much the same way as you would think of planning a wedding. First, you decide what time of the year works best — will it be a spring wedding, a summer affair, or a winter event on a tropical isle? You also need to decide what time of the day or night you'll hold the event — will you have a noon-time wedding or an evening ceremony as the sun sets? When you get the general details in order, you also have to decide how long in advance you need to send out your invitations to give your respondents time to plan to be there with proverbial bells on (and plenty of wedding gifts!).

When you make these plans, you probably consider your invitees, their life-styles, their schedules, their preferences, and so on. The same holds true for online surveys. As you plan to launch your online survey, you have four key factors to consider: seasons, vacations and holidays, the day of the week, and the time of day. The following sections examine these factors in detail.

A survey for all seasons

When you set out to pick an online survey launch date, you need to consider the seasons. Your would-be participants are likely busier at certain times of the year than others. For example, you wouldn't want to try to survey an accountant during tax season. You wouldn't want to survey a retailer during the holiday shopping season. You wouldn't want to survey a chocolate maker around Valentine's Day, and so on. You get the idea.

For some industries and for some surveys, the season might not make a bit of difference. But if you don't at least consider this factor, your online survey could get rained out.

Who needs a vacation or holiday?

You might have a little extra time on your hands in the summer, when most of your clients go on vacation. And that's exactly why you shouldn't send an online survey during that time — your respondents might not be around to answer it. The point is this: Vacations and holidays are typically less-than-ideal times to launch online surveys because people are busy focusing on relaxing and spending time with family — not answering surveys.

Try to avoid sending out your online surveys in November, December, and January because this is prime-time holiday season. People are preparing for Thanksgiving, Christmas, Chanukah, and other holidays, and your response rates will suffer. Likewise, three-day weekends aren't the ideal time to send surveys because people are out of the office, and when they do return, they're going to be heavy-handed on the Delete button of their e-mail program. Granted, some surveys might need to be conducted during these periods. But if it's not vital to send surveys during these periods, for the sake of the survey itself, hold your horses until after these peak periods.

Rainy days and Mondays

You can find all sorts of songs about Monday. It's been said that rainy days and Mondays can get you down, that you can't trust Mondays, and even that Mondays are downright manic. When it comes to sending online surveys, stick with the songwriters' wisdom: Don't do it! Mondays are a poor choice of survey launch days because people are just getting back to the office and they're too busy to deal with your curiosity. On Fridays, people want to get home for the weekend and are too distracted to deal with your queries. The middle of the week — Tuesday, Wednesday, and Thursday — is the best time to send your online survey.

Watching the clock tick

If you're a worm catcher (that is, you arise early in the morning and get right to work), you might be tempted to send out your online survey first thing in the morning. However, most people don't want to answer a questionnaire when they first log in to the computer; they have a long to-do list and can't afford the distraction. Sending online surveys near quitting time is also a no-no. No one wants to get home late for a steak dinner because she was answering your questions about frozen pizza.

The best time to send your online survey is in the middle of the day. People might take a few minutes during lunchtime (or even when they return from lunch before diving into their next task) to respond.

Maximizing Your Online Survey Distribution

When you set out to launch your online survey, you obviously want the largest possible sample you can get. The more responses you get, the more insights you get. The more insights you get, the more direction you have about your next step on the road to a new product, new service, new campaign, and so on.

Most people who launch online surveys fall back on one method: sending a survey invitation. That's a good place to start, but it's not the best place to end. Your e-mail list — whether it's a list you bought or a list you built — limits your sample size by default. In other words, you aren't reaching as many people as you could because every possible respondent is not on your list — no matter how big your list is.

If you want to maximize your online survey distribution — and your online survey responses — launch your survey in as many ways as you can think of. The following sections provide five ways to get you started.

Send a survey invitation

E-mail survey invitations are fundamental. For effective survey invitation development strategies, read Chapter 16. In a nutshell, your survey invitation should be simple, short, and sweet; offer information about your survey objectives; tell folks how long it will take them to complete it; spell out any incentives you are offering; and of course, include a link to the survey itself (see Figure 11-2).

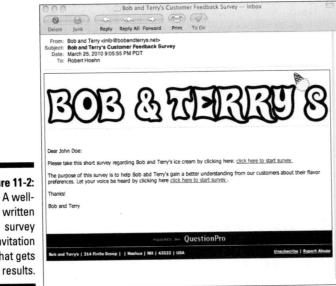

Figure 11-2:
A well-written survey invitation that gets results.

Ask at strategic times

At certain times, your customers or members are primed for the online survey pump, so to speak. For example, when your customer completes a purchase, it's an ideal time to launch a short customer satisfaction survey. By the same token, if someone bailed on your site in the midst of a transaction, it's an ideal time to send an e-mail follow-up with a quick survey that aims to get to the bottom of why the visitor left. Maybe it wasn't your fault at all. Maybe his browser just crashed. But maybe there's room for improvement with your Web site design. This is a good time to find out.

Add a survey link to your Web site

If you have a Web site, you should definitely leverage the traffic you get to drum up respondents to your online survey. And don't bury the link some-where obscure. Trumpet the online survey on your home page and perhaps also in other places on the site that are a natural fit. Use graphics and head-lines that get the attention of your visitors.

If you're running a clothing Web site and you're conducting an online survey about men's shirts, it would be natural to put a link to your online survey on the page where you display these products. If you're a nonprofit that's conducting a survey on issues important to your donors, you might also include a link to your survey on the donation page.

 Check your Web Analytics report to see which pages on your Web site get the most traffic. These are prime pages to include a headline, short blurb, and link to your online survey. To find out more about Web Analytics, pick up a copy of Wiley's *Web Analytics For Dummies,* by Pedro Sostre and Jennifer LeClaire.

Add a survey link to all communications

Take advantage of every form of communications possible to publish a link to your online survey. One easy option is your e-mail newsletters. You can remind folks of upcoming surveys and active surveys, and even offer a link to the survey results to keep your faithful newsletter subscribers in-the-know. You can also publish a link to your survey on electronic sales receipts, news-letter registration confirmations, or any other opt-in e-mails you send out (see Figure 11-3) for any legitimate purpose under the sun. You can even add the URL to your survey on your direct mailers, flyers, or other printed materials.

Put the social media factor into play

Blogs and social media sites such as Facebook, MySpace, and Twitter (see Figure 11-4) are potential gold mines of survey respondents, especially if you've taken the time to build up your readers, friends, fans, and followers. Social networkers might be more prone (by nature) to participate in your online survey because they're, well, more social than others. Blogs and social networks also offer a prime vehicle for publishing your survey results.

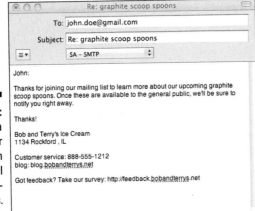

Figure 11-3: Placing a link to your survey in your e-mail communications.

Figure 11-4: Sending out a Twitter message about your survey.

Creating the Survey E-Mail Invitation

Are you ready to create your survey e-mail invitation? Don't worry. You don't have to do anything as fancy as those expensive wedding invitations you've no doubt received. You don't need any special design skills, or any special skills at all, really. Your online survey software does the heavy lifting for you.

Here's how to create the invitation that can get your survey into the hands of people who can give you the answers you need using the free QuestionPro license you received with this book:

1. **Log in to your QuestionPro account by entering your username and password.**

2. **Click the first tab you see when your account opens — My Surveys. Then select the survey you want to work with.**

   Be sure that you select the right survey. If you've created several surveys with similar names, it's easy to choose the wrong one, so go ahead and double-check. The active survey name is displayed in the upper-right corner.

3. **Click the Send Survey tab.**

4. **In navigation bar at the left, click the Send Email Invitation link in the Email Invitations section to access the Email Invite.**

5. **Click the Edit Email Invitation link.**

   This is the area that lets you set up the text for the e-mail invitation. You can either enter plain text or you can use HTML formatting for the e-mail invitation. This section also allows you to specify or change the Name (the name of the person the e-mail is from), Email Address (the address the e-mail is being sent from), and Subject for the survey e-mails, as shown in Figure 11-5. You might discover that some subject lines are more successful at getting people to open the survey than others.

6. **Click the Insert Survey Link button (refer to Figure 11-5) to access the drop-down menu and select the survey link you want to include with the invitation.**

   Most online survey software applications have a section similar to QuestionPro's Edit Email Invitation section, where you are required to include the survey link.

7. **Click the Preview button to preview your invitation or the Exit without Saving button if you've decided to hold off sending the invitation; if you are happy with what you see in Preview mode, click the Save button so that you don't have to do double duty.**

The Insert Survey Link button

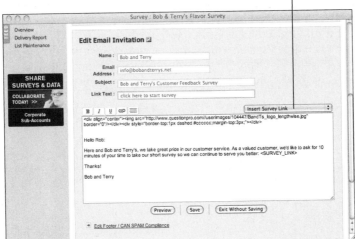

Figure 11-5:
Editing
your survey
invite.

If you want to test the survey invitation before you send it to the masses, your enterprise-level online survey software paves the way. But be sure to clear the data from the survey when you're ready to send out the survey to your real respondents so that you don't skew your data.

Uploading Your E-Mail Addresses

You've probably built a substantial e-mail mailing list in your day, or perhaps you've purchased an e-mail mailing list from a reputable organization. Either way, you have to upload those e-mail addresses before you can finally launch your survey through your online survey software. This quick task takes you one step closer to getting the results you need. Here's how to upload your e-mail addresses using your free QuestionPro software license:

1. **Log in to your QuestionPro account by entering your username and password.**

2. **Click the Send Survey tab.**

3. **In the navigation bar at the left, click the Manage Email Lists link in the Email Invitations section.**

4. **From here you have two options: You can either create a new e-mail list or click the Edit link to upload e-mail addresses in an existing e-mail list.**

You can make your e-mail list available to all your surveys or only to a specific survey. Just click Advanced Options and choose from the Type drop-down menu; you choose either Survey Specific List or Global List to suit your specific needs. Most enterprise-level online survey software vendors allow you to designate certain groups within your master list as survey recipients.

5. **Click the Bulk Upload link to upload the e-mail addresses.**

   A pop-up window appears and asks you to browse for the correct path for the file on your hard drive. When you find the file, click the Upload File button (see Figure 11-6).

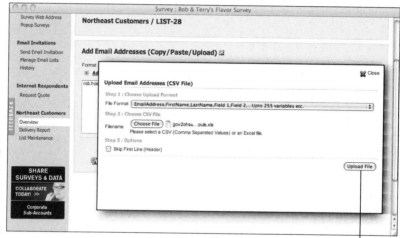

Figure 11-6:
Uploading a list of e-mail addresses.

Click this button
to upload the file

Reminding Your Respondents to Respond!

It's a busy world, and even the people with the best intentions of responding might readily forget in the face of deadlines, family pressure, and, well, you get the picture. Sometimes a friendly reminder in the form of another e-mail can offer that gentle nudge they need to complete your survey. This is where respondent tracking comes in handy.

If you chose to enable respondent tracking when you were setting up your online survey, you can send *e-mail reminders* (a resend of your survey invitation to people who have not completed the survey). After all, maybe they're on vacation and need a little computer-based warm-up before diving back into the world of work. Your simple survey could create that buffer between the vacation world and the real world as they limber up for another week answering business e-mail.

Here's how to send reminders using your free QuestionPro license that came with this book:

1. **Log in to your QuestionPro account by entering your username and password.**

2. **Click the Send Survey tab.**

3. **In the navigation bar at the left, click the Manage Email Lists link in the Email Invitations section.**

4. **Choose the e-mail list to which you have already sent the survey, and click the Edit link.**

5. **Click the Send Reminder link for the e-mail batch to which you want to send the reminders.**

    The reminders will be sent only to the e-mail addresses for the respondents who have not completed the survey. An example e-mail reminder is shown in Figure 11-7.

Figure 11-7:
Sending
e-mail
reminders
for your
survey.

A word about paid surveys

You've probably seen paid surveys out there. Maybe you got some spam e-mail inviting you to participate in a survey in exchange for a dollar or even $25. Online survey panel companies offer to pay people to participate in surveys, but you can cut out the middle man if you're willing to put the cash directly in your participants' pockets. The question is whether you should. First and foremost, it depends on your budget. If you don't have the cash to buy a list, you might not have the cash to pay your own list for answers. Although you'd probably pay less to participants if you pay them directly instead of going through a panel company, you also have to administer all the payments, which could ultimately be more costly and time-consuming.

One thing is certain: Some consumers rake in big bucks sitting and doing surveys all day. That might or might not be the type of participant you want to respond to your questions. The upshot is that they're familiar with online survey questionnaires and are less likely to jump ship halfway through the survey. They're also more likely to wade through longer online surveys because there's a cash incentive at hand. But the downside is that these participants might be so eager to collect the cash that they rush through the surveys without giving enough thought to the responses. Of course, that could be true of any participant. Only you can decide whether to pay or not to pay.

After You Send the Survey . . .

After you send the survey, you might feel like a kid on Christmas Eve, anxiously awaiting the opportunity to see what's inside the box. You want an up-to-the-minute heads-up on the survey completions, as well as a way to thank respondents for their valuable time after they selected the last *radio button* (a button on a Web page that can be chosen by the respondent). With online survey software, you have a quick-and-easy means to do both tasks in its browser-based interface.

Sign up for e-mail notifications

If you want to know each time someone completes the survey you toiled over, enable Automatic Email Notification for your survey. (Most enterprise-level vendors offer this feature.) That way, when respondents complete the survey, you'll receive an e-mail with the completed response attached. You can have the e-mails sent to the survey administrator's e-mail address, or if you have multiuser accounts, the e-mails can be sent to all users for the organization at the same time.

Don't forget to say "thanks"

Don't you hate it when people don't say "thanks" after you've done a good deed? Don't repeat that etiquette no-no. When respondents take the time to complete your survey, be sure to thank them for offering their valuable feedback. Once again, online survey software makes it easy. You can set up your survey to automatically send out e-mails thanking your faithful respondents. Here's how, using your free QuestionPro account that came with this book:

1. **Log in to your QuestionPro account by entering your username and password.**

2. **Click the Edit Survey tab.**

3. **In the navigation bar at the left, click the Email Notification link in the Survey Control section.**

4. **Click the Edit link next to the Thank You — Respondent.**

5. **Select the Email Type option from the drop-down menu and edit the subject and body of the e-mail (see Figure 11-8).**

6. **Be sure to save your changes when you're done by clicking the Save Changes button.**

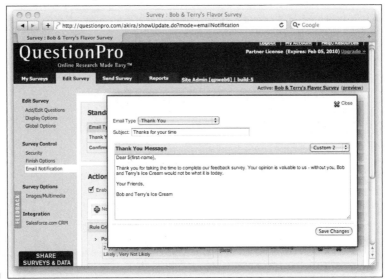

Figure 11-8:
Sending a
thank you.

Chapter 12

Surveying Survey Administration

. . . .

In This Chapter

▶ Inhibiting users from taking your survey

▶ Safeguarding your survey with a password

▶ Requiring user passwords

▶ Creating a quota for your survey

▶ Stopping repeat users

▶ Constructing multiple-user surveys

▶ Manually adding in paper-based responses

▶ Understanding custom variables

▶ Grasping fulfillment and compensation strategies

. . . .

Survey administration might not be the sexiest topic in the book, but it's a necessary read if you want to do all you can do with your online surveys. As the survey administrator, the power is in your hands — and so is the responsibility. There are lots of things you could do, some you might want to do, and some you want to avoid doing at all costs.

As survey administrator, you're charged with doing everything possible to ensure a smooth experience for your participants. You're also charged with gathering as many respondents in the shortest possible amount of time. And you're empowered to set rules on how many users can respond, the deadline for responding, how many users can take the same survey, and many other details that could possibly have a dramatic impact on your online survey results.

As you can see, survey administration is not for the faint of heart! But don't panic. This chapter offers valuable insights that steer you toward online survey administration success. From security issues to establishing parameters around your survey and from setting quotas to preventing repeat users, this chapter shows you how to implement any back-end decisions you need to make before you launch your online survey.

You also get some time-saving advice on tinkering with time zones and survey compensation strategies. And if you need to conduct a hybrid survey, we show you how. Get ready to soak up this information, because this is what separates the online survey administration men from the boys.

Preventing Users from Taking Your Survey

When you read this section's title, you probably thought we were nuts. After so much focus on finding online survey participants and optimizing your e-mail invitations and survey questions for a maximum response rate, why on God's green earth would we attempt to prevent users from taking the survey? Well, believe it or not, we have some good reasons:

✔ You want to keep the online survey top-secret. Therefore, you need to make sure that not just anybody and everybody who stumbles onto — or who is forwarded a link to — your online survey will offer responses.

✔ You want to control the time period during which users can take the survey. Perhaps some sort of time sensitivity applies to the survey, such as attitudes about online shopping before Black Thursday.

✔ You want to prevent the same person from taking the survey more than once. If someone takes the survey more than once, it can skew your data.

✔ You have an employee ID or some other existing ID you want to use to correlate each response in your survey data.

✔ You're conducting human subject research, and an oversight board (for example a university ethics committee, IRB, and so on) requires you to assign an anonymous ID to each respondent.

You have many ways to prevent users from taking your online survey. You can use a simple password, mandate an e-mail address and password, require a username and password, or issue a participant ID. There are pros and cons to each method.

Protecting Your Survey with a Password

The notion of using a password to protect your survey might seem put-offish. Well, it's supposed to be. Passwords are designed to let certain respondents in and keep others out. One way to protect surveys from unauthorized users is to use global password protection. When you enable global password protection for your online surveys, respondents share a common password.

The advantage of offering one password is clear: It's simpler to manage on the administrative side of the survey. You don't have to create an individual password for the 100, 1,000, 10,000, or 100,000 or more respondents you invite to take your online survey. However, a downside to issuing a global password is just as clear: Respondents can share it with folks you didn't invite to take your survey, potentially leaking sensitive market research data or somehow skewing your survey results.

Generally, a global password is sufficient when no monetary incentives are involved in taking the survey. Think about it for a minute. Why would someone want to take a survey over and over again? The most logical reason is to cash in on the reward you offer. If you feel that you need an additional level of security, see "Requiring an E-Mail Address and a Password" later in this chapter to find out how to batten down the hatches even more.

Here's how to password-protect your online survey using your free QuestionPro license that came with this book:

1. **Log in to your QuestionPro account by entering your username and password.**

2. **Click the My Surveys tab, and then select the survey you want to password-protect.**

3. **Click the Edit Survey tab.**

   You'll see three main sections in the navigation bar at the left: Edit Survey, Look and Feel, and Survey Control.

4. **Under the Survey Control section, click Security.**

   The screen now displays several different option boxes.

5. **In the Survey Authentication box, select Global Password Protect from the drop-down menu.**

   The drop-down menu offers several options, including Global Password Protect, Email/Password Authentication, User/Password Survey Authentication, Participant ID (Unique Key) Survey Authentication, and Facebook Connect Authentication, but for this exercise, choose Global Password Protect.

6. **In the Survey Password field, enter a password that all your respondents can use (see Figure 12-1).**

   Be sure to write down your password and keep it in a safe place.

7. **Click the Save Changes button in the lower-right corner and you're finished.**

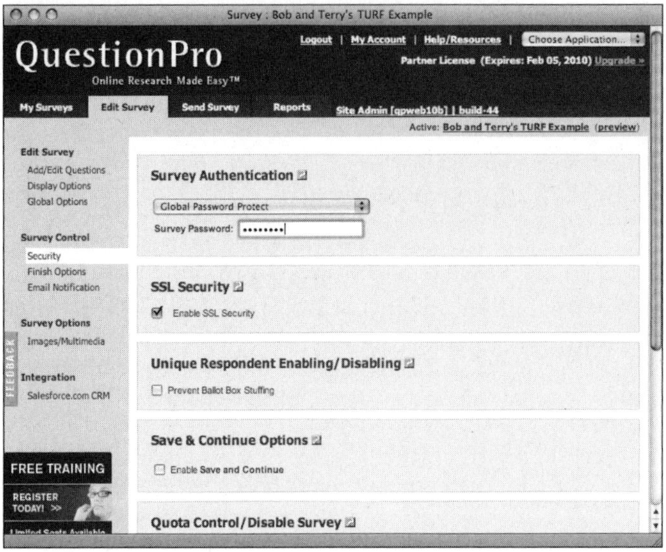

Figure 12-1:
Enable a
global
password
for your
survey.

Choosing Strong Passwords

If you've never had the five-minute seminar on choosing strong passwords, listen up. The following sections not only help you secure your online survey, but they could also help you protect your identity. If you choose a weak password, your survey could be hacked, or at least completed by people you didn't intend to have respond. The best passwords take on the appearance of a string of characters that are difficult to remember.

Characteristics of solid passwords

If you've never considered what makes a solid password, it's time to give it some thought right now. You have three areas to consider as you set out to create a solid password: length, complexity, and memorability versus guessability. Keep the following security truths in mind:

✔ **The longer your password, the more secure your online survey.** A three-letter password is much easier to guess than a 10-letter password. Ideally, security researchers suggest at least eight characters, but 14 characters — or even longer — are recommended.

✔ **The more complex your password, the more secure your online survey.** By complex, we mean using different types of characters, such as letters, numbers, and symbols. The best passwords make use of the entire keyboard, mixing uppercase and lowercase letters, numbers, and symbols.

✔ **The harder your password is to guess, the more secure your online survey.** That goes without saying. The challenge is not making it so hard to remember that you forget your own password. One way to avoid forgetting your password is to write it down and keep it in a safe place.

Avoiding password-creation mistakes

You find quite a number of pitfalls down your road to creating a strong password. If you follow the rules in the sections that sandwich this one, you won't fall into those pitfalls. But we figure you should at least know what they are. Some of them seem simple, while you might not have considered others. For example:

✔ **Avoid using your personal password.** It might be tempting to use the same password you use for your e-mail, social networking site, or other online account. But don't do it. You don't want to compromise the integrity of your personal information. You can't be too careful.

✔ **Avoid using personal information.** You should avoid using your name, social security number, birthday, or other personal information. It might be easy to remember, but it might also compromise your personal identity. If hackers can get into a database and steal millions of dollars, they can certainly crack your codes if you use personal information.

✔ **Avoid strings of repeated or sequenced characters.** With so much else to do, it's easy enough to settle on a password that looks something like "12345678" or "222444666." You want to avoid using those types of passwords or even adjacent letters on your keyboard.

✔ **Avoid the dictionary.** Don't use the dictionary as a password-builder. Even if you use rare words in foreign languages, hackers have a knack for breaking those types of codes. You can't trick them by using common misspellings or writing the word backward, either. These are not secure practices.

✔ **Avoid using symbols for similar letters.** Using symbols to replace letters is smart, but you want to avoid making it too easy. You could spell password like "p@$$w0rd," but that's easy to guess.

✔ **Avoid storing passwords on your computer.** Don't keep a list of passwords on your hard drive. Hard drives can be compromised remotely in any number of ways. Instead, keep them written down on an old-fashioned piece of paper and securely store it.

Building your bulletproof password

Of course, no password is completely bulletproof. But you can bulletproof your online survey passwords in the figurative sense of the word by following a formula that security experts agree helps shut out those you don't want to let in:

✔ **Construct a sentence that's easy for you to remember.** For example, "I've been married to my wife for 22 years."

✔ **Translate that sentence into a password.** Take the first letter in each word of your sentence and turn it into a secret code. Our example here would translate to "ibmtmwf22y."

✔ **Mix it up.** You can make your online survey password even stronger by mixing things up a bit. Use uppercase and lowercase letters to create a case-sensitive password. Using the previous example, it might look like "iBMtmWf22Y."

✔ **Use special characters.** When possible, trade your alphanumeric characters for special characters. The letter *S* could turn into a dollar sign ($), for example, or the letter *I* could turn into an exclamation point (!). In our example, your password might look something like "!BMtmWf22Y." Again, those simple substitutions are easier to guess than other characters you might choose. But in this example, it would be very difficult to guess.

Requiring an E-Mail Address and a Password

If you want to increase the level of security beyond the global password, you can take your efforts another step forward by requiring both an e-mail address and a password. Mandating an e-mail address and a password adds a second layer of security. Respondents will have to enter their e-mail address, along with the individual password, to access the survey. The downside is that your respondents will have to remember their password — this will inevitably require increased survey administration support to help people retrieve lost passwords.

Here's how to require an e-mail address and password using your free QuestionPro license that came with this book:

1. **Log in to your QuestionPro account by entering your username and password.**

2. **Click the My Surveys tab, and then select the survey you want to password-protect.**

3. **Click the Send Survey tab.**

4. **In the navigation bar at the left, click Manage Email Lists and then click the Create New Email List button to create a new e-mail list.**

5. **In the next window, give your list a name and click Create New List.**

6. **Click the Advanced link to select a custom data format (see Figure 12-2).**

Advanced link   The Custom Data Format drop-down window

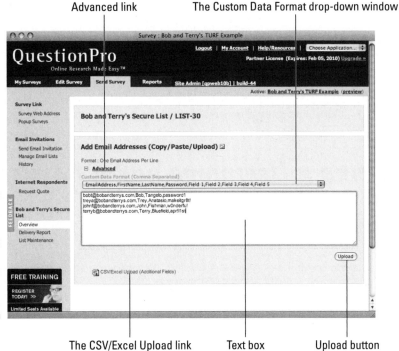

Figure 12-2:
Uploading
your list
of e-mail
addresses
with
passwords.

The CSV/Excel Upload link   Text box   Upload button

7. **Select EmailAddress,FirstName,LastName,Password . . . from the Custom Data Format drop-down menu (refer to Figure 12-2).**

   This lets QuestionPro know how your data is arranged (the order of your columns of data).

8. **In the text box (refer Figure 12-2), enter the e-mail addresses, first names, last names, and assigned passwords of the people who are allowed to take your survey.**

   Separate each element with a comma.

   You don't have to type in all the e-mail addresses manually. If you have more than a few, you can save a lot of time by uploading data directly from a CSV or an Excel spreadsheet file. Looking back at Figure 12-2, you can see the CVS/Excel Upload link at the bottom of the screen. When you click this link, it allows you to upload a file from your hard drive. Remember to follow the order of the columns in your spreadsheet as illustrated in the drop-down menu.

9. **In the lower-right corner of the screen, click the Upload button (refer to Figure 12-2) to save your changes.**

10. **QuestionPro gives you a confirmation screen where you can verify that the data was uploaded successfully. Click Finish if the data is correct.**

Now all you need to do is enable this security method for your survey.

11. **Click the Edit Survey tab, and then click the Security link under the Survey Control section in the navigation bar at the left.**

12. **From the drop-down list in the Survey Authentication box, select Password (Email Detected Automatically).**

13. **Choose the e-mail list that you created in the previous steps (select the name you gave it in Step 5), and then click Save Changes to finish.**

Requiring a Username and a Password

If you don't want to base your security on individual recipients' e-mail addresses — maybe you don't even know what their e-mail addresses are because you haven't met them yet — you can add a layer of security by requiring a username and password. This is especially helpful if you're posting an online survey on your Web site, blog, or somewhere else online and want to restrict access to the survey.

We don't recommend this option unless you don't have your respondents' e-mail addresses. If you have your respondents' e-mail addresses, it's better to use the e-mail address and password security method that we discuss in the previous section. That's mainly because you'll have more respondent tracking options available in your analysis phase, such as e-mail reminders, domain analysis, completion rates, and so on.

Here's how to require a username and password using your free QuestionPro license that came with this book:

1. **Log in to your QuestionPro account by entering your username and password.**

2. **Click the My Surveys tab, and then select the survey you want to password-protect.**

3. **Click the Send Survey tab.**

4. **In the navigation bar at the left, click Manage Email Lists and then click the Create New Email List button to create a new e-mail list.**

5. **In the next window, give your list a name and click Create New List.**

6. **Click the Advanced link to select a custom data format.**

7. **Choose Username,Password from the drop-down menu.**

   This lets QuestionPro know how your data is arranged (the order of your columns of data).

8. **In the text box, enter the usernames and passwords of the people who are allowed to take your survey (see Figure 12-3).**

Advanced link   The Custom Data Format drop-down menu

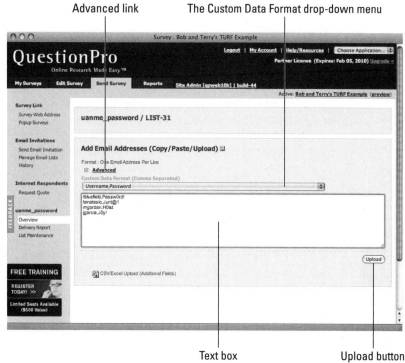

Figure 12-3:
An example
of a list of
usernames
and
passwords.

Text box   Upload button

Separate each e-mail address and password with a comma but no space.

9. **In the lower-right corner of the screen, click the Upload button (refer to Figure 12-3) to save your changes.**

10. **QuestionPro gives you a confirmation screen where you can verify that the data was uploaded successfully. Click Finish if the data is correct.**

   Now you need to enable this security method for your survey.

11. **Click the Edit Survey tab, and then click Security under the Survey Control section in the navigation bar.**

12. **From the drop-down list in the Survey Authentication box, select Password (Email Detected Automatically).**

13. **Choose the e-mail list you created in the previous steps (select the name you gave it in Step 5), and then click Save Changes to finish.**

Issuing a Participant ID

Enterprise-level online survey software also offers the ability to issue a *participant ID,* a unique identifier for each participant. If you're conducting an employee survey, this might be an employee ID. If you're conducting a B2C (business to customer) survey, this might be a customer ID. Alternatively, you can issue participant IDs for a broader survey to identify and track individual participants. Only those who have the participant ID can access the survey.

The advantage of using the participant ID is that the participant doesn't need a separate password — in effect, the participant ID serves as both the username and password. All the participant has to do is enter his participant ID to access the survey (see Figure 12-4). The downside is that if your base of would-be survey respondents don't already have some sort of identifier associated with the relationship, this is a time-consuming and potentially costly road to travel. Therefore, we don't recommend it in those cases.

Figure 12-4:
Requiring a participant ID at the beginning of the survey.

Here's how to require a participant ID using your free QuestionPro license that came with this book:

1. **Log in to your QuestionPro account by entering your username and password.**

2. **Click the My Surveys tab, and then select the survey for which you want to add the participant ID.**

3. **Click the Send Survey tab.**

4. **In the navigation bar at the left, click Manage Email Lists and then click the Create New Email List button to create a new e-mail list.**

5. **In the next window, give your list a name and click Create New List.**

6. **Click the Advanced link to select a custom data format.**

7. **Choose Participant ID from the Custom Data Format drop-down menu.**

8. **In the text box, enter the list of participant IDs on each row.**

   Separate each e-mail address and password with a comma but no space.

9. **In the lower-right corner of the screen, click the Upload button to save your changes.**

10. **QuestionPro gives you a confirmation screen, where you can verify that the data was uploaded successfully. Click Finish if the data is correct.**

    Now you need to enable this security method for your survey.

11. **Click the Edit Survey tab, and then click Security under the Survey Control section in the navigation bar.**

12. **From the drop-down list in the Survey Authentication box, select Participant ID.**

13. **Choose the e-mail list you created in the previous steps (select the name you gave it in Step 5), and then click Save Changes to finish.**

Terminating Your Survey Immediately

It's hard to imagine having too many responses to your online survey, but there might be times when you decide enough is enough and you want to stop the flow of new survey participants. With many folks putting off taking your survey or falling behind on e-mails (which might include opening your e-mail invitations), participants could continue to slowly trickle in past your market research deadline. Online survey software allows you to set parameters around your survey, such as closing the survey's virtual doors.

Here's how to set a deadline parameter around your survey using your free QuestionPro software license that came with this book:

1. **Log in to your QuestionPro account by entering your username and password.**

2. **Click the My Surveys tab, and then select the survey for which you want to set parameters.**

3. **Click the Edit Survey tab.**

4. **Under the Survey Control section in the navigation bar at the left, click Security.**

    A page appears with a subsection called Quota Control/Disable Survey (you might have to scroll down the screen to see it; see Figure 12-5). You'll also see a Current Status drop-down menu that allows you to make your survey active or inactive.

5. **If you're sure that you want to deactivate your survey, select InActive from the Current Status drop-down menu (refer to Figure 12-5).**

6. **Click the Inactive Message link (to the right of the Current Status drop-down menu) and write a note to your would-have-been respondents to explain why the survey is closed.**

You might write something like this: "Oops! We're sorry. Our market research on this topic is finished. We're currently tallying the results and will issue them soon. Of course, we do value your opinion. Check back with us again soon for the next survey. You can find out about upcoming surveys by joining our mailing list. Thank you for your interest." You can even use HTML formatting in your message.

7. **In the lower-right corner of the screen, click the Save Changes button to save your changes.**

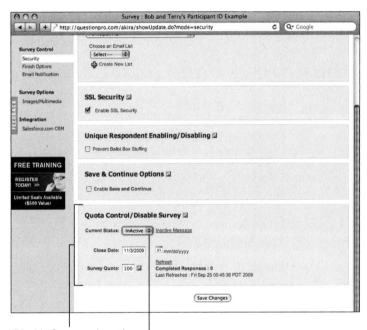

Figure 12-5:
Setting
the survey
status to
inactive.

Quota Control/Disable Survey subsection

The Current Status drop-down menu

If you want to automatically shut off access to your online survey on a particular date, you can do that, too. You can enter the date in the Close Date field just beneath the Current Status drop-down menu. For example, if you set the date as 12/12/2010, respondents will be able to take the survey until 11:59 p.m. on 12/11/2010. People who try to take your survey at 12:00 a.m. on 12/12/2010 or later will get your inactive message.

Setting a Quota for Your Survey

If you only need 1,000 responses to get a strong sample for your market research and you've already received 1,000, you don't need to wait any longer or weed through any more responses than necessary to get your answers. Your online survey software vendor offers tools that let you set quotas for your survey, automatically disabling the survey after a set number of respondents have taken it.

Here's how to set quotas for your online survey using your free QuestionPro software license that came with this book:

1. **Log in to your QuestionPro account by entering your username and password.**

2. **Click the My Surveys tab, and then select the survey for which you want to set a quota.**

3. **Click the Edit Survey tab.**

4. **Under the Survey Control section in the navigation bar at the left, click Security.**

   A page appears with a subsection called Quota Control/Disable Survey (you might have to scroll down the screen to see it). You'll also see a Survey Quota field that allows you to enter the quota number for the survey.

5. **In the Survey Quota field, type the quota number (see Figure 12-6).**

6. **In the lower-right corner of the screen, click the Save Changes button to save your changes.**

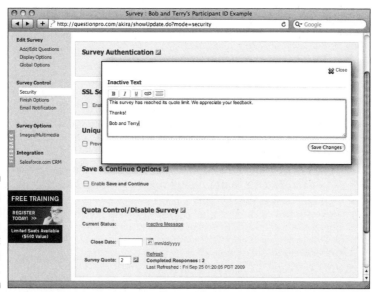

Figure 12-6:
Setting
the quota
over-limit
message on
a survey.

Preventing Repeat Users

Repeat users are a major no-no in the online survey world. Think about it for a minute. What if half your respondents took your survey twice? That would significantly skew your survey — whether they answered the same way both times or not.

If only 25 percent of your respondents took your survey twice, it would make an impact. Even if 10 percent took the online survey twice, it could cause your results to lean slightly more in one direction than another. And when you're trying to make major decisions based on your survey data, you can't afford that scenario.

When an individual responds to your survey more than once, it's called *ballot stuffing.* This might be unintentional — maybe the respondent didn't realize that the survey was accepted the first time he or she took it. Or it could be intentional — the respondent might want to reap more than his fair share of the incentives you're offering for completed surveys. Who knows? It could even be a sinister plot to skew your survey results out of spite for your brand.

By default, respondents can take a survey multiple times from the same computer. That default is there to let individuals in families or in workplaces with only one computer take the survey. If you want to want to prevent this, you'll have to use the appropriate tools from your online survey software vendor, and we cover these tools in the following sections.

Putting a stop to ballot stuffing

Online survey software vendors typically offer safeguards to prevent ballot stuffing, at least on fee-based accounts. Those safeguards include the following:

- ✔ Notifying the respondent that her survey has been received and assigning the respondent a unique ID number.

- ✔ Sending cookies to a respondent's computer when the first survey is submitted. This *cookie* — a small piece of text stored on a user's computer by a Web browser — contains information that identifies the respondent and the survey and prevents her from retaking the particular survey.

- ✔ Using respondent-tracking mechanisms to check whether a particular e-mail address has a completed response recorded. If a completed response exists for the particular e-mail address, the online survey software will not allow another response to be submitted.

You could shoot yourself in the foot if you enable these tools prematurely. These measures can't distinguish between the survey owner's PC and the PC of an actual respondent. In other words, if you enact these measures, you'll only be able to test your survey once. So if you plan to do multiple rounds of testing, make sure that you enable these settings when your survey is complete and ready to launch.

Enabling anti-ballot box stuffing tools

Most enterprise-level online survey software offers some way to prevent ballot box stuffing. Here's how to enable the feature using your free QuestionPro license that came with this book:

1. **Log in to your QuestionPro account by entering your username and password.**

2. **Click the My Surveys tab, and then select the survey for which you want to prevent ballot stuffing.**

3. **Click the Edit Survey tab and you'll see four sections in the navigation bar at the left: Edit Survey, Survey Control, Survey Options, and Integration.**

4. **Under the Survey Control section in the navigation bar, click Security.**

   A page appears with a subsection called Unique Respondent Enabling/ Disabling and a Prevent Ballot Box Stuffing check box.

5. **Select the Prevent Ballot Box Stuffing check box to enable anti-ballot box stuffing for the selected survey.**

   When enabled, the respondent will see the message shown in Figure 12-7 if he tries to take the survey more than once.

   If you change your mind later, just deselect the check box.

6. **Remember to save your changes by clicking the Save Changes button, or your efforts to preserve the integrity of your online survey will be in vain.**

Figure 12-7: Preventing a respondent from answering a survey more than once.

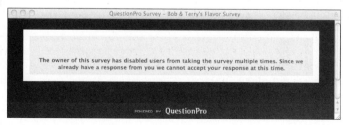

Creating Multiple-User Surveys

You can allow multiple people to complete different portions of the survey that you create. This is common if you have a survey that needs to be completed by different departments within a large organization.

Here's how to create multiple-user surveys with your free QuestionPro license that came with this book:

1. **Create a survey as you normally would.**

   If you need a refresher, read Chapter 3.

2. **Create page breaks at the desired points in your survey (where you'd like one user to hand off the questionnaire to another user) by clicking the PageBreak toggle link provided for the question on the Edit Survey page. (You access the Edit Survey page by clicking the Edit Survey tab.)**

   The page break is inserted after this question, and the rest of the questions show up on the next page.

   Here's how to determine the placement of your page break. If you have a survey with ten questions and you want the first user to answer the first three questions, create a page break after the third question.

   The page break feature is available for every question, and you can insert a page break at any point in the survey.

3. **Under the Survey Controls section in the navigation bar at the left, click Security.**

4. **Make sure that the Enable Save and Continue check box is selected.**

   This allows the first user to save his response.

5. **Offer clear instructions.**

   Make sure that you give instructions to the respondents to click Save and Continue after finishing their part of the survey. When they do, their response will be saved. They can then enter the e-mail address of the next person who needs to finish the survey. Specifically, when the respondent enters the e-mail address of the next participant in the chain, the online survey software sends an e-mail with a URL to continue the survey where the last user left off. The current user will not be able to see the answers of the previous user.

6. **Complete the survey.**

   The next respondent can then click the link and finish the survey.

Manually Adding In Paper-Based Responses

In some cases, you might need to conduct a *hybrid survey* — a survey in which you use more than one technique to gather responses. This could be a headache for survey administrators, unless online survey software plays the middleman.

For example, perhaps you need to print a survey and have people fill in the responses the old-fashioned way because some of your valuable customers don't have access to a computer. You can go back into your online survey software program and add these answers in manually. This way you can still use the powerful analytics engines on the back end of your online survey software to dissect your responses.

If you choose to manually add in paper-based responses, be sure that the survey tool you're using is configured to accept responses from the same computer multiple times. This concept is discussed earlier in the chapter.

Here's how to configure your survey to help you manually add in responses using your free QuestionPro license that came with this book:

1. **Log in to your QuestionPro account by entering your username and password.**

2. **Click the My Surveys tab, select the survey you want to complete, and click the Edit button.**

3. **Copy the URL from the Survey Link box at the top of the screen.**

4. **Under the Survey Control section in the navigation bar at the left, click Finish Options.**

5. **In the Finish Options box, paste the survey URL in the Website Address box and then click the Save Changes button (see Figure 12-8).**

6. **Start taking the survey, either by clicking the Preview link or pasting the URL of your survey into a new browser window.**

7. **Each time you complete the survey, click the Thank You for Completing This Survey link — this takes you back to the beginning again.**

Be careful of human error when entering data. It's easy to not pay attention while you're listening to the baseball game on the radio and entering results.

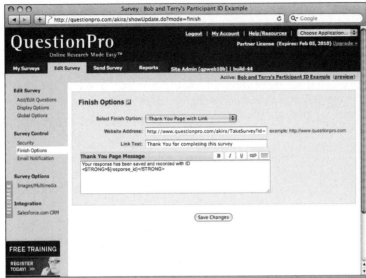

Figure 12-8:
Setting
the finish
options to
return to the
beginning of
the survey
again.

Understanding Custom Variables

If you want to be a superstar survey administrator, becoming familiar with *custom variables* (or hidden questions) is an absolute must. *Variables* are used to store additional information that's passed to the survey to create a more personalized survey experience.

For example, you can use variables in your online survey e-mail invitations to address would-be respondents by name. You can use variables to segment your e-mail list, sending the survey only to customers, for example, who purchased a certain product type recently based on internal data. You can use these same variables to address them by name during the actual survey or to reference the respondent's previous answers.

You can even use variables in the analysis process. Specifically, you can set up grouping based on the custom variables. For example, if you've uploaded a department within your organization as a custom variable, you can set up groups for each department and run a separate analysis for each department; you can then compare one department to another to determine how different user groups view the organization, its products, services, and so on.

Here's how to upload variables using your free QuestionPro license that came with this book:

1. **Log in to your QuestionPro account by entering your username and password.**

2. **Click the My Surveys tab and select the survey for which you want to add custom variables.**

3. **Click the Send Survey tab and then click Manage Email Lists in the navigation bar at the left.**

4. **Click the Create New Email List button to create a new e-mail list.**

5. **In the next window, give your list a name and click Create New List.**

6. **Click the Advanced link to select a custom data format.**

7. **Choose a file format (see Figure 12-9) for your data (usually in the form of EmailAddress,FirstName,LastName,Customer1,Customer2, and so on).**

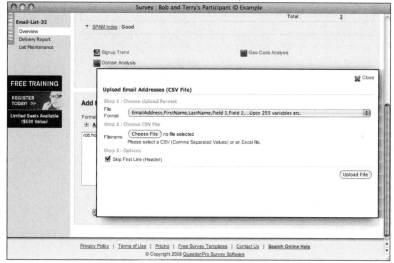

Figure 12-9:
Uploading custom variables to Question-Pro.

8. **Click the Upload File button to load the data into QuestionPro.**

9. **In the data upload confirmation screen, click Finish if the data is correct.**

10. **Click the Send Email button.**

    Your data set is populated with these custom variables, and you can later use them to personalize survey e-mail invites or analyze the data using real-time summary reports.

Your file needs to be in Excel (.xls) or CSV (.csv) file format. If you have Excel 2007, you need to save the file as a .xls file (an Excel 2003 or earlier format). All spreadsheet application software products have the option for saving files as .csv files.

It's very common in spreadsheets for the first row to be headings. If the first row in your list of data includes a header, select the Skip First Line (Header) check box; refer to Figure 12-9. This keeps QuestionPro from getting confused with the data you upload.

Tinkering with Time Zones

What if you could turn back time? You can, with online survey software. Well, sort of. Most online survey software vendors have a default setting for time zones. Typically, it's the time zone where the company is headquartered or where its servers are located. If the online survey software firm is headquartered in Miami, the default time zone will probably be set to Eastern Standard Time. If the firm is in Seattle, it's probably set to Pacific Standard Time. You get the picture.

However, as a survey administrator, you can change the default setting to match your home time zone. This might be less confusing for you as your results start coming in, especially if you're monitoring results in real time. You could easily confuse yourself thinking that the results came in three hours earlier than they actually did, for example. This, in turn, could lead you to think that you launched your survey at a less-than-optimal time to generate the greatest initial response when the truth might be just the opposite — your timing might have been perfect.

Here's how to customize your time zone using the free QuestionPro software account that came with this book:

1. **Log in to your QuestionPro account by entering your username and password.**

2. **Click the My Surveys tab and select the survey for which you want to set the time zone.**

3. **Click the My Account hotlink in the upper-right corner of the screen.**

4. **Under the Account Overview section in the navigation bar at the left, click User Profile.**

   A screen appears that displays your billing information, login details, and (at the bottom of the screen) your User Profile information.

5. **In the User Profile information area, click the Update User Profile link that appears next to your name.**

6. **In the User Profile dialog box that appears, select the time zone of your choice from the Time Zone drop-down menu (see Figure 12-10).**

7. **In the lower-right corner of the screen, click the Update User Profile button to save your changes.**

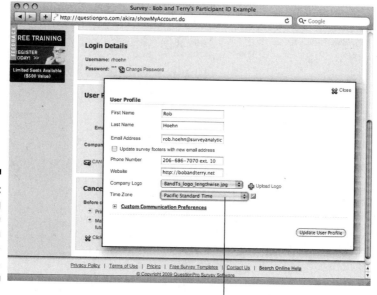

Figure 12-10:
Updating
the time
zone in
Question-
Pro.

The Time Zone drop-down menu

Understanding Fulfillment and Compensation Strategies

Response rates are a vital part of online surveys. Without responses, you have no results. And without results, your labor was in vain. This book addresses time and again how the length of the survey can impact response rates. Longer surveys typically see lower response rates because people lead busy lives. If you want answers, keep your survey short.

Now it's time to understand the second driving force in response rates: the compensation strategy. Here's the deal: In some cases, you have far more control over the compensation strategy than you do over the length of the survey. Sometimes — large *tracking studies* (studies that track consumer behavior over long periods of time) being a good example — you can't keep your survey as short as you'd like. When your survey is longer than your respondent's right arm, the only way to reliably guarantee that you'll meet your research quota is to offer an attractive incentive.

Our research indicates that offering incentives to each respondent results in better response rates than offering the entire base of participants one chance to win a larger prize. In other words, you're better off offering one dollar to 250 respondents than you are offering a $250 gift certificate to one in every 250 members who complete the survey.

This is called the *pay everyone* approach, and while it might seem obvious to some, many organizations still don't use this approach because it drives up administrative costs. That's understandable. It takes time and money to mail out $1 checks to 250 online survey participants. The good news is that advances in online survey software now make it possible to lower survey administration costs via instant gratification. By leveraging technology tools and platforms, you can compensate participants for their time immediately after they complete the survey.

Making online payments via PayPal

Can you remember e-commerce before PayPal? It was almost impossible for people without credit cards to do online shopping. Now, PayPal is being used far and wide — even in online survey participant compensation. Forward-thinking online survey vendors are exploring how to integrate PayPal's "pay anyone with an e-mail address" system to offer instant payments.

Admittedly, it's still not cost-effective to make micropayments in its strictest sense. After all, someone from your organization still has to physically respond to an automatically generated request for payment. But you can set up rules. For example, you can set funds to be released at predetermined amounts, such as when the participant has earned $20, and then automatically approve the payment.

Personal accounts with PayPal are free, and funds can be transferred to and from bank accounts using PayPal. What's more, an enormous number of online sites accept money from PayPal. The point is this: People are comfortable with PayPal. If you want to find out more about how to use PayPal to your advantage, pick up a copy of *PayPal For Dummies,* by Victoria Rosenborg and Marsha Collier (published by Wiley).

Facing the music

The online survey software world is ultracompetitive. Savvy online survey software companies are investigating all sorts of ways to tackle the compensation challenge as effectively and efficiently as possible. One notion that Survey Analytics is exploring is a partnership with Apple's iTunes Store to offer coupons for song downloads as compensation for taking online surveys. With the immense popularity of legal music downloads, this is a very lucrative option. With this option, participants would be offered a song download code worth 99 cents that they can use immediately at iTunes. They could choose any song that's provided by the store to download and listen to. Expect more creative compensation solutions from online survey software companies in the years ahead.

Providing coupons and discounts for your own product or service

One of the easiest ways to compensate participants for taking your survey is to offer a discount or a coupon for a product or service that you already sell. This is a viable alternative to expensive payouts — and it also encourages participants to use your product. It's a win-win for you and your customers. Custom coupon codes can be uploaded into the panel management interface of your online survey software for automatic delivery when your participants complete the survey. This approach also fits well along the lines of instant gratification.

Part IV

Analyzing Your Online Survey Results

The 5th Wave   By Rich Tennant

"I understand you've found a system to reduce the number of complaints we receive by 50 percent."

In this part . . .

In this part, we show you how to dive into the reports your online survey software generates. In fact, you don't even have to wait until all the results are in to start gleaning insights. That's because we show you how to dissect real-time data reports as the responses trickle in. You also discover how to understand special reports, review respondent reports and participant stats, analyze open-ended answers, and deal with individual responses individually.

By the time you've done all this, you should have most of the answers you need. But in case you need more in-depth reports, we show you how to get advanced with survey analytics by tapping into the power of special functions like banner tables. We also illustrate ways you can share your reports with colleagues so they can get in on the analytical fun, how to group and segment your data, and how to dig out survey trends dummies might never see.

Finally, we cover the ins and outs of exporting your raw data. If that sounds tricky, well, that's because it is. But don't worry — we walk you through the steps that will allow you move your data into external files so you can backup data or run reports in other programs such as Excel.

Chapter 13

Diving into Your Online Survey Reports

*N*umbers don't lie, but unless you understand how to read the reports that display the numbers, you could end up basing your next marketing campaign on erroneous information. The good news is that online survey software helps you make the most of your data with easy-to-read reports that get to the bottom line in a hurry.

Whether you're the type that can't wait until the final whistle blows to start peeking at the responses or the one who likes to see the data from a dozen different angles, online survey software applications let you decide how to digest the data. You can get the numbers in real time with an *RSS reader* (a software program that aggregates data from Web sites). You can group your respondents into any number of different categories. You can even put a spotlight on certain respondents' answers and share them with key stake-holders in the organization to prove a point.

What's more, analyzing data can give you distinct clues into the survey-building process. If your respondents repeatedly failed to answer a certain question, it's possible it wasn't clear. If most of the people you sent the survey to got halfway through and quit, your survey could have put them to sleep because it was too long, too wordy, or too something else. Your online survey statistics give you insight into not only how your respondents feel about issues, products, or services, but also how they feel about the way you asked them your questions.

In this chapter, we show you how to clean your data to ensure high-quality results and dissect real-time data reports in a jiffy. You also find out how to use online survey software filters, review participant stats, and access your open-ended question responses. We even throw in some best practices for analyzing your data for good measure.

Before You Begin . . .

If you have read the earlier chapters in the book, you know how important it is to have clear objectives for your survey before you start developing questions. Now, it's time to look at your results through that same lens. So before you dive into your statistics, take some time to review your survey objectives.

You need to have a clear understanding of what you're trying to discover so that you don't spend a lot of time getting lost in interesting — but not particularly useful — data points. Sure, your online survey results might offer some bonus revelations. But first and foremost you need to get to the bottom of the insight barrel you set out to explore.

It's vital to keep your survey objectives in mind as you approach the analysis phase of your project because analyzing your data isn't merely a matter of looking at the reports that your online survey software generates. Although the reports can offer a wealth of data in and of themselves, if you don't know what you're looking for, you probably won't find it.

Not every angle on your responses is automatically served up in a handy-dandy report. So while you won't have to calculate the percentages, the scales, and the tables in your pretty little head, you will have to know what you want to see with your big blue eyes or you'll overlook it. If you need to draw specific analysis from the report, you might need to process it with filtering tools that slice and dice the data in various ways.

Some online survey software vendors (typically at the enterprise level) allow you to export your raw data into other, more sophisticated analytical software programs. A free survey tool like SurveyMonkey, for example, can offer some rudimentary results. Enterprise-level tools like Vovici can drill down so deep that you might strike oil. See Figures 13-1 and 13-2 for a comparison of the typical report screens of SurveyMonkey and QuestionPro.

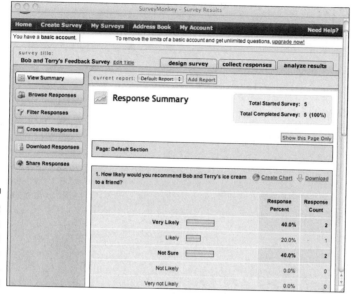

Figure 13-1:
A basic report in Survey-Monkey.

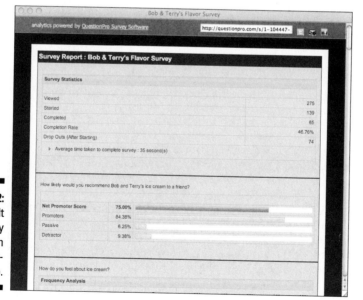

Figure 13-2:
The default summary report in Question-Pro.

Tracking your survey responses

It's ultra-important for you to keep track of your survey responses as they come in. You need to monitor your response rates and be ready, willing, and able to send follow up e-mail invitations with friendly reminders about your all-important quest to gather opinions. The good news is this: With online survey software, tracking your survey responses is simple. The software automatically offers insight into which e-mail addresses have responded and which haven't.

This function relegates paper-based surveys to dinosaur status. Can you imagine keeping track of surveys you mail out in an envelope with a stamp? Even sending the survey out via e-mail itself can lead to problems because you never know whether the e-mail actually arrived in your would-be participant's inbox. With online survey software, you can review which e-mails were delivered, which ones were opened, who answered, and who needs a little nudge to respond.

Data Cleaning 101

Just as nobody likes to do the dishes, *data cleaning* (the process of detecting, correcting, and removing data from your online survey results that's either inaccurate, corrupt, incomplete, or irrelevant) isn't exactly the most exciting part of analyzing your survey results. But just as washing the dishes is an integral part of serving your next meal, data cleaning is vital to serving accurate insights to the conference room table. After all, you don't want to eat a filet mignon on dirty dishes, and you don't want to analyze your results based on dirty data.

Understanding the benefits of quality data

If you aren't sold on the need for high-quality data, consider a study by The Data Warehousing Institute. According to the study, there are three key benefits to maintaining high-quality data: greater confidence in analytic systems, less time spent reconciling data, and a single version of the truth. Noteworthy is the fact that customer data, product data, financial data, and sales contact data top the areas where data quality is prone to problems.

With that in mind, consider the common characteristics of high-quality data:

✔ **Accuracy:** Data that represents a clean match between the target population and the sample. If your market research examines senior citizens and your sample contains middle-aged folks, your data isn't accurate.

✔ **Completeness:** Data that answers the objectives of the survey. If data related to key objectives is missing from the survey, the data set isn't complete and you can't benefit fully from the results.

✔ **Consistency:** Each analyzer sees a consistent view of the data, including visible changes made by the user's own transactions and transactions of other users. If more than one person in your group is analyzing the data in separate sessions, it's important that nothing is removed, renamed, or modified without all parties knowing.

✔ **Density:** *Density* refers to data without missing values. For example, if people didn't answer certain questions in your survey (or they responded with "I don't know"), it weakens the density of the data.

✔ **Integrity:** Data that maintains information exactly as it was input to a system, free from alteration or unauthorized disclosure, or if it has been modified, that modification was carried out in a secure and auditable fashion.

✔ **Uniqueness:** Data without any duplicates. If one person took your survey more than once, your data would not stand the uniqueness test.

✔ **Validity:** The survey measures what it intends to measure. If your survey questionnaire is poorly designed, your data is likely not valid.

Skimming over your initial results

You'll be tempted to start diving into the data at a deeper level when you open your online survey software dashboard to view the results — but don't! Before you spend hours analyzing your data from beginning to end, spend a few minutes skimming through the results.

If you see any major flaws in the design of your questionnaire that caused confusion among your participants, it's better to find out now before you spend too much time with the data. If the participants don't represent the sample you need to drive the insights you must have, again, it's better to know that now.

Who's answering your survey?

As you skim through your data, (see Figure 13-3) check to see whether the results are generally what you expected them to be. If you sell pantyhose and your data shows that most of your respondents were male, you have a problem with your data. If you're conducting a survey of your nonprofit membership and you discover that only a handful of your respondents are paid up on their dues, it might signal that your data isn't reliable because your participants aren't active members — you get the idea. A quick skim can help you make sure that you have the right answers from the right people. If your survey isn't valid, the results don't mean much.

Who's not answering your survey?

A quick scan through your responses (see Figure 13-3) might also reveal another problem. What if half of your respondents are only making it halfway through your survey? That could signal a major flaw in your questionnaire — most likely, it's too long. Before you conduct your next online survey, you need to take a deep breath and review Chapter 6 for some tips on how to develop questions that get responses.

You might also discover a terribly low response rate. If only 45 percent of the invitees responded to your survey, it could mean that your e-mail invitation didn't do its job (go back and read Chapter 11 for some instructions on how to create the survey e-mail invitation). It could also mean that your e-mail invitations are landing in junk mail or being reported as spam. In that case, review Chapter 10 and find out how to avoid those spam filters.

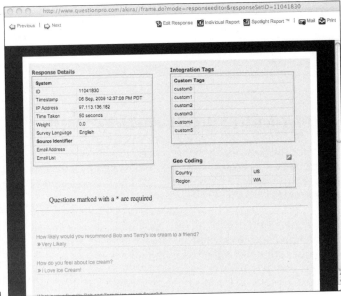

Figure 13-3: Viewing completed responses to your survey.

Screening, Diagnosing, and Treating Your Data

Now that you're convinced of the need for high-quality data, it's time to jump into the process. Much of what we've discovered about data cleansing (see Figure 13-4) comes from a marvelous paper called "Data Cleaning: Detecting, Diagnosing, and Editing Data Abnormalities," written by Jan Van den Broeck, Solveig Argeseanu Cunningham, Roger Eeckels, and Kobus Herbst. Of course, this paper is a high-level dissertation written in a sophisticated language that's not appropriate for our format. Therefore, in the following sections, we offer our interpretation as well as our own experiences in screening, diagnosing, and treating online survey data.

Data Stage	Sources of Problems: Lack or Excess of Data	Sources of Problems: Outliers and Inconsistencies
Questionnaire	Form missing	Correct value filled out in wrong box
	Form double, collected repeatedly	Not readable
	Answering box or options list left blank	Writing error
	More than one option selected when not allowed	Answer given is out of expected (conditional) range
Database	Lack or excess of data carried over from questionnaire	Outliers and inconsistencies carried over from questionnaire
	Form or field not entered	Value incorrectly entered
	Data erroneously entered twice	Value incorrectly changed during previous data cleaning
	Value entered in wrong field	Transformation (programming) error
	Inadvertent deletions and duplications during database handling	
Analysis dataset	Lack or excess of data carried over from database	Outliers and inconsistencies carried over from database
	Data extraction or transfer error	Data extraction or transfer error
	Deletions or duplications by analyst	Sorting errors (spreadsheets)
		Data-cleaning errors

DOI:10.1371/journal.pmed.0020267.t001

Figure 13-4:
The basic data cleaning process.

If you're using a free online survey software tool, you probably won't have much control over data editing. Therefore, if you're conducting research on issues that demand laser precision, enterprise-level software tools are the route you need to take because they allow you to have far more control over your data in every respect. Chapter 4 offers an in-depth look at free, low-cost, and enterprise-level tools.

Screening your online survey data

You don't have to wait until all your data is in to begin screening it. You can go ahead and start this process as your results start to pour in. In fact, that's a best practice because the sooner you've screened your data, the sooner you can move on to analyzing it (see Figure 13-5).

Even better, if you screen your data early enough, you might be able to make quick adjustments to your survey in response to poor questionnaire design or some other problem you discover. If you notice that people are consistently skipping the fifth question, for example, you probably need to rephrase that question. Or, it could be some sort of issue with the software presentation itself. Now is the time to get to the bottom of it before thousands of surveys come back without responses.

Here's what you need to look for during the screening phase:

✔ **Too little data:** Look for any questions that have noticeably fewer answers than the other questions in the survey. If you don't have enough answers to offer a sample, you might need to cut that question out of your results.

✔ **Too much data:** Look for duplicate surveys. If one person takes your survey more than one time, it skews the sample. Perhaps some participants started the survey, didn't finish, and restarted the survey again. You might need to parse the incomplete or duplicate surveys from your data.

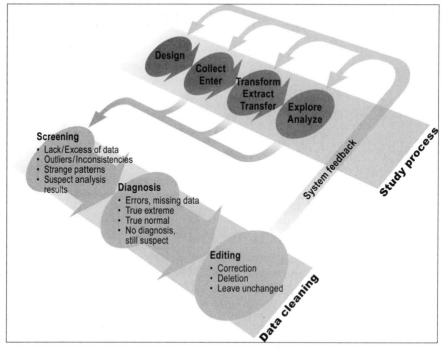

Figure 13-5:
Issues to
consider
when
reviewing
your survey
data.

✔ **Inconsistent results:** Malcolm Gladwell wrote a best-selling book called *Outliers* (published by Little, Brown and Company) that explores factors that contribute to high levels of success. People who offer results that are so far out of line with the general population (individuals that Gladwell calls *outliers*) can skew your survey. So, look for those inconsistencies and be prepared to cull them from your data.

✔ **Unlikely responses:** If the answers to some of your questions seem like they came out of left field, they probably did. If the answers seem unlikely to come from your sample — maybe a respondent said he had a cat but indicated he only bought cat food once every six months — get ready to throw them out. They won't help you produce a more marketable cat food.

✔ **Oddball patterns:** You have outliers and then you have liars. You have no punishment for participants who offer less-than-honest answers, but you don't have to let them skew your data. Look for patterns in your online survey data that might indicate participants who were just trying to get through the survey as fast as possible to earn the incentive. Perhaps they *Christmas-treed* (answered the questions without any real thought) the survey or just answered "yes" or rated "best" for every question without taking the time to think it through. You don't want those responses.

Diagnosing your online survey data

The screening phase might be considered the manifestation of symptoms that your data isn't all you had hoped. But just as you wouldn't cut off your toe because you thought it might have gangrene without getting a doctor to confirm the problem, you shouldn't cut out parts of your data without spending the time to take a closer look and diagnose it.

In some cases, the diagnosis is so obvious that seeing the data in context shows the root cause of the symptom. For example, if your respondent says she goes to the movies 20 times a month, she either wasn't paying attention, was lying, made a typo, or has a serious movie addiction and doesn't accurately represent the sample population. But other times, the diagnosis isn't quite as straightforward. That's why you need to put on your survey stethoscope and diagnose the data.

Here are some possible results of your head-to-toe online survey exam:

- **Missing data:** If you're missing data, it can skew your survey. Maybe your percentages are whacked because a large number of people skipped questions or just didn't want to share that information. You need to take this as a learning experience and find out what might have gone wrong so that you don't repeat the mistake. Was the question too personal? Was it offensive? Was it too complicated to understand? Get to the bottom of it now.

- **Survey extremes:** Sometimes extreme answers are perfectly valid. That's why you need to explore the context of the answers. If your respondent says he dines out 75 times a month, for example, that might sound extreme. But when you realize that you're dealing with a single male who works 80 hours a week, the extreme answer begins to make sense. You don't want to cut out the data — you have a valuable food critic on your hands.

- **Human error:** Everybody makes mistakes. If you've asked respondents to type in a number to indicate some frequency or other value, they might have typed in 13 when they meant to type in 31. They also might have clicked the wrong radio button on a value scale or misunderstood the ranking system (ranking 1 as good and 10 as poor instead of the other way around). Don't be too quick to blame your respondents for human error, though. Maybe you could do a better job of explaining some of your questions.

- **Honest answers:** Your survey results might not be what you expect, or what you hoped for, but if the answers appear to be honest, they're valid. That might leave you with results you don't like, but your goal is to get the truth, not merely what you'd like the truth to be.

- **Iffy answers:** Sometimes — even after you've diagnosed the answers — you still can't discern whether the symptoms you first recognized earlier are really a painful boil on the back of your data or just data that seems a little out of the norm.

Treating your online survey data

It's decision time. The treatment phase is when you get your digital data shears and cut out the invalid extremes, duplicates, human errors, and other problems with your online survey data. Perhaps you can save the data by following up with your participant and asking him to answer the questions he skipped. Maybe you can even rephrase the question for him. This is a painful process, but it might be necessary to save your survey. However, it's not always as easy as putting your virtual data shears to work. When the answers are iffy, it's tough to know what to do.

Here are three time-tested suggestions for the testing phase:

- **Don't change a thing:** Some people don't believe in cutting out any data. If you're in this camp, your decision is easy — don't change a thing. If you have thousands of responses, a few bad apples aren't going to spoil the cart. But keep in mind that if you have 10 bad answers in a 100-person survey, your results might suffer the consequences of symptomatic data.

- **Fix the issue:** If you can loop back around with your respondent, by all means make the attempt to fix the symptomatic data. You might even take the opportunity to ask her why she didn't answer the question or what she thought you meant so that you can hone your question-development skills for future online surveys.

- **Cut it out:** In cases where the data just doesn't seem at all likely, delete the data. Some will argue that this dilutes the integrity of your survey. Some people in the survey world would consider it blasphemy to cut out responses, no matter how far afield they seem. Others don't have a problem with it. This is ultimately your decision. Consider the consequences and use wisdom.

Dissecting real-time reports

Our society is hooked on real-time data. You can get real-time NBA scores on the Internet, real-time headlines on your cell phone, and real-time reports on your online survey software. The best online survey software vendors hook you up with what's called the real-time summary report. *Real-time summary reports* provide basic statistical analysis on your survey questions as they come in. The data is actually collated in real time as the respondents are completing your survey. This can be an exciting experience, and it can also alert you to any problems in your survey design.

You probably won't find real-time summary reports (see Figure 13-6) in the freebie category, but most low-cost and enterprise-level online survey software providers offer this feature. (Read Chapter 4 to discover more about the various levels, features, and functions of online survey software providers.)

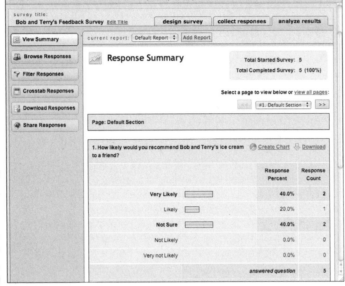

Figure 13-6:
An example
of a
real-time
summary
report.

Defining the stats

One thing is certain: If you don't know what the various stats mean, you probably won't rank as most improved. Some of the stats are obvious; others aren't. Here are some quick definitions to get you on the fast track to survey optimization. If you need more, go back and read Chapter 2.

✔ **Viewed:** The total number of users who click the link to access the survey. Every time your survey is requested, the view count is incremented and updated. The respondent does not necessarily have to start the survey for the click to be counted as a view.

✔ **Started:** The total number of respondents who have started the survey. A response is recorded as Started if the respondent clicks the Continue button on the first page.

✔ **Completed:** The completed count is all respondents that have gone through the entire survey and clicked the Finish button on the last page of the survey.

✔ **Completion rate:** This is the number of Completed survey responses divided by the number of Started survey responses.

✔ **Drop-outs:** The number of respondents who start the survey but do not complete it.

✔ **Terminated via branching:** If you have set up branching in your questions to terminate the survey for specific criteria, the number of terminated respondents will be displayed.

Reviewing respondent reports and participant statistics

Whether or not you like stats, you'll appreciate all the options that online survey software dashboards offer to help you make the most of your online surveys. Beyond the answers themselves — like how many people prefer your brand of soap — you need to keep tabs on how many people are actually taking your survey, how many only make it halfway through, how many never open the e-mail, and other telling statistics.

Let's face it, a survey doesn't count for much if only three people respond. You might be losing respondents with the subject line of your e-mail or with the choices of questions. Most online survey tools provide some type of *respondent reports* or *participant statistics* (see Figure 13-7) that can give you the skinny on why people aren't filling out your awesome survey. These tools also give you some clues you might need to improve future surveys. You can find these stats on the Reports tab of your online survey software.

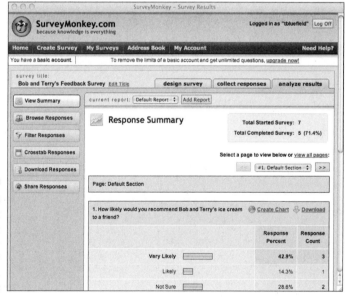

Figure 13-7: Participant statistics in a Survey-Monkey survey.

Filtering Your Online Survey Report

If you like to slice and dice the data to get fresh perspectives on your survey results, you have plenty of options with online survey software. You can filter your reports by various criteria with the click of a graphical button. In fact, if you don't use filters to segment your data, you could be missing out on valuable insights that you can't access any other way.

Filtering your report is a valuable online survey amenity because it amplifies the good, the bad, and the ugly. If you have a slew of respondents who aren't completing the survey, a filter can magnify that unpleasant reality. If most of your respondents answered at noon, that could impact the month of the year you send out future surveys.

Pay close attention to the online survey software filters. They offer analytics that could help you boost your conversion rates, enhance your customer service, drive greater responses to your next fundraiser, sell more products and services, and much more. Filters let you compare groups on whatever data points you've collected in a flash.

Response-based filtering

If you want to segment your respondents into groups based on their answers, response-based filtering can do the job. Typically, your online survey software tools allow you to filter the report by the status of each response, such as completed, incomplete, and terminated. Or, you could filter by male and female. You can even filter the report based on monthly income — you get the idea. Filtering your responses based on these types of attributes can help you drill down into the immediate responses you need quickly.

Time-based filtering

Time-based grouping is just what it sounds like — creating segments of data based on time, such as when the survey was completed. You could, for example, create a time-based group called March that includes all survey data from 3/1/2010 to 3/31/2010. You'd then have totals for the month of March that you could then use to compare with those of other months.

System variable–based filtering

If you send out surveys on a regular basis, you could get bogged down in the details — unless you use *system variable–based filtering* (grouping surveys based on variables). Enterprise-level online survey software applications typically offer built-in system variables that make it easy to group your surveys on almost any variable you can think of.

When you're at the reporting stage, these system variables are usually something you've already collected as part of your list of potential respondents.

These might be important data elements such as Employee ID, Project ID, Representative ID, Customer Number, or some other ID descriptor. So perhaps your company assigns a customer number to each survey response it collects. You would use variable-based grouping to filter out your survey data, looking at only certain custom IDs.

Grouping and filtering in action

Online survey software takes the heavy lifting out of grouping and filtering. If you want to see just how easy it is to group and filter, follow these simple steps using your free trial of QuestionPro software that came with this book:

1. **Log in to your QuestionPro account by entering your username and password.**

2. **Click the My Surveys tab, and then select the survey you want to work with.**

3. **Click the Reports tab.**

   You see options for various different types of reports, online tools, and advanced analysis in the navigation bar at the left.

4. **Click the Data/Segmentation link.**

   The screen in Figure 13-8 is displayed.

Figure 13-8:
Response-
based
grouping in
Question-
Pro.

5. Click the New Data Filter button.

This will launch the Data Segmentation Wizard (see Figure 13-9).

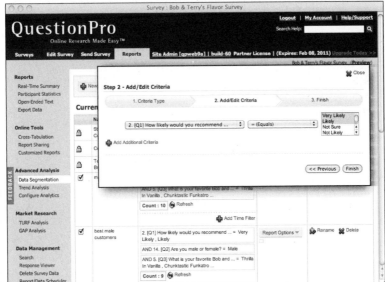

6. Give your criteria a name.

Type a name for your filter criteria in the text input area next to Name. Then, click the radio button next to Responses to the Survey. Finally, click the Next button in the bottom-right.

7. Enter the desired filter criteria.

Choose the question you want to filter by in the first drop-down box. In the next drop down box, we'll choose = (Equals). In the last selection box, choose the answer that you want to filter the responses. Click the Finish button in the bottom-right, and then the Continue link in the bottom-left.

8. Run the filtered Summary Report.

You'll see the filter you just created in the list. Now execute the Summary Report based on this filter by choosing Summary Report from the Report Options drop-down menu to the right of the screen (See Figure 13-10).

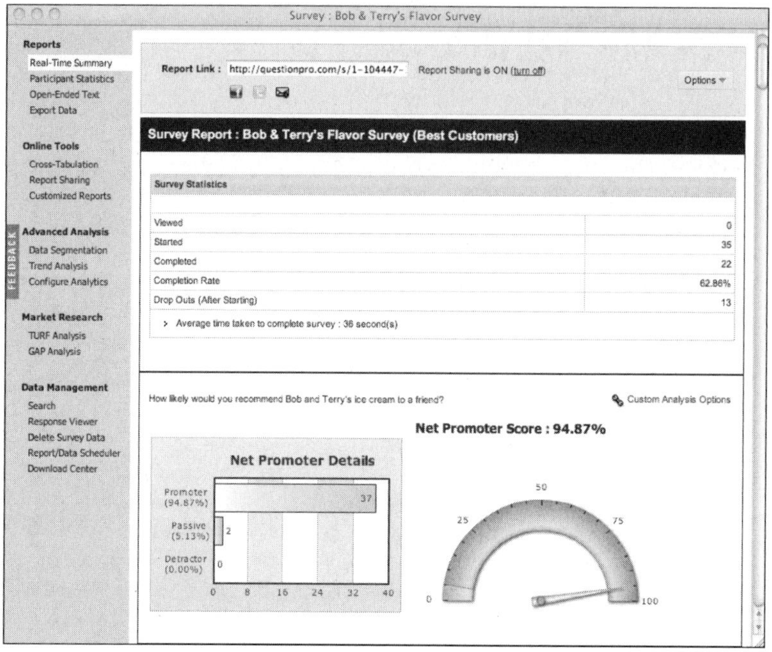

Figure 13-10:
The
Summary
Report.

Exploring Best Practices for Online Survey Data Interpretation

We love best practices, and you will too when you realize how much time they can cut off the learning curve. When it comes to online survey data analysis, best practices are not only a must-have, but they're also a godsend. What you're looking for are the results that really matter: results that answer the questions you set out to answer when you developed your survey objectives. Sure, you might find some tasty gravy when you dive into your data, but you want to first and foremost look for the meat and potatoes.

Your mandate is to focus on actionable insights that can drive real value for your organization. It can be intimidating to try to interpret survey data, but you have an advantage with online surveys. Think about how much work you would have if you conducted paper-based surveys. You'd have to come up with coding and do plenty of data entry just to get to the point where you are right now. So don't look at how difficult you think it might be to interpret your data. Think about how much easier you have it compared to your counterparts of 20 years ago, and dive in with a smile.

Get the 50,000-foot view

If you're a little nervous about interpreting your data, start off by getting familiar with the types of reports your online survey software offers. At a glance, you can see some interesting results that can give you some quick takeaways to chew on before you get into the deeper waters. Start with asking yourself these questions:

- ✔ **How many people finished your survey?** If you got a low percentage of responses, your first interpretation is that something, somewhere went wrong. You'll have to analyze the data more closely to figure out what it is, but at least you know there's reason to investigate. If you got a high percentage of responses, congratulations. That's a welcome revelation.

- ✔ **What was the response rate?** The *response rate* is the proportion of those who actually participate in a survey. This is a measure of whether the data you collected accurately reflects the views of the population you surveyed. The response rate can also help you determine whether weighting or other methods might improve your data quality. If you skipped the section on the benefits of high-quality data earlier in this chapter, this is a good time to go back and review it.

- ✔ **How long did it take respondents to take the survey?** With this data, you can determine whether perhaps your survey was too long or the questions too complicated. You might find some correlation between the time it took participants to finish the survey and the response rate. Longer surveys tend to get fewer responses and a greater number of survey abandonments.

Take a sneak peek at the core questions

After you've gotten your feet wet, it's time to wade a little deeper into the water. Rather than starting with all the qualifying questions, jump right into the core questions of your survey and get a feel for what your participants are thinking. The core questions relate directly to your survey objective.

For example, if you're trying to find out whether your target audience has the appetite for a new line of Italian frozen dinners, jump straight to the questions that relate to preferences. You can go back later and look at who did the answering to determine where the thinnest slice of your target market is. For now, it's just good to know whether anybody wants another frozen pizza.

Dive into the demographics

After you've gotten a feel for the general direction of your responses, take another step forward and examine your demographics. At this level, you're trying to find out whether males aged 18–34 are hungrier for a new pizza product than females aged 34–45, and so on. In other words, which demographic is most likely to plop down $4.99 for the exotic pizza you've brainstormed in the boardroom?

The goal here is to pinpoint your target market so that you can determine whether it's potentially large enough to make research and development of a new pizza flavor worthwhile, and later to develop marketing messages to that slice of the broader population so that they'll buy what you've just produced.

Tackle open-ended answers

If you started with open-ended answers, you might not get to the nitty-gritty of your results for hours, or even days. It can be time-consuming to read through open-ended answers — and you must take the time to do it. You can get some great insights from open-ended answers: answers to questions you might not have asked outright but could ask more directly in your next survey. Customers might also suggest answers to problems you didn't know you had or couldn't solve on your own.

Roll up your sleeves and get to work

Conducting an online survey for the sake of gathering the data is an exercise in futility. You need to take action on your data. For more on how to report your survey results with others in your organization so that you can devise an action plan, read Chapter 15.

Avoiding Common Analysis Temptations

Whether you've been conducting surveys for decades or are just getting started with this powerful opinion-seeking method, you should be aware of the three data-analysis temptations known to man. Avoid these like the swine flu because falling into these traps is like injecting a harmful virus into your survey results.

Temptation 1: Assuming the answers

If you sat down at the beginning of the online survey process and developed survey objectives, you'll probably never have to face the temptation to assume the answers — unless your questions didn't line up with those objectives.

Of course, if you set out on one course and changed course mid-survey, your questions might not answer your newfound objectives, either. That's why you need to pick your survey objectives and stick to them. If you get a flash of surveying brilliance midway through your current survey, save it for the next survey.

The bottom line is this: Don't try to find answers to questions that weren't asked by reading between the proverbial lines. It can be tempting when it seems like you failed to ask a question that you sorely need an answer to — and now. But don't fall into this trap — you know what they say about people who make assumptions. If your results are based on guesswork, your actions might lead you into adversity.

Temptation 2: Changing the data

We repeat, never change the data. If you launched a poorly designed online survey questionnaire, you can't make up for it on the data analysis side of the survey. Your attempts to avoid a disaster in the way you asked a question could lead to just as big a catastrophe when you present skewed results that your boss believes are accurate, launches a new product based on those skewed results, and flops on his face.

Here's an example: analyzing a multiple-choice question as if it's a single-choice question. Making inferences about what people really mean in open-ended questions when their answers are ambiguous (or even putting on your rose-colored glasses when you review the open-ended questions so that you see only the good and not the criticisms) is another temptation.

Temptation 3: Applying results with a broad brush

Most surveys ask demographic questions of some sort, such as age, race, location, or household income. These demographic questions are important to pinpoint in your market research so that when you launch a product or service (or when you otherwise target efforts of a campaign, membership drive, charity fundraiser, or some other cause), you have the right information about the right audience.

For example, you can't apply the results you get from males aged 18–34 to females aged 45–60. Young males are likely to have much different perspectives on the subject at hand than middle-aged females, especially if the product or service is targeted to a specific age group. In an employee survey, workers that are near retirement might have a different perspective on benefits packages than workers who recently joined the company. Married couples might have a different perspective on home ownership than single college kids.

Here's the lesson: Don't take results from one group and use them to paint a picture that includes other groups. If you try to target Generation Z based on responses you gathered from Generation Y, you might be left wondering what the X factor was in your failed campaign.

When it comes to honing your data-analysis skills, remember this: Be humble. If you don't know, ask somebody. You can learn from other peoples' mistakes so that you don't have to walk down the same errant path. We can hear what you're thinking: "Nobody is going to give me that kind of access to his or her internal surveys." Maybe you're right, and maybe you're wrong. But it's worth asking. At the very least, you can ask your enterprise online survey software vendor to spend a few minutes reviewing your analysis techniques so that you can make the most of your market research.

Chapter 14

Daring to Get Advanced with Survey Analytics

*I*f a simple analysis doesn't satiate your desire for survey data, online survey software offers more advanced tools that slice your responses in colorful ways. In fact, these tools can save you hours of time that you might otherwise spend number crunching. They can also offer insights that you might not otherwise have thought to dig out. Taking advantage of these tools can make even the simplest data profound by offering comparisons that tell a deeper story about your respondents' opinions.

As you discover how to dig deeper into your data, always keep actionable results top of mind. Some statistics might be quite interesting, but that doesn't mean they'll necessarily translate into a tangible action item. It could be something you need to keep your eye on, but not necessarily something you can wrap your arms around this quarter. The value of online surveys is that they provide information on which you can base decisions about employees, products, services, and other issues your organization is facing — right now.

In this chapter, we show you how to leverage the power of banner tables, how to group and segment your data at new levels, how to dig out all-important survey trends that can identify trends you never considered, and how to deal with nonrespondent bias. We even throw in a bonus: combining online surveys with Web Analytics.

Betting on Banner Tables

Everybody likes pretty pictures. Most enterprise-level online survey software providers offer banner tables to satisfy your taste for visual data that has real meaning. *Banner tables* give you a picture of the data that corresponds to individual survey questions.

Pretend that your survey asks respondents where they're from, and the answer options are East Coast, West Coast, and Midwest. You can use the banner table option to generate a visual representation that shows you how respondents from each region answered the other survey. This way you can identify regional trends, if they exist, without having to create groups and segments for each option.

The question you use to segment the rest of the survey is called the *pivot question,* and it can be based on any number of criteria. In addition to location, you could segment by age, income, or some other demographic. An example of a pivot question might be, "Please select your age from the following group: 18–24, 25–32, 33–45, 46–54, 55–62, 63–80, and 80 and over."

Creating a Banner Table Report

Creating a banner table report offers a great return on your time investment. With just a few clicks, you can save yourself hours of work. Here's how to create a banner table report using the free QuestionPro license that came with this book:

1. **Log in to your QuestionPro account by entering your username and password.**

2. **Click the My Surveys tab, and then select the survey you want to work with.**

3. **Click the Reports tab.**

4. **Under the Online Tools section in the navigation bar at the left, click Cross-Tabulation.**

5. **In the Step 1 section of the Banner/Pivot Tables box, choose your pivot question from the Pivot Question (Required) drop-down menu (see Figure 14-1).**

Indicate your pivot question here

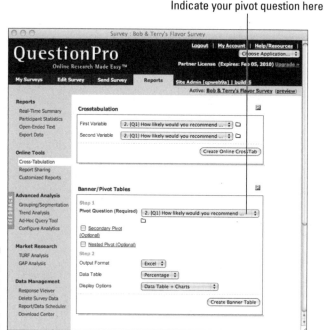

Figure 14-1:
Choosing
the question
to pivot.

You can choose a custom variable, such as sales regions or project ID. If you decide to use a custom variable, your online survey software will produce a banner table for each distinct item for that custom variable. For example, if you're capturing Sales Region as one of the custom variables, choosing that custom variable will automatically segment your data based on every distinct region in your data set.

6. **In the Step 2 section of the Banner/Pivot Tables box, make your selections for the various output options for your banner table.**

7. **Create your banner table by clicking the Create Banner Table button.**

Voila! Easy, yes? As soon as you click the Create Banner Table button, your report is placed into the job queue. As is the case with most online survey providers, you'll receive an e-mail with the completed report (see Figure 14-2) attached. In other cases you'll be able to click Refresh after a few minutes and access a link to download the report.

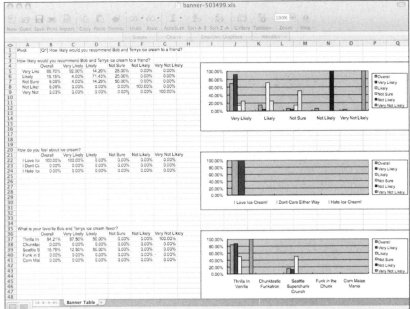

Figure 14-2:
A typical
banner
report in
Excel.

Grouping and Segmenting Your Data

If you're looking for power tools, look no farther than the Grouping/
Segmentation feature. This is one of the most powerful and underused features in an online survey software application's reporting tool set — and
you're about to discover how to use it.

A *group* (or segment) is one or more filters on your data set. A group can
be a simple filter like "all male respondents" or complex like "all female
respondents, aged 18–25, that drink orange juice but hate vanilla ice cream."
After you've created a group, you can save it for later use in various reports
throughout your analysis.

Never forget the power of grouping and segmenting your data. The technique
has been around for a long time, and to this day it hasn't lost its importance.
Being able to examine discrete groups within your data gives you insight
about your respondent that you'd never have otherwise.

How to create a group

Are you ready to tap into the power of grouping and segmenting? You don't
even have to wear goggles or gloves to operate this power tool. Here's how

to set up segments and groups using your free QuestionPro license that came with this book:

1. **Log in to your QuestionPro account by entering your username and password.**

2. **Click the My Surveys tab, and then select the survey you want to work with.**

3. **Click the Reports tab.**

4. **Under the Advanced Analysis section in the navigation bar at the left, click Grouping/Segmentation.**

   In the resulting screen, verify that the Response Based Grouping tab is active, as shown in Figure 14-3.

Figure 14-3: Preparing to create a response-based group.

5. **In the Create Data Segments box, make the following selections:**

   a. Choose the question you want to filter/select from the Choose the Question drop-down menu.

   b. Choose one of the operators for the answer from the Comparison Operator drop-down menu.

   Most people choose the = (equals) operator.

   c. Choose the answer for the selection criteria from the Choose the Answer to Filter On drop-down menu (this is the drop-down menu that shows AND selected in Figure 14-3).

6. **Click the Add Filter button in the Create Data Segments box to filter the data according to the criteria you selected.**

7. **Repeat Steps 3–6 if you want to add more criteria to the filtering process.**

8. **After you're finished applying filters, give the group a name and click the Save Filter to Group button.**

That's it. You can now run the Summary Report or Advanced Reports page and view the data and charts for this selection criteria.

Digging Out Survey Trends

Did you wear bell-bottoms in the 1970s (or the 2000s)? Whether or not you consider yourself a trendy dresser, you'll certainly want to be a trendy surveyor. In other words, you'll want to dig out the trends buried in the mountains of data your online survey software collects for you. Trends play an important role in your decision-making process — and so does monitoring how trends change over time.

Most enterprise-level online survey software tools offer a downloadable "trend report" that computes the analysis of your data over the long haul.

Imagine that you're running the same survey multiple times a year, or even on a continual basis. You can view the data for different time segments side by side, such as January versus June. Here's how to generate a trend report using your free QuestionPro account that came with this book:

1. **Log in to your QuestionPro account by entering your username and password.**

2. **Click the My Surveys tab, and then select the survey you want to work with.**

3. **Click the Reports tab.**

4. **Under the Advanced Analysis section in the navigation bar at the left, click Trend Analysis to access the data set filters.**

5. **Click the Data Set Filter link to choose an optional grouping.**

6. **Choose a survey result you would like to focus on for the trend.**

   This can be something like a demographic or the answer to a specific question.

7. **Enter the start and end dates into the box.**

8. Choose the frequency.

Although you will automatically generate a report in this process, you can choose to generate a trend report weekly, monthly, or quarterly in this section so that you can keep tabs on the trends.

9. Click the Download Trend Report button.

The report will be generated and e-mailed to you when it's complete (see Figure 14-4). If you're anxious to receive the report, wait right where you are and refresh your browser. In moments, you'll see a link to download the report.

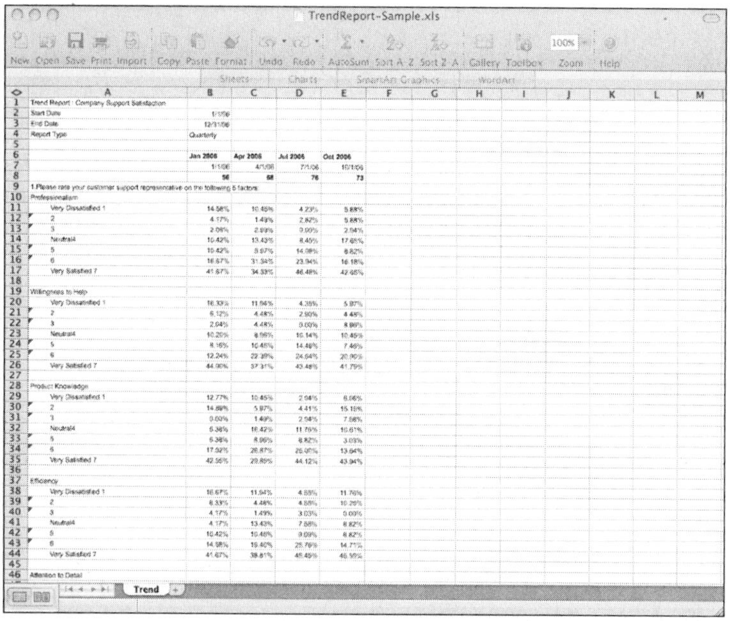

Figure 14-4: An example of an Excel trend report from QuestionPro.

Analyzing Trends over Time

Modern essayist and novelist John Ralston Saul once said, "With the past, we can see trajectories into the future — both catastrophic and creative projections." Within this quote lies the wisdom of conducting trend analysis over time. In other words, it's not enough to just pick up on the trends in your data from one survey.

The smartest market researchers save past survey data so that they can compare and contrast responses over the long haul — and not just over the long haul of multiple surveys, but over the long haul of a single, long-running survey. For example, by analyzing trends over time, you can measure the differences in how respondents perceive your brand, product, or service at the launch of a new initiative, three weeks after the launch, and three months after the launch.

You can accomplish this long-term trending by keeping a link to the same survey on your Web site, in your e-mail newsletter, in your pop-ups, in your online advertising for a long period of time, or by sending out the same survey at regular intervals to new customers or members who are just getting familiar with your brand. For more information on the methods mentioned, read Chapter 9.

Proactive data analysis can help your organization stay in touch with customers and business partners. Trend analysis provides an easy mechanism to monitor the aggregate response data, filtering out the noise so that you can make informed decisions.

Warning: Your customers are upset!

Analyzing trends over the long term is more than just a fun exercise. It holds real value for market researchers. For example, a trend analysis can be extremely valuable as an early warning indicator of potential problems and issues with product line and service-level changes that impact customers.

If you see a dip in the average among survey respondents who say they are "satisfied" or "very satisfied" with your products and services and you see a sharp increase in the number of respondents that are "not satisfied," you had better get busy investigating what's causing the trouble. If you ignore these warning signs and fail to explore the causes of declining customer satisfaction levels, you're heading for trouble.

Trend-hunting 101

As you hunt for trends, your online survey software application gives you some convenient tools to track them down. Indeed, your online survey software is like a hound dog looking for the trail of valuable insights that can save your organization time and money — and sometimes even face. For starters, you can measure the *mean* and *mean percentile,* which offers you the approximate average of your survey respondents. This might tell you, for example, that your average respondent likes chocolate ice cream or that 85 percent of your respondents like chocolate ice cream. Analyzing trends over time also means paying attention to deviations from what you expect to see in your survey results. You can root out these deviations and variances with online survey tools that let you hunt for trends based on time factors such as daily, weekly, monthly, quarterly, or yearly.

Pulling cross-survey reports

When it comes to customer service, pulling *cross-survey reports* (reports that aggregate data across multiple surveys) can help you in more ways than one. One online survey software tool called Cvent offers strong cross-survey reporting capabilities that let you show progress or regression in feedback ratings from customers who call your customer care center. Management can use this data to help find poor-performing shifts and motivate employees to provide better service through incentive plans that reward workers for high ratings. With trending in mind, you can look at your cross-survey reports and compare them against each other to determine how your customer care center is performing over time. If your feedback ratings have declined since last quarter, you need to find out why so that you can fix the problem before it grows worse. If your feedback ratings have risen, you also need to find out why so that you can keep up the good work.

Gauging response to marketing events

Another way to use the trend analysis report is in conjunction with marketing events, such as a new Web site launch, a new television commercial, a new fund-raising drive, or some other promotion. One example is a Web site usability upgrade. Many organizations go to great lengths to make their Web sites more usable but fail to assess impacts before and after the upgrades.

If you want to gauge the response to your Web optimization efforts, start with an online survey about your current Web site. But don't stop there. After you spend weeks — or even months — giving your site a "Web lift" in response to the issues your customers point out in the online survey, send an announcement that your new site has launched and include a second online survey.

This "customer pulse" survey should ask visitors to rate the Web site on a seven-point scale. A rating of 4 would indicate no change in the usability of the site after the upgrade. A rating of 1, 2, or 3 would mean that the changes you made backfired. And a rating of 5, 6, or 7 would indicate that you've improved some of the issues and should see your sales reflect your efforts. In this case, the trend analysis reveals a jump or decline in customer satisfaction with your Web site.

The trend analysis in marketing events can also be used to simulate the potential increase or decrease in satisfaction levels by using focus groups or a representative sample. This data can be further used to conduct a cost-benefit analysis on your investment in the marketing events. With this knowledge, you can decide whether to do similar events or try something new.

The limitations of the trend analysis

For all the virtues of the trend analysis, it has limitations. For example, a trend analysis can only be performed on quantitative question types. *Quantitative questions* include multiple-choice, rank order, and constant sum. By contrast, *qualitative questions* (questions that explain perceptions or opinions using text instead of numbers) can't be used for trend analysis. For a better understanding of question types, read Chapter 6.

Understanding the Spotlight Report

Everyone likes to be under the spotlight. Well, almost everyone. Online survey software vendors typically offer what's called a *spotlight report,* or something similar. This report lets you share the survey results with each respondent so that he can see how his answers compare to the rest of the respondents'.

Offering a spotlight report might be a key incentive for getting people to participate in your survey to begin with. Some folks are just curious by nature. They wouldn't take you up on a free luggage tag for filling out your survey about Hawaii as a summer destination, but they'll respond to your survey so that they can see how their views compare to others.

If you use a spotlight report, you don't have to worry about your respondents getting stage fright because the report has an audience of one. In other words, you aren't violating anyone's privacy and you can assure them that you aren't.

You can offer the spotlight report at the end of the survey. Just direct users to a public version of your summary report. Your online survey software should encircle, highlight, or mark your respondents' answers with a star so that they can quickly see how they compare. It's easy to put your respondents in the spotlight, so to speak. Follow these quick steps using your free QuestionPro license:

1. **Log in to your QuestionPro account by entering your username and password.**

2. **Click the My Surveys tab, and then select the survey you want to work with.**

3. **Click the Edit Survey tab.**

4. **Under the Survey Control section in the navigation bar at the left, click Finish Options.**

5. **Select Spotlight Report from the drop-down menu and save your changes.**

   You can see a sample spotlight report in Figure 14-5.

QuestionPro Spotlight Report ™   🖨 Print

Spotlight Report™ and QuestionPro® are registered trademarks of Survey Analytics

■ Your Choice
☐ Overall

Which game do you like the most?

	Answer	Count	Percent	20%	40%	60%	80%	100%
Frequency Analysis								
☆1.	BaseBall	3	50.00%					
2.	Soccer	2	33.33%					
3.	Golf	1	16.67%					
4.	Tennis	0	0.00%					
5.	Other	0	0.00%					
	Total	6	100%					

Which games do you like to watch?

	Answer	Count	Percent	20%	40%	60%	80%	100%
Frequency Analysis								
1.	Hockey	5	45.45%					
☆2.	Soccer	2	18.18%					
☆3.	Golf	3	27.27%					
4.	Tennis	1	9.09%					
	Total	11	100%					

Figure 14-5:
An example of a spotlight report at the completion of a survey.

Dealing with Nonrespondent Bias

With the online survey process, long and unwieldy online surveys are becoming very popular. It's relatively easy and tempting to create long surveys so that granular data points are collected. While on one hand this gives you all the data you need to make and affect business decisions, it also introduces an important concept in online research called *nonrespondent bias* (the bias that results from limiting the survey analysis to the available data).

Nonrespondent bias occurs when people who don't respond to your online survey have different experiences than those who do respond. Your survey winds up biased toward those who responded because they don't represent a full sample of the population. How do you prevent this from having an impact on your survey? Continue reading the following sections to find out.

Nonrespondent bias in action

We now look at nonrespondent bias in action. Here's an easy-to-understand scenario: You have 200 customers. You send out a customer satisfaction survey to all of them. You get a response rate of 20 percent, meaning that you have 40 responses to the survey.

Now consider these questions to determine whether you're dealing with non-respondent bias:

- ✔ **Do these 40 customers speak for all your customers?** If your answer is no, unfortunately you might be dealing with nonrespondent bias. You need to try to drum up more responses from the 160 who didn't answer your survey. Ideally, you would have at least 150 responses to feel comfortable about a balanced survey result.

- ✔ **How confident are you that the responses the 20 percent of your customer base are offering can be taken and applied to most of your customers?** It could be that when you do a skim of your data, you feel pretty confident that the 20 percent who responded are strongly representative of your customer base. Only you can make that decision. However, a number upwards of 60 percent would be a stronger foundation on which to base your market research.

- ✔ **What if only the "very satisfied" or the "very dissatisfied" customers took the time to complete the survey?** This is an interesting question. If your dissatisfied customers are crying out for help, you should address their concerns and let them know you did so. If your very satisfied customers are taking the time to respond, by contrast, that's a good sign. If between the two groups you have a majority of your responses, you might not be as concerned about the middle-of-the-roaders — if this is the case, you probably aren't dealing with nonrespondent bias.

How to avoid nonrespondent bias

Again, *nonrespondent bias* is the bias or the skew in the analysis and interpretation of your data due to the fact that a large percentage of your respondents didn't complete the survey. The more important question to ask is what you can do about this online survey nemesis if you do discover it in your results. Consider the following solutions:

- ✔ **Use a good survey design.** You can avoid nonrespondent bias to begin with (in most cases) if you offer a well-written, well-designed survey. For more tips on how to do this, read Chapters 5 and 6.

- ✔ **Offer your objectives.** Making your respondents aware of your objectives at the get-go can encourage more respondents to participate in your online survey. If your objective is to improve customer service, tell them so. If your objective is to develop a new product and you need their insights, be sure to share that with them.

- ✔ **Keep your survey short.** Surveys that run on and on can lead to online *survey abandonment* (when a person who began taking your survey decides not to finish it). This could lead to nonrespondent bias.

✔ **Keep it private.** Some consumers are hypersensitive about personal privacy online. Assuring your would-be respondents that their information will be kept confidential can help you avoid nonrespondent bias.

✔ **Offer incentives.** Offering incentives for consumers to take your survey could help you avoid nonrespondent bias. A simple token of appreciation, such a discount coupon, can go a long way in getting survey responses.

✔ **Send follow-up invitations.** Sending reminder survey e-mail invitations can help you reduce nonrespondent bias. People might have had good intentions of completing your survey but then became busy and forgot about it.

Although you have many effective ways of making sure that your response rates are high enough to avoid nonrespondent bias, our experience and research has shown that the primary factor responsible for not completing surveys is the length of the survey. While promotions and incentives will always increase the response rates, they're mechanisms for working around the core issue instead of fixing the core issue. If you want our advice, keep your surveys short and simple.

If you don't get many responses to your survey no matter what you've tried, you can send out a follow-up survey to the nonresponders asking why they didn't respond. It might seem like a long shot, but a two-question survey that first asks whether they received the questionnaire followed by a multiple-choice question that offers several reasons why they didn't respond (for example, was the survey too long, were they too busy to complete it, was there a lack of interest, and so on) might offer some interesting insights.

Analyzing Open-Ended Answers

If you included *open-ended questions* (questions that seek to explore the qualitative, in-depth aspects of a particular topic or issue) in your survey, you obviously need to review the text responses manually and take them into consideration based on general trends you find in the responses. You'll find a list of each open-ended text question and response for your reading enjoyment in the results panel of your online survey software.

Surveys are often associated with analytics. Almost all surveys are heavily weighted toward collecting what market researchers call *closed-ended data* — when users are typically asked to choose among a set of choices (either discrete choice or a rating scale, for example). *Open-ended text data* (also called *free-form text*), however, is different in the sense that there's no concrete question — users are asked to give their opinions on a subject via free-form text.

A blessing or a curse?

Open-ended comments on surveys are a curse and a boon for conducting customer perception and satisfaction studies. They're a curse because they can't be consolidated and analyzed easily. Although some textual analysis programs claim to be a by-product of artificial intelligence, we've yet to meet a serious market researcher who uses these automated text analysis tools for real decision making. An open-ended comment is a boon because it allows your respondents to "open up" and give you comments, ideas, and suggestions that you weren't even asking them.

It's generally considered good survey design/practice to have a "catch-all" open-ended comment question toward the end of a survey. Even if you don't really want users to give open-ended comments for your research, a simple open-ended comment question can give you valuable insight into areas of research you've not even thought about. Users might even give you feedback on the survey itself — they might point out grammatical inconsistencies or even offer suggestions on how you can structure your survey better. Trust us on this one — we're speaking from experience!

So, if you're putting together a survey and you don't have an open-ended comments section, think about the valuable data that you're missing out on. You already have a respondent's attention — why not give him the opportunity to express himself in his own words in addition to conforming to your structured survey?

Analyzing the mountain of text

The question is how to tackle the actual analysis. Hopefully you didn't include too many open-ended questions or you'll be knee deep in analysis for some time to come. But, by the same token, hopefully you added one or two questions so that you can get deeper inside the heads of your participants. Here are a few ways to go about it:

✔ **Eyeball browsing:** Believe it or not, the easiest way to analyze open-ended comments is (you guessed it) reading them! If you have a ton of responses, it might make more sense to download the Excel report and read through the comments. Reading through the comments while having the analytical data in the back of your head gives you a complete picture of how to interpret the overall survey.

It's generally prudent to support the analytical data with representative quotes from some comments when preparing an executive summary. This allows a personal, impact-oriented analysis and summary of the survey. This is why journalists typically quote an established figure — to personalize or put a face on the survey data.

✔ **Grouping/segmentation:** In some cases, you might want to isolate the comments for a particular data segment. The most commonly used technique is when respondents are asked a closed-ended question and you want to segment it based on that. For example, if you're running a customer satisfaction survey and you ask your customers to choose the region (or department) that they interacted with, you'll probably have a question that asks users which department they interacted with as a closed-ended, multiple-choice question.

The idea is to filter the results of the open-ended comments and view the ones that are associated with some key departments. This is fairly simple to do within online survey software. The system can filter the open-ended comments for the data segment you choose.

✔ **Keyword searching:** This technique can be used if users are specific about a particular topic. The big question here is what to search for. Because open-ended comments can be all over the map, you need to know what kinds of phrasings your respondents will be using.

A classic example is a satisfaction survey given to all the attendees of a conference. They had the basics of conference surveys, for example, "Did you like the schedule, the speakers, the hotel accommodations," and so on. It turns out that one of the big issues was that the restroom was dirty, and a huge line was apparently there as attendees shuttled among presenters. Keyword-searching open-ended questions could show you what percentage of the comments had to do with that one issue.

This is a good example of having context, and the only way to determine the specific issue is to read the first few comments and decide whether the issues can be framed using a set of keywords. If that's the case, the data can be analyzed in the aggregate and deeper insight can be extracted.

✔ **Text categorization:** If you've been in the market research business, you would call this *coding*. This is where you pay someone to analyze each text response and categorize (or code) the responses into a set of predefined buckets. Quite frankly, we don't believe this is a reasonable cost-efficient model. Numerous flaws are associated with this methodology, and the model is very cumbersome. The first issue is that someone (either within or outside your company) needs to get trained to understand the categorization model.

This is not cheap and really doesn't scale well (it's a linear cost model). For example, the cost to categorize 1,000 comments would be 10 times the cost to categorize 100 comments. The Web is all about exponential scaling, not linear scaling, and you wouldn't be doing online surveys if you didn't buy into the exponential scale concept — would you? This model fits in with the paper survey or the phone survey model, where the cost to conduct a survey is linear — simply because the costs associated with these surveys are time based — where human beings need to spend time as data-entry operators.

Of course, you can find many valid arguments for using a text categorization model, in certain situations, such as when you're paying through the nose for a niche target demographic (doctors, IT decision makers, and so on). In such cases, we think it makes sense to spend the time and effort to analyze the comments using a text categorization model.

Leveraging Excel for quick analysis

For more information on the best use of open-ended questions, read Chapter 6. If you're ready to get started with your open-ended question analysis, follow these steps:

1. **Download your survey responses.**

   You'll need to gather the responses to your open-ended survey in another format. We recommend a Microsoft Excel spreadsheet because it's easy to navigate from one field to another. If you aren't familiar with how to use Excel, pick up a copy of *Excel 2010 For Dummies,* by Greg Harvey, Ph.D. (published by Wiley).

2. **Set up your spreadsheet.**

   Create a column using the random function. This lets you randomly generate codes for each response.

3. **Sort the columns.**

   Sort the columns of your random codes, and select the first 50 rows of responses to begin your analysis.

4. **Develop response categories.**

   Using the first 50 rows as a starting point, begin sifting through the first responses and develop appropriate categories. Look for keywords such as *user-friendly* or *low price,* and group your responses in line with those categories.

5. **Categorize all responses.**

   Repeat Steps 3 and 4 until you have categorized all your responses. Use as many categories as you need to distinguish between the general sentiments in the responses.

6. **Review your categories.**

   Go back through the categorized responses and make sure that each response truly fits into the category you originally put it in. You might decide to drill down even deeper at this point and create some new categories. Or, if results are slim in some categories, you might choose to combine them, such as Value/Cost instead of Value and Cost.

Liar, liar, data on fire!

It was Mark Twain who once said, "There are three kinds of lies: lies, damned lies, and statistics." Twain probably never foresaw the advent of online survey software — or the Internet, or come to think of it, even the computer, for that matter — but he understood the issue of lying statistics. It's vital to understand the statistics and modeling behind survey data so that you can make common (empirical) sense of it.

Here's a good example of how data can lie: Consider that you're conducting a survey to find out what students want out of a Master of Business Administration (MBA) program. You might offer a question that allows potential students to select their top three reasons for attending a specific college. Your choices might include academic, alumni, career, community

service, networking, and social responses. When the results come in, the verdict seems clear: 26 percent of students are pursuing an MBA to further their career and 21 percent chose networking.

Here's the lie: The question was a *multiple-select question,* one that allows participants to select more than one option. If you analyzed the data using a reach analysis or TURF analysis, as opposed to a regular *frequency analysis* that calculates how often a particular choice is selected, your results would be much different: A full 80 percent of users selected career as one of the options. Between networking and career, you have almost 100 percent of the users covered! This tells you what to focus on in your marketing efforts.

With these steps completed, you can sift through your open-ended responses much more quickly. Of course, nothing replaces reading your open-ended responses. You can't get the big picture or maximize the value of the information if you don't digest it. But analyzing open-ended questions is much easier when you take it one step at a time.

Combining Online Surveys and Web Analytics

Online surveys are powerful tools for gaining insights into your target market. You can figure out the core demographics of folks visiting your Web site, why they came online, why they bought what they did, how satisfied they were with the purchase, and so on. But online survey software alone can't tell you certain things. That's when it's time to get daring with your analysis and bring in Web Analytics. For a primer on how to make the most of Web Analytics software, pick up a copy of *Web Analytics For Dummies,* by Pedro Sostre and Jennifer LeClaire (published by Wiley).

Automating your survey analysis

Usually an online survey tends to include both quantitative and qualitative questions. Analysis of the quantitative is obviously quite easy, using such tools as a real-time summary report, grouping/segmentation tool, pivot tables, and so on. The qualitative analysis, however, is much more challenging. You can take numerous routes, most of which involve expensive software or a great deal of time spent coding and tagging the data by hand.

One creative way to handle the workload of analyzing qualitative data is to integrate your online survey software with Amazon's Mechanical Turk. If you haven't heard of this service yet, it's pretty smart: Anyone can submit a request for a task to be completed, while workers can select from the tasks that they would like to get paid to complete. Mechanical Turk offers an API interface, so naturally, the concept of linking your online survey software to this API to tag your open-ended data is the next logical step.

When you combine online surveys with Web Analytics, the possibilities are downright amazing. When you add Web Analytics to the mix, you can drill even deeper to discover how those attitudes reflect actual site usage. Consider the insights you can gain when you combine Web Analytics and online surveys:

- ✔ Did visitors who are more satisfied with your site return more often than those who expressed dissatisfaction during your online survey?

- ✔ What did the dissatisfied visitors actually do while they were on your site? Did they get caught up in a long shopping cart process? Did they have trouble with your product search engine?

- ✔ Did your dissatisfied customers do anything different from your satisfied customers while they were on your site? Were they looking for products you just don't have, for example?

Web Analytics software gives you insights into actual visitor behavior that you can compare with your online survey results to find out what's really going on. Enterprise-level online survey software typically allows you to integrate your applications with Web Analytics software so that you can uncover these powerful connections.

Chapter 15

Reporting Your Online Survey Results

*Y*ou aren't conducting online surveys in a bubble. You have people all around you — colleagues, department leaders, and the general public — that are chomping at the bit to see the results of your online survey.

Your final stop on your market research journey is reporting the results of your questionnaire, including the analysis. After all, if you don't act on the results of your market research, you won't get the business results you hoped to achieve when you started down this path to begin with. Taking it a step further, if people don't understand the *management report* (a summary report of the survey data covering the highlights or key findings), they won't be compelled to act.

Whether or not you like giving presentations, if you've been charged with administering a survey, you're going to need to display your results. That might mean full-out PowerPoint-driven presentations in the conference rooms. Or, it might mean creating a PDF file with pretty charts and graphs that folks can review as you explain the takeaways. But you should know the ins and outs of reporting your online survey results to the powers-that-be within your organization who are trying to make decisions.

You can present reports in written form, verbally, or with charts, graphs, and tables in an interactive presentation. You find out when you should do what and why in this chapter. But you should also brush up on your understanding of statistics, so we give you a primer that will get you off and running. We also show you how to share your reports with colleagues in Excel formats and leave you with some inspiration to put your results into action.

Going Back to Statistics 101

When you saw this headline, you either panicked or felt very confident. Some folks are great with numbers and others aren't. Even if you are a statistics wizard, you are still charged with reporting survey results to folks who might not be.

Whether you're reporting on a customer satisfaction survey to the customer service department, relaying an employee satisfaction survey to the HR department, or reporting the results of some other survey type to some other group within your organization, you need to have a working knowledge of statistics. What's more, you need to be ready to share this working knowledge with others when you present your reports.

If you're deathly afraid of statistics, you could probably use some good news right about now. We have some for you: Your online survey software crunches all the numbers for you. You don't need to figure out the mean, median, and other calculations, but you do need to understand what those terms mean (no pun intended). Without this working knowledge, your results won't work for you because you won't know how to put them into action.

Consider the following a quick education in statistics. You might even call it Statistics 101. These definitions come courtesy of Berkeley University:

- **Association:** Two variables are associated if some of the variability of one can be accounted for by the other. You can have positive associations and negative associations. For example, if you're grouping and segmenting your responses, you might find that different age groups share an association with one another or behave completely differently from one another. Maybe all respondents in your survey shared the positive association of liking vanilla ice cream, but the 25–34 age group tended not to like chocolate sprinkles on top. You have a positive association and a negative association that can help guide your decision making.

- **Mean:** The sum of a list of numbers divided by the number of numbers. This is also called the *average,* and that's a little easier to digest. Through the lens of the online survey world, the average number of people who used your soap products doesn't offer laser precision on which to base your product development decisions, but it does offer a bird's-eye view that might signal the need to drill down farther.

- **Median:** The median is the middle value of a list of values. Put another way, the median is smack dab in the middle. At least half the numbers in the list are no greater than the median. If the list has an odd number of entries, the median is the middle entry in the list after sorting the list into ascending order. If the list has an even number of entries, the median is the smaller of the two middle numbers after sorting. The median represents the middle-of-the-road responders in your study. In online surveys, it can be used as a baseline that can signal a red flag for customer service or disinterest in a new product idea.

- ✔ **Mode:** For lists, the mode is a most common, or most frequent, value. A list can have more than one mode. For example, in your online survey's multiple-choice questions, you might find that the mode was choice C, meaning that respondents chose the answer that corresponded to choice C more often than any other answer.

- ✔ **Population mean:** The population is clearly the people being surveyed. The population mean is the average of the numbers in a numerical population. For our online survey reporting purposes, the *population mean* is the average number of people who responded in a specific way to a specific question.

- ✔ **Range:** The range of a set of numbers is the largest value in the set minus the smallest value in the set. Don't let the standard definition of range fool you. As a statistical term, the range is a single number, not a range of numbers.

- ✔ **Standard deviation:** This describes the probability of the data set's distribution. For our purposes in the online survey world, a high standard deviation signals that the data is spread out. A low standard deviation signals that the data points are close to or identical to the mean.

- ✔ **Variance:** This shows how spread out the distribution of a data set is.

The Written Report

Even if you plan to give a verbal presentation, we recommend that you prepare a written report of your online survey results first. There are a few reasons for this. First, you need to have all your facts straight before you build your presentation. Developing a written report forces you to think about all the elements you need to present. Second, you might also want to provide your audience with a copy of the written report on which they can take notes or reference later. And if you need one more reason, here's a good one: A written report can serve as a study that highlights your organization's history on a topic, such as a customer satisfaction poll. You can use the stats you've recorded in a report as a benchmark for future comparisons.

Written reports let you get into a level of reporting detail that would take you hours to explain in a verbal presentation. When you develop a written report, you can focus your verbal presentation on the high-level overview and the "wow" results that provide people with the information they need to make decisions and the motivation they need to take action on them.

Keeping your target audience in mind

Before you type a single keystroke on your computer, take a minute to consider your target audience. The idea is to tailor your report to the specific information needs of that audience — and you might have several different potential target audiences in your organization.

Although you can certainly create one master management report that drills down into every aspect of the survey, departments within your organization will appreciate not having to read through metrics that don't matter to them. By the same token, your written report to an internal department and your written report to outside audiences (such as investors and consumers) might take on a different tone and share or emphasize different results. So keeping your target audience in mind is critical as you set out to write your management report.

Some audiences to whom you're delivering your report might even have strict guidelines on how to prepare and submit management reports. For example, universities might have different citation styles than the media, and the media might have different length requirements than other audiences. How you present that data might also change based on audience requirements. Investors might require charts and graphs that demonstrate return on investment (ROI), while governments might demand tables that track results over time. You also need to use language that your target audiences are comfortable with, and that might change from one group to another.

Organizing your management report

Like any writing project, your management report needs to be logically organized so that your audiences can make a natural progression through the important points in the survey. Organizing your management report also allows different audiences to jump to the part of the report that matters most to them, whether it's a summary, the methodology, the results, or some other aspect of the online survey.

If you're planning to submit the results of your survey to a professional journal or trade magazine, be sure to get submission guidelines. You'll find different writing styles and formatting styles, such as Chicago, Associated Press, American Psychological Association, and Modern Language Association. With all this said, there's a fairly standard way to format your management reports, and the following sections spell it out.

Leveraging the title page

Don't skimp on the title page. This is your first impression — and you know what they say about first impressions. The title page should include the name of your study, the name of the survey administrator, the name of your company, and the date the report was prepared. If you didn't give your online survey a proper title when you launched it — or if you were just using a working title as a descriptor — now is the time to carefully consider an accurate headline for your report. Consider the following tips:

- ✔ **Use as few words as possible while still conveying the thrust of your survey.** You don't want the title to be so long that you bore people before they even begin reading the report. Keep it short, like you did your online survey.

- ✔ **Keep the keywords near the beginning of the title.** When you use the keywords that describe your online survey near the beginning of the title, you give the reader an immediate clue to the topic of the report.

- ✔ **Brainstorm.** Beyond the two previous tips, you just need to brainstorm. Look at how other studies — especially studies and reports from competitors — are titled to get some clues as to what works and what doesn't. You'll know it when you see it. Write down a page-long list of potential titles and even get some input from your colleagues before you make the final decision.

Offering acknowledgments

You might be the survey administrator, but that doesn't mean you didn't have plenty of help along the road to a successfully completed online survey. This is the area of the management report where you acknowledge the folks who helped you along the way, both personally and professionally. If your online survey had financial sponsors or companies that donated incentives to your participants, this is the most appropriate place to recognize those contributions as well.

All about the abstract

An *abstract* is a short summary of the management report. It's usually a paragraph or two long, up to about 200 words. This is where you share information such the purpose of the study, participant demographics, sampling methods, the relevant results, and the overarching conclusions of your research.

You'll probably need to write the rest of the report and come back and do this at the end. After all, you can't summarize what you haven't yet completed writing.

Executing the executive summary

An *executive summary* is a short document that summarizes a longer report so that readers can draw conclusions without reading the entire document. This is where you highlight the purpose, the methodology, the rationale, and the key findings. This is sort of like a glorified abstract. Instead of 100 words or so, it might run as long as a page. Using bullet points is an effective way to call out key points in the executive summary.

Tackling the table of contents

The table of contents is another aspect of the management report that you won't be able to complete until the writing is finished because you need to correlate the sections of the report with the page numbers on which they begin. Within your table of contents, you might also list tables and figures.

Most report authors include separate lists of tables and figures so that graphics junkies can reference them quickly.

Introducing the introduction

The introduction is another place where you can make a strong first impression. This is the text you use to introduce the survey report itself. If your introduction is boring, people might not want to read your report. Some target audiences might have no choice but to read the report, but others (such as the media) might not have to.

The introduction of your survey should convince readers that the research you've conducted is important. You need to be clear about the objectives of the study and how valuable the insights are.

Be careful not to run on and on, though. Most people will want to move into the actual study quickly and don't want to get bogged down in the introduction. And sure, some folks will skip the introduction altogether. Those who do read your introduction should move on with anticipation to see the results.

Glossary

If your online survey — or its results — relies on technical terms or industry jargon, it's vitally important that you include a glossary with your study. (That's the same reason why we've included a glossary with this book and painstakingly defined terms throughout the chapters.) If you use acronyms or abbreviations, you should clearly define those in your glossary too. In the world of management reports, you do this up front rather than at the end because you want the reader to be familiar with the jargon before he dives into the full body of the report.

Methodology

Including your methodology is important. *Methodology* is the collection, the comparative study, and the critique of the individual methods that are used in a given discipline or field of inquiry. Put another way, it's the method you used to conduct your online survey. In a nutshell, it lays out who was involved, the vehicles on which you conducted your survey, and the types of questions that were asked.

The idea here is to allow others to conduct duplicate surveys that validate or annul your results. That's not bound to happen with customer and employee surveys. But recording the methodology is still important so that the next time you want to conduct the same kind of survey, you can use the same methodology and then compare results over time. Here's what you should include in your methodology:

- ✔ **Survey vehicle:** Online or hybrid. A *hybrid* is survey in which you use more than one technique to gather responses. For example, if you manually entered in paper-based surveys for folks who couldn't go online, you need to make that clear here.

- ✔ **Survey limitations:** You should clearly spell out the limitations of online surveys. This is fair and just, because limitations exist on every survey type, including online surveys. If you want to read more about the limitations of online surveys, as well as other types of surveys, read Chapter 1.

- ✔ **Survey question types:** You should offer examples of the types of questions you asked, or at least indicate what question types you relied on. If you relied heavily on open-ended questions or scales, you want to make that clear. You can read more about question types in Chapter 6.

- ✔ **Response types:** You find many different response types, such as drop-down menus, comment boxes, and checklists. Your methodology should spell out your response types.

- ✔ **Incentives offered:** If you offered incentives, whether money, product discounts, coupons, or some other prize, you need to make that clear in your methodology. If you didn't offer incentives, you need to make that clear too.

- ✔ **Distribution methods:** Even with online surveys, you still need to indicate how you found your participants — whether you used your e-mail list, hired a survey *panel company* (a company that gives you the list of people willing to participate in surveys like yours), or used some other method. You can read more about recruitment methods in Chapter 9. You also want to indicate how you dealt with folks who didn't respond to your survey invitation — whether you followed up, how many times, and so on.

- ✔ **Informed consent methods:** Consent is vital. You need to indicate how you addressed this issue. This is usually handled with a question on the first page of your survey that asks "Do you consent to taking this survey?" See Figure 15-1 for an example of an informed consent question.

Use survey branching to exit the survey if your respondent chose not to consent to take the survey. For more on survey branching, see Chapter 7.

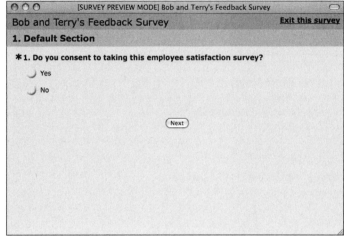

Figure 15-1:
An informed
consent
question
using
Survey
Monkey.

✔ **Validity:** *Validity* is whether the survey measures what it intends to measure. You need to discuss how you ensured that your responses were valid. For more information on validity, read Chapter 6.

✔ **Survey construction:** You need to address how you built the survey; the software program used; the languages in which you launched it; whether you included graphics, photos, or videos in the survey; the reading level of the questions; and so on. For more about building surveys, read Chapter 5.

✔ **Anonymity:** You need to indicate as part of the methodology whether the survey respondents offered anonymous answers or whether the participants can be identified.

✔ **Sampling:** You need to indicate what sampling method you used to conduct your survey. To find out more about sampling methods, read Chapter 11.

✔ **Incompletes:** Your methodology should also indicate how you handled incomplete surveys — whether you ditched the entire survey or pulled the answers from the survey into the overall results for particular questions.

Results

Finally . . . the results portion of your management report. This is one of the most exciting parts. It's where you get to share all the keen insights you learned from your online survey. You'll probably want to use a good number of charts, tables, and graphs in the results segment of your report. We talk about those in the section "Counting on Charts, Tables, and Graphs," later in this chapter. Your results section should incorporate the following information:

 ✔ A summary of key findings with charts when possible

 ✔ Relevant observations and conclusions based on the data

 ✔ In-depth analysis of the data, with plenty of figures and explanations

Try to avoid interpreting the results or offering actionable insights in this section. Here you stick to just the facts, ma'am. You can observe associations or interesting trends, but you shouldn't attempt to give them meaning at this stage of the report.

Recommendations

With the results all in, this is the section of your report where things finally get action-oriented. This is where you interpret the results of your online survey. Be sure to show plenty of facts and figures to support your conclusions. However, this is not the time to make assumptions or engage in guesswork. You need concrete evidence that demonstrates why you're recommending a specific course of action for your organization.

Maybe your results didn't line up with what you were expecting. If that's the case, try to demonstrate why that might have occurred. Consider what external forces — such as time of year, world events, competitor product launches, or some other issues — might have impacted public opinion during your online survey window. If you found pleasant surprises in your online survey results, highlight those as well. Sometimes you discover helpful answers to questions you didn't even think to ask.

References

If you relied on other research to supplement your management report, to put key concepts into context, or to draw comparisons between your study and others, cite those sources in the reference section.

Appendix

If you have additional information that wasn't immediately relevant to the core study but might be helpful for putting the study into a broader context or better explain your methodology, then insert this into an appendix. You might offer screen shots of some of your questions, for example, or in-depth demographic data.

Counting on Charts, Tables, and Graphs

Charts, graphs, and tables — everybody loves them. In the world of data analysis, charts, graphs, and tables offer the eye candy that breaks up mundane rows of numbers and otherwise helps people digest your reports more easily. When it comes to using charts, graphs, and tables in your online survey reports, you need to know where you're heading before you take off. In other words, take the time to consider how you want to present the data when you begin analyzing it. It could make a major impact on how you proceed.

Ideally, you'll have thought about your survey analysis in terms of the sampling methods before you launched the survey. Random sampling methods are the preferred way to conduct online surveys because random samples introduce less bias. A *random sample* is one in which every element in the population has an equal chance of being selected. If you want to find out more about sampling methods, read Chapter 11.

Defining the different charts, tables, and graphs

Charts are vital to your survey reports, whether written or verbal. Charts are the most viewer-friendly way to see results. But just because you can and should use charts in your online survey management report doesn't mean that you should do so with reckless abandon. First, you need to understand the various uses of charts. Then, you need to understand the do's and don'ts about them. We now explore the wonderful world of charts, tables, and graphs.

Bar chart

A *bar chart* uses bars (big surprise) to show frequencies or values for different categories (see Figure 15-2). You find horizontal bar charts and vertical bar charts. If you're surveying consumers to find out how much money they spend on various household budget items, a bar chart would break down the results into category bars such as house payment, car payment, groceries, and so on. The tallest or longest bars would signal the highest proportion of income allotted to that category.

The advantage of using a bar chart is that comparisons are quick and easy. The results are represented by bars that are staggered according to the results. At a glance, you can quickly see the top results, the bottom of the barrel, and the middle, and you can make quick comparisons among the bars. Bar charts are also ideal for showing how data changes over time and express trends better than tables. The downside to bar charts is that they tend to require some additional explanation, they might yield false impressions if further interpretation isn't offered, and they don't reveal causes, effects, or patterns.

Figure 15-2:
A bar chart using FluidSurveys.

Histogram

A *histogram* typically shows the quantity of points that fall within various numeric ranges. The histogram displays *continuous data* (quantitative data that's measured in intervals on a number line) in ordered columns. It's used to measure categories in time, inches, temperature, or some other continuous measure. The advantages of histograms are that they're visually strong and they make it easy to compare one result to another. The downside of histograms is you can't see the exact values because the data is grouped into categories. If you don't have continuous data, you can't use this chart.

Line graph

A *line graph* is a two-dimensional *scatter plot* (a plot that displays the relationship between two factors) of ordered observations, where the observations are connected following their order. These graphs are sometimes called *line charts* or *plot graphs*. A good use of a line chart is to make strict comparisons. For example, you could compare your customer satisfaction survey results from the last quarter to your customer survey results from this quarter.

The line graph (see Figure 15-3) offers quick analysis of data. You can compare multiple continuous data sets easily. The disadvantage is that you can only use the line graph with continuous data. It wouldn't be appropriate in our household budget example in the "Bar chart" section, earlier in this chapter.

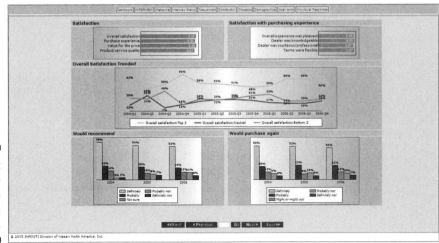

Figure 15-3: An example of a line graph using ConfirmIt.

Pie chart

A *pie chart* shows percentage values as a slice of a pie. If you are surveying consumers to find out how much money they spend on various household budget items, a pie chart would break down the results into categories, such as house payment, car payment, groceries, and so on.

Pie charts (see Figure 15-4) make it easy to see relative proportions of multiple classes of data. They help to summarize the data in a virtual form, and they require minimal explanation. The pie chart is easy to understand, and most people are familiar with them. The downside to pie charts is that they don't offer specific values and they don't reveal causes, effects, or patterns. If you aren't careful, you can draw incorrect conclusions from pie charts.

Table

A *table* is a set of data arranged in rows and columns. The only time you really want (or need) to use tables is when you have so much data that you can't spell it out in the text without a page-long narrative. A table (see Figure 15-5), for example, might be effectively used to compare the responses of males and females who said they were very satisfied, satisfied, unsatisfied, or very unsatisfied. With a table, you can portray meaning in your data, whereas if you tried to explain it in prose alone, you would bore your readers.

While you can find many other types of charts, tables, and graphs, these are the most common to the online survey world.

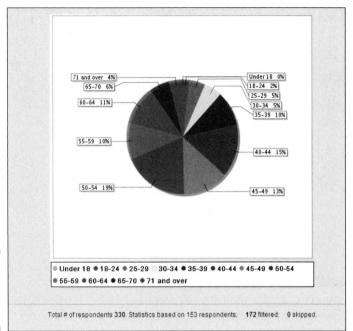

Figure 15-4:
A pie chart in KeySurvey.

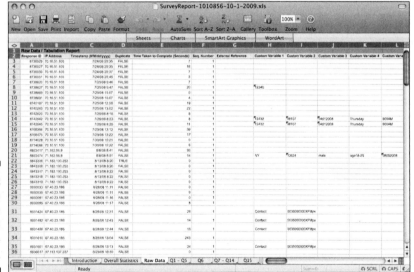

Figure 15-5:
Survey data in table form via an Excel spreadsheet.

Using charts, graphs, and tables the right way

You can make a mess with charts, tables, and graphs if you aren't careful. But you can also use them to make your point in a way that words couldn't describe with nearly as much impact. Sometimes, visuals are the best way to make a point. There are some do's and don'ts we want to explore here.

Avoid 3-D charts

Charts dress up your management report and add spice to your verbal presentation. But you don't want to overdress your report or add so much spice that it overwhelms your audience. 3-D charts qualify as overdressing. That's because they can throw off the viewer. 3-D charts tilt the graphs and skew your perspective. You worked so hard not to skew your data, so don't start now by using a 3-D chart.

Title your chart

Just as you titled your online survey management report, you also need to title your charts. At a glance, your readers should be able to get the gist of the purpose of the chart. If you fail to title your chart or otherwise describe it, you're leaving your readers in a dimly lit room.

Use colors appropriately

When it comes to charts, you need to use contrasting colors so that people can clearly distinguish one area of the chart from another at a glance. If you use navy blue next to black, you're forcing your viewers to work too hard to see the results. Get out a color wheel if you have to and use colors on the opposite sides of the wheel to make a contrast.

Explain yourself

Don't forget to offer an explanation. Offer a one- or two-line description that tells readers why they should pay attention to this graph, point out the significance of the data, and tell them what conclusions it offers — but do it quickly!

Sharing Your Reports with Colleagues

After you get the survey results and all the customer revelations about your products and services that come with them, one of two things will happen. You'll be so excited at the opportunities the survey represents, or you'll be disappointed that your organization hasn't lived up to its reputable brand name. Either way, you'll be eager to share the results of your reports with colleagues so that the decision makers can do what they do best: make decisions on how to respond to the results.

You can share your reports with colleagues via e-mail, Twitter, or Facebook, or through report-sharing links. You can even export them as PDFs or plug them into PowerPoint presentations. You can share them with everyone, or you can provide a password that allows a select few to view the reports. Your online survey tools give you plenty of options for sharing your reports with colleagues. You might even find that some prefer one method over another. Whatever it takes to make the boss happy!

Here's how to allow your colleagues to see the results of your online survey using the free QuestionPro license that came with this book:

1. **Log in to your QuestionPro account by entering your username and password.**

2. **Click the My Surveys tab, then select the survey that contains the data you'd like to share.**

3. **Click the Reports tab at the top of the screen.**

4. **Click the Real-Time Summary link in the upper left under the Reports section.**

5. **Turn Report Sharing on.**

   At the top of the screen, the report sharing status will be displayed (Report Sharing is ON or OFF).

   You see a text box with the link to your report (see Figure 15-6).

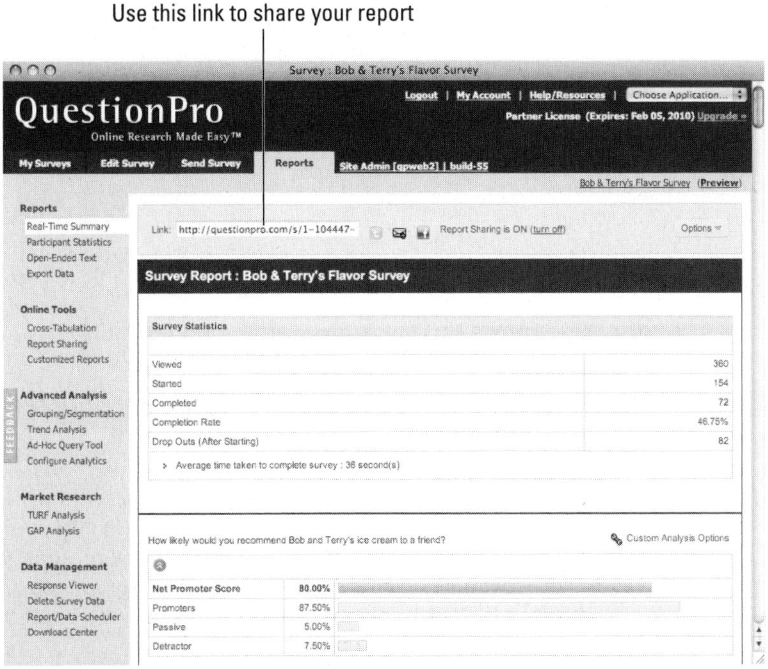

Use this link to share your report

Figure 15-6: Report-sharing tools in Question Pro's real-time summary report.

6. **Copy this link to share with your colleagues.**

   You can also click the Twitter or Facebook icon (just to the right of the text box with the report link) to share with your social network.

If you'd like to restrict the report to the people within your organization who are on a need-to-know basis, click Report Sharing in the upper left, enter a password in the Password field, and click the Save button. You can then share the password with the appropriate people within the organization and keep others who don't need to know out of the know.

What If 1 Need an Excel Spreadsheet?

If you need to export your raw data out of your online survey software and into another file format, even the free tools make that possible. We highly recommend exporting your raw data into an Excel spreadsheet. That's because sometimes you need to have the data in another format, and it's always a good idea to have a backup.

If you don't like working with Excel, you can use comma-separated values (CSV) files or SPSS files. A *CSV* file is used for the digital storage of data structured in a table of lists form, where each associated item (member) in a group is in association with others also separated by the commas of its set. *SPSS* is a computer program used for statistical analysis.

Your online survey software lets you export the raw data from your survey to any of these common external file formats. Here's how to export your raw data using your free QuestionPro license that came with this book:

1. **Log in to your QuestionPro account by entering your username and password.**

2. **Click the My Surveys tab, then select the survey that contains the data you'd like to export to an Excel spreadsheet.**

3. **Click the Reports tab at the top of the screen.**

4. **Under the Reports section in the navigation bar at the left, click Export Data.**

5. **In the Raw Data Export box (see Figure 15-7), select the exporting options you want and click the Download button.**

   Now hold tight — QuestionPro will take a minute to generate the file. Each time you request a file, a link is displayed for you to download it. Also, files are e-mailed or made available in the processing queue for your convenience. When you receive the files, you can put them in a safe place for storage, conduct additional analysis, or share them with your colleagues.

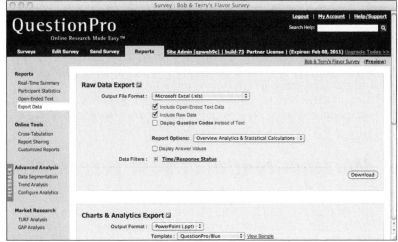

Figure 15-7:
Preparing
to export
your data
to an Excel
spread-
sheet.

Making Live Presentations

If you thought you were going to escape the lesson on making live presentations of your management report, think again. Some folks just shiver and shake at the notion of giving live presentations. But things can go much more smoothly if you take the advice offered in this section. Just as with written reports, you need to keep your target audience in mind.

Your oral presentation will have a different format than your written report. You'll introduce the survey, give the meat of the results, and offer a conclusion that presents some interpretation. You should spend most of your time on the main message — diving into the numbers and showing visuals that drive your points home. Your visuals could be handouts, PowerPoint presentations, or even videos. The most common tool, however, is the PowerPoint presentation.

If you want to find out more about PowerPoint, pick up a copy of *PowerPoint For Dummies,* by Doug Lowe (published by Wiley). In the meantime, here are some quick tips for putting together a PowerPoint presentation to bring your live presentation to life.

Communicate clearly

Make sure that your slides communicate your most important points. You do this not only through text but also through presentation tools. First, outline your copy in a word processor before putting it into the slide tool. You can set up and use the templates that Microsoft offers, for example, for more visual appeal.

Use space effectively

After you have your message and your template, it's time to put your copy into the slides. Use space effectively. Don't crowd the slides with too much information. Less is more in PowerPoint. Include only the key points you want to make, and maybe a graph or chart to accompany them. You can hide notes in the bottom of the tool that only you can see. These notes can guide your live presentation, helping with your verbal explanation to what is seen onscreen.

Maintain control of your presentation

If your presentation crashes, it won't do anybody much good. Be sure that your file sizes aren't so large that they load slowly. Use smaller picture and graph sizes. You can do this with file-compression tools and by using native PowerPoint features like tables and charts whenever possible.

Don't parrot PowerPoint

This is something we've seen time and again. The presenter sits and reads the copy from the PowerPoint presentation. This doesn't make for an effective presentation. Your PowerPoint presentation should be a visual aid only, supporting the points you're making instead of making them for you. You might even want to insert some blank slides to pull the audience's attention back to you when you don't have a specific graph or chart to show.

Sharing Your Results with Participants

After you're certain that you have the answers you need — and that the answers are accurate — one of the first things you should do is share them with the respondents. After all, you couldn't have done it without them, and many of them are probably eager to know the results. But you have another reason to offer the results to your participants: You're likely to get even more valuable insights when you let them in on the findings. You have a few options here. Consider these benefits of sharing your online survey results with the masses:

- ✔ **Generating leads:** You might generate more leads and close more sales. You can even pull anonymous quotes from clients who offered positive feedback about your product and service for use as testimonials.

- ✔ **Positioning yourself as an expert:** You can position yourself and your company as an industry leader and expert in your field by associating your brand with online surveys. Your company is on the cutting edge, is forward thinking, and cares about client feedback. That's the image you want to portray.

> ✔ **Marketing new services:** Publishing your online survey results could even be a marketing tool. When you distribute survey results about customer satisfaction, it can serve as a reminder of what you offer or help introduce loyal customers to new products and services they might not have tried.

E-mail survey results to your list

If you sent your online survey to a distinct e-mail list, you can announce the results the same way. Just work up an e-mail that thanks the participants once again for taking the survey and gives a recap of the results. Use bullet points to share key findings, and be sure to share your action plan with your participants. In other words, tell them how you're going to move forward based on their valuable feedback.

Share survey results on your Web site

You can also use the e-mail that contains the recap of the survey results (see the preceding section) to entice participants to click the link to your Web site, where the results are displayed in greater detail. Or, you can just publish them on your Web site for all to see with or without an invitation. You might choose to set up a separate e-mail address and invite people to comment on the results, whether they took the online survey or not. You might get a lot of congratulations, or you might get some folks who fill your ear with why your survey results are wrong. Either way, you get more valuable feedback.

Share survey results on your blog

A surefire way to encourage additional comments about your online survey results is to post the results to your blog. Two-thirds of the world's Internet population visit social networking or blogging sites, accounting for almost 10 percent of all Internet time, according to a Nielsen report. That number is expected to grow. Sharing your survey results on your blog encourages visitor interaction. Who knows? Maybe some other bloggers will pick up on your survey results and you'll build some additional buzz around your brand.

Share survey results on social networks

Social networking has become a fundamental part of the global online experience, according to Nielsen. Nielsen Online CEO John Burbank commented that while two-thirds of the global online population already access member community sites, their vigorous adoption and the migration of time show no signs of slowing. If your company is active on social networks like Twitter and Facebook, posting your survey results there is a smart move. You can generate even greater awareness for your company as one that cares about its clients and customers.

Distribute a press release about your results

If your online survey results might be of interest to a broader community, distribute a press release that features the key findings. Perhaps you run a travel agency and you received some insights about customer preferences for vacation spots. Distributing a press release about your findings positions your company as a leading-edge knowledge center for industry trends. You might even get journalists calling you to ask your expert opinion on fall get-away spots. The point is, a press release — you can even distribute it over a free service — broadens your audience and could pay dividends via positive brand exposure.

Are You Ready for Action?

Now that you've reported on the results, your organization should be ready to put the findings into action. To fail at this point would make the entire journey into the world of online surveys a waste of time. After all, you set out to make business decisions based on this data — now it's time to run with it.

If you conducted a customer satisfaction or an employee satisfaction survey, it's now your job to determine the most effective ways to make improvements within your organization. If you launched market research around a new product or service, it's time to decide whether you want to take the plunge, whether you need more market research, or whether you should hold off on your bright idea. Whatever kind of research you were doing, you need to take a good hard look at how your results lined up with your assumptions and make a move. Of course, sometimes making a move means sitting still.

Whatever your course of action is, be sure to share it with the people who took the time to take your online survey. If you're improving call center processes, let them know and invite them to let you know if they don't see improvements. If you're going to launch a new product, let them know and offer to send them a sample or offer a coupon so that they feel special. After all, they are special — they traveled with you on this journey, and you want them to keep traveling with you as you embark on your next online survey.

Part V
The Part of Tens

The 5th Wave   By Rich Tennant

"I like getting complaint letters by e-mail. It's easier to delete than to shred."

In this part . . .

*N*ow that you've got the basics of online surveys under your belt, this final part of the book helps you implement best practices, avoid embarrassing survey mistakes, and offers strategies for increasing your response rates.

We discuss a number of pitfalls that are common in the online survey realm. There are plenty of stumbling blocks on the road to online survey success, and we help you avoid them.

Of course, it's one thing to avoid pitfalls. It's another thing to find a road that's been freshly paved (as is the case with the relatively young field of online surveys). That's why we illustrate some online survey best practices in this part. These approaches to creating and launching surveys are tried and true and will work for you just like your favorite cake recipe.

Finally, we offer proven ways to wring more responses out of your e-mail list, Web site visitors, and other potential survey respondents. After all, at the end of the day it's all about getting the answers you need. We show you how to make the most out of your survey.

Chapter 16

Ten Ways to Increase Your Response Rates

*Y*ou've defined your audience. You've developed strong questions. You've built a user-friendly survey. You even launched it to your e-mail list, your Web site, and in a few other places you were sure would draw respondents in droves. Hopefully, your strategy paid off, and you received an overwhelming response to your online survey that gave you all the insights you needed — and more. But if you didn't, don't fear. We have some good advice to help you boost your response rates.

If you're reading this chapter *before* you launch your online survey, you can maximize your response rate because some of our suggestions (such as targeting the right audience) require implementation from the get-go.

In this chapter, we share ten strategies for increasing your response rates. Some of them might seem like no-brainers, but others might be less obvious. Either way, if you employ these ten tips you're almost guaranteed to increase the response rates on your online survey.

Targeting the Right Audience

Whether you're designing a new product, launching an ad campaign, or conducting an online survey, your success always begins with targeting the right audience. If you want to increase the response rates of your online survey, you need to make sure your survey is presented to the people who have some interest in your brand.

In other words, your target audience should be made up of people who are interacting with your products or services specifically, or your product category generally. Your audience members must have some connection with your organization or they won't bother to take your survey. In fact, one of the biggest points of failure in the online survey world is sending surveys to the wrong audiences.

Knowing what audiences to target with your survey begins with understanding the objectives and scope of your survey. That's why preparation is so vital to a successful survey. (To find out more about how to prepare a successful survey, check out Chapter 5.)

If you're launching a survey about how visitors to your hotel chain perceive your customer service, you need to target consumers who have actually visited your hotel chain in order to get accurate responses. By the same token, if you're launching a survey that compares your hotel chain with other leading brands, you need to target consumers who have frequented all the hotel chains in question; otherwise, you won't get valid responses.

Don't be overwhelmed wondering how to effectively reach your target audiences with your online survey. You can find qualified respondents in a variety of ways. You can start with your own e-mail list. Presumably, folks who have opted to receive communications from your company have some interest in seeing you provide the best products and services possible. You can also post your online survey on your Web site, to newsgroups, or in other Web communities your target audience frequents.

With the rise of social networking, your company fan pages are a smart place to insert links to your survey. Company blogs are also an ideal place to post your online surveys. If you're unsure how to navigate these waters, check out other Wiley book titles such as *Facebook For Dummies,* by Carolyn Abram and Leah Pearlman; *Blogging For Dummies,* by Susannah Gardner and Shane Birley; *WordPress For Dummies,* by Lisa Sabin-Wilson; or *MySpace For Dummies, 2nd Edition,* by Ryan Hupfer, Mitch Maxson, and Ryan Williams. It's time to get on the social media bandwagon. You can glean tremendous insights from conversations that take place on social networking sites.

Personalizing Your E-Mail Invitations

The sender and the subject line are the first two things your recipient sees, but you can pretty safely assume that your recipient is getting flooded with e-mails. If you want to avoid the perils of the Delete button, you need to connect with your potential respondents quickly. For example, send your e-mail to "Dear Mr. Wright" rather than "Dear Valued Alumni." Addressing recipients by name signals that they already have a relationship with you. This is a proven way to increase your response rates. Figure 16-1 shows a personalized invitation.

Figure 16-1: A personalized survey invitation.

Dear John Doe,

Please take this short survey regarding Bob and Terry's ice cream by clicking here: <u>Start Survey</u>

Thanks.

The Bob and Terry's Team
1134 Rockford, IL

Survey Analytics | 3518 Fremont Ave N #598 | | Seattle | WA | 98103 | USA   <u>Unsubscribe</u> | <u>Report Abuse</u>

While you're at it, you might want to try personalizing your subject line, too. The personalized salutation in the interior of your digital invitation won't take you very far if the recipient doesn't bother to open the e-mail. Your subject line should hint at what's inside the e-mail but with enough creativity to pique the reader's interest.

Your subject line needs to be catchy. Some winning subject lines include "Your Feedback is Needed," "Help Us Serve You Better," and "Learn What Your Peers Think About [Insert Topic]." You might need to test what works better with your customer base by sending half the e-mail invitations with one subject line and half with another. It's not a scientific test, but this technique gives you a chance to explore which subject lines seem to best encourage recipients to open the e-mail.

People are weary of spam. The source of the survey itself can factor into whether the reader opens the file or hits the Delete button. Using a `noreply@ companyname.com` address is one way to make your online survey seem impersonal before the reader ever knows what your survey is all about — or what incentives you might be offering for completing the survey. Instead, use the name of the person who is managing the survey, the corporate brand name, or some combination of the two.

This part of online surveys has parallels to e-mail marketing. If you want to go deeper into ways to get people to open your e-mails, check out *E-Mail Marketing For Dummies,* by John Arnold. *E-Mail Marketing For Dummies* can help you send your message to the inboxes of the world while observing professional standards, improving your deliverability, and executing your e-mail invitations in line with current laws.

Keeping Your Invites Short and Sweet

If you want to increase your response rates, you absolutely must keep your e-mail invitation short and sweet. The first line of your survey is the most important because, as any good journalism teacher will tell you, if you don't capture the reader's interest in the first couple of lines you've probably lost him forever.

Although your e-mail invitation should be brief, it does need to make a few clear, convincing points to lead your reader down the digital road to your online survey. Here are some things to clarify in your e-mail:

- **Who and why:** Right off the bat, you need to tell the reader who you are and the purpose of the study. Be clear about how the survey can benefit the recipient. "Your feedback will help us provide you with better quality service" is a good example of what we're talking about.

- **What:** Be sure to let the reader know the specific subject of the survey, such as "This online survey examines your views on the dog food industry."

- **Duration:** It's absolutely vital to let your readers know how long the survey will take to complete. People are busy, and they want to understand the time commitment involved before making that time commitment. If the survey will only take a few minutes, emphasize that. Whatever you do, be honest about the length of the survey. People are more likely to stick with longer surveys if they know roughly how much time they will take. But if you deceive the reader by suggesting the survey is short when it's really long, you'll breach a trust that's hard to regain.

- **Incentives:** If you are offering incentives, be clear about what they are and how to get them.

- **Anonymity:** If the survey is anonymous, briefly mention that in a single sentence as well.

- **Privacy statement:** If your organization requires a privacy statement, be sure to include it.

All in all, this e-mail is only a couple of paragraphs and leads to a call to action: Take our survey now!

One tried-and-true way to increase response rates is to include the link to your survey more than once in the e-mail invitation, as shown in Figure 16-2. The best way to do this is to insert the link at both the beginning and the end of the e-mail.

Multiple links to a survey

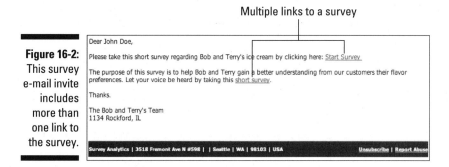

Figure 16-2:
This survey
e-mail invite
includes
more than
one link to
the survey.

Dear John Doe,

Please take this short survey regarding Bob and Terry's ice cream by clicking here: Start Survey

The purpose of this survey is to help Bob and Terry gain a better understanding from our customers their flavor preferences. Let your voice be heard by taking this short survey.

Thanks.

The Bob and Terry's Team
1134 Rockford, IL

Survey Analytics | 3518 Fremont Ave N #598 | | Seattle | WA | 98103 | USA   Unsubscribe | Report Abuse

Keeping It Simple

Much the same way you kept your e-mail invitation short and sweet, you need to keep your survey instructions short and sweet. After people have decided to take your survey, they'll want to get started. Studies show that most people don't read extensive instructions. If you want to increase your response rates, decrease the length of your instructions to a sentence or two. If your survey demands more explanation than that, it's probably too complicated.

Trumpeting Your Privacy Protections

Existing laws and regulations mandate securing the personal information of consumers and employees. What's more, privacy concerns are top priority in the minds of many online consumers. A 2008 survey by information security research company Ponemon Institute and Internet privacy trustmark TRUSTe revealed that over 70 percent of consumers surveyed ranked personal privacy protection as "important" or "very important."

With the advent of technologies that track people's online behaviors in order to serve up relevant ads, privacy advocates are up-in-arms over Internet privacy. Although some consumers might not be too concerned — about 30 percent if you consider the preceding survey results — it's better to be safe than sorry when it comes to explaining privacy protections. If you want to increase your response rates, be sure to trumpet your privacy protections.

Here's how you do it: Include information about how you will be using people's responses on the first page of the survey. Even with online privacy concerns rising, people are typically comfortable sharing information on the Internet if they know how it will be used. Are they anonymous? Is the information confidential? Shared with others? How long do you keep the data? How is it secured? In a few lines, you need to be able to clearly answer those types of questions and put your respondents at ease.

If your organization doesn't already have one, create a Web page that states your privacy policies and terms of use. Then place the link to these policies in the footer of your survey.

Sending Friendly Reminder E-Mails

Some people will take your survey right away. Others will be too busy to take it at all. Still others might have every intention of completing your online survey as soon as they get through their next big deadline.

In any case, you can increase your response rate by sending follow-up e-mail reminders that include the survey link. Some studies show that you can more than double your response rate with reminder e-mails; you can see a spike in new respondents each time you send the reminder. Resending the survey is an important technique if you didn't get enough responses for a proper sample after the first invitation or if you're trying to reach out to unhappy customers to address their concerns.

A best practice is that reminder e-mails should be even shorter than the original e-mail invitation and should emphatically remind recipients what they stand to gain from completing the survey.

Enterprise-level online survey software can automatically send reminder e-mails only to potential respondents who haven't yet completed the survey. (Sending a reminder to someone who has already completed the survey would be downright annoying.) You can set up your online survey software to send reminder e-mails at the intervals you desire. Typically, you don't want to send more than three e-mail reminders. If your recipients haven't decided to take the survey after you've contacted them four times, they likely aren't interested. You don't want to aggravate customers or potential customers. Maybe they'll take the next survey. Also, be sure to filter out e-mail addresses of people who replied with an "unsubscribe" or some other indication that they don't want to be contacted again.

Offering Compelling Incentives

If your survey is lengthy, if it covers a boring subject, or if your company doesn't have an established relationship with the respondents, offering an incentive to complete the survey might be your best way to increase response rates. To be clear, in these instances you need to offer a tangible gift that will be mailed at a defined time rather than a sweepstakes with a chance to win a prize. Sweepstakes work well when you're sending online surveys to large audiences who have vested interest in seeing you improve your products and services. But otherwise, compelling incentives are your best bet for getting responses.

If your budget allows it, give incentives to all your respondents — not just a lucky few via a sweepstakes or random drawing. Studies show that you can get increased response rates when you guarantee a gift or prize with all completed surveys.

The good news is that studies show incentives don't have to be large to increase response rates. In fact, you can see better results by offering 1,000 people a small incentive than offering 100 people a large incentive. A small token, gift certificate, or something similar can increase responses considerably. To limit your expenses, you can choose to limit the incentive to the first X number of respondents. That limit gives respondents a sense of urgency to complete your online survey.

Consider making your incentive optional. A large number of people complete a survey to share their information rather than to receive an incentive. Some respondents might prefer to remain completely anonymous, or perhaps they have no interest in the incentives you're offering. Let your respondents choose to be included in a raffle rather than automatically entering them when they complete the survey.

Make sure your incentives are as relevant as possible for your respondents. If you're surveying math geeks, a free gift certificate to the ESPN Shop probably wouldn't woo them. Similarly, giving out free pocket protectors to football players would make little sense.

Using Graphics Strategically

Surveys generally don't need fancy graphics, and sometimes graphics can distract from the content of the survey or influence answers. Adhering to the "Keep It Simple" rule from earlier in this chapter, use graphics strategically and purposefully so the reader can focus on the questions.

Respondents may also subconsciously interpret the questions based on the images you've used. If an image shows a product in question, that might enhance the respondent's ability to offer an accurate response. But if the graphic is merely to make the page pretty, it stands to distract the respondent and might even lead to *survey abandonment* — which means respondents fail to complete the survey at some point along the way.

That said, here are a few ways to use graphics to improve your survey responses:

✔ You probably want to use your company logo (as shown in Figure 16-3) because it helps recipients quickly identify with your brand and it breeds credibility.

✔ You can use a graphic in a survey to clarify the product that you're referring to. Some people can relate more to pictures than words.

✔ You can provide an image and Web link for a prize or an incentive that shows the recipient exactly what she'll get.

The company logo

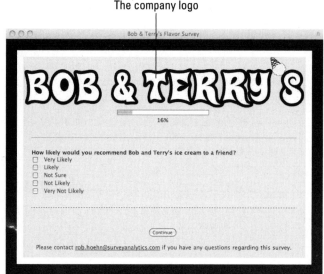

Figure 16-3:
A company logo in a survey.

Leveraging the Viral Effect

With Web 2.0 technologies encouraging content sharing, savvy online survey developers are increasing response rates by using friends, family, and colleagues to help them spread their online survey to others. You can employ this strategy by offering respondents an opportunity to send the survey to others when they have completed your questionnaire. Specifically, you can offer the respondent an incentive, such as an extra entry in your sweepstakes, for providing additional e-mail addresses of people who might also be interested in taking the survey.

Encourage respondents to share the link to your survey on various social networking sites like Facebook or Twitter. This is a great way to reach out to additional respondents who might not exist in your own contact list.

Publishing Your Results Online

No one likes to think that he has taken the time to complete an online survey only to have the results go into a black hole. People who respond want to see results and find out how their responses stack up against others who took the survey. Offering them a chance to see these results encourages would-be respondents to complete the survey. Figure 16-4 shows a report that respondents see at the end of a survey.

Of course, this doesn't mean you have to publish them for the entire world to see. Most online survey providers let you share the results publicly, with only the respondents of the survey, or with a private group of people you specifically choose. Even if you plan to publish your survey results to the masses, offer your respondents a sneak peek at the results before the rest of the world sees them.

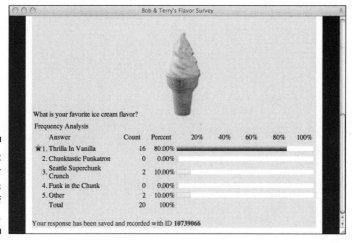

Figure 16-4: A report for respondents at the end of a survey.

Chapter 17

Ten Common Survey Mistakes to Avoid

Mistakes. Nobody likes to make them, but everybody makes them. When it comes to online surveys, though, making simple mistakes may actually justify crying over the proverbial spilled milk.

That's because one simple mistake can derail your entire online survey before you ever send an invitation. Other mistakes aren't as drastic, but they can still make your organization look pretty silly or can even irritate, offend, or annoy loyal followers. Still other mistakes can dampen response rates so much that you don't get the full picture and wind up making decisions based on a blurry image and a list of assumptions you were trying to avoid when you got the bright idea to launch an online survey in the first place.

Large or small, you don't have to stumble into the same perilous online survey pitfalls that have snagged many others who have gone before you. You can learn from the experience of online survey veterans that have fallen to rise again and conduct many insightful online surveys since.

In this chapter, you discover ten common online survey mistakes. Believe us, these are far from the only mistakes you could make. But because this book isn't called *Online Survey Mistakes For Dummies,* we had to narrow it down to the ten most common — and perhaps most detrimental — faux pas we've seen and experienced.

Failing to Determine Survey Objectives

Why are you conducting an online survey? If your answer is, "Because my boss said I have to," your motivation is only half right. Your real motivation for conducting an online survey is to get answers, insights, perspectives, and opinions on a topic in order to drive value for your organization. That means you have to first determine the topic and then determine the objectives of conducting an online survey.

You'd be surprised at how many people we see set off down the road to online survey launch without taking the time to stop and think about the survey objectives. You may also be surprised at how many people try to do so much in one survey that they overwhelm the respondent and fail to get the answers they need because their objectives were too broad.

By pinpointing the specific objectives of your survey and developing just enough questions to lead you to that objective, you increase your chance to get the answers you're searching for. Otherwise, your questions may lack the relevancy needed to yield useful answers.

It's easy for us to tell you to stay focused on objectives, but that focus is difficult to achieve when you lack experience in building effective online surveys. Of course, that's why you're reading this book.

Avoiding question fluff

If you could sit down face-to-face with a celebrity, you'd probably be tempted to ask a list of questions longer than your right arm. But if you only had 15 minutes with that celebrity, you'd have to force yourself to eliminate the "I'd like to know this" questions (which we call *question fluff* for our purposes here) and focus on the "I absolutely must know this" queries. If you don't have a specific objective, you'll waste a lot of your valuable, once-in-a-lifetime face time with your celebrity and walk away with regrets that you didn't chat about more substantial topics.

It's the same story with survey questions. If you don't have well-defined survey objectives, you'll run your respondents around the wrong mountain and miss the opportunity to get the answers you really need. Because long surveys breed fewer responses, avoid question fluff by narrowing your questions to a list that directly relates to your objectives. Ask yourself whether you can get the answers somewhere else, how much detail you really need, and how well your questions map to your objectives before launching your online survey.

Sometimes staying focused on your objectives is a matter of narrowing down a larger objective to several smaller ones that become a series of shorter, more manageable surveys. Here are a few common survey objectives to give you an idea of the drivers for launching an online survey:

✔ Improve customer satisfaction or customer loyalty.

✔ Compare your customer service against a competitor's.

✔ Discover how to best market your company to potential customers.

✔ Find out what clients perceive as your unique value proposition.

✔ Boost the attendance at your events by determining what potential attendees might want or what past attendees found most valuable.

✔ Find out more about your target audience members' likes and dislikes.

✔ Improve retail store traffic with a Web site usability survey that reveals where customers are getting confused.

✔ Measure the quality of your products and services.

✔ Determine how to improve the online customer experience at your Web site.

✔ Track changes in your service quality over time.

✔ Identify dissatisfied customers so you can fix the issues.

✔ Find out how to make your nonprofit more responsive to member needs.

✔ Discover which new products and services your customers are most interested in.

Failing to Invite People to Participate

Just because you build your online survey, that doesn't mean people will actually take the time to complete it. Much like your Web site, unless you do something to promote it — for instance, put your URL on your business cards and letterhead, search engine optimize your site, and/or shell out bucks for search engine marketing — few will visit you online. Failing to invite people to participate in your survey might be characterized as a near fatal flaw in the online survey world.

Inviting people to participate is more than just blasting out the survey to your e-mail list. You need to literally *invite* people to take the survey (see Figure 17-1). The invitation, then, becomes the call to action. The invitation makes your would-be respondents feel special. The invitation shows that you respect their time and makes the whole process more personal. (For more information on creating the survey e-mail invitation, see Chapter 11.)

Using survey software to send invites

One of the beauties of survey software is that it has a built-in contact manager that makes sending invitations — and resending invitations to folks who didn't respond the first time — as easy as clicking a few buttons. That means if you don't have an e-mail marketing list subscription, you can upload your e-mail contacts into the survey software and allow the vendor to send them for you. That also means there's absolutely no excuse not to send an invitation. The e-mail will come from you, is spam compliant, and the software allows you to easily track who has responded and who hasn't so you can either remove them from your list or send a follow up invitation. To find out more about spam compliant survey invitations, see Chapter 10.

If you want to be really classy, try sending out an e-mail from the president or CEO of your organization a couple of days before you actually e-mail the survey to give your list a heads-up. Let the list members know how important their opinion is, how you'll use the information to improve their experience with your products and services, and how long you expect the survey to take. If you're offering an incentive, spell that out in the e-mail.

Figure 17-1:
An e-mail invite to an online survey.

Failing to Write Clear, Concise Questions

Failing to write clear, concise questions can cause you problems aplenty with your online survey initiatives. If your questions are difficult for readers to understand, they might answer them inaccurately or skip them altogether. (We'll let you decide what's worse. Either leads to a potentially skewed survey.)

By the same token, run-on questions with multiple clauses can also be confusing. The goal is to phrase the question in as few words as possible and with clarity. If the participant has to read the question three times in order to determine what you're really asking, the question is too complex.

Let your colleagues read through your questions and even take a sample survey so you can determine whether there are any issues with the questions before you send your survey to the masses. Also, try reading the questions out loud so you can flag any potential confusion yourself.

Okay, so you want specific examples. We don't blame you. Much of question confusion comes from the way the queries are phrased. Here are some do's and don'ts to follow as you develop your questions:

- **Don't stray from everyday language.** Most people don't speak like a professor and many don't read at the college level. So unless your target audience is university scholars, keep your language simple. Use everyday language that doesn't leave room for reader interpretation. Avoid using vague phrases like *many, most,* and *several*.

- **Limit the number of options.** If you're ranking items in order of importance or using multiple-choice questions, limit the number of options to no more than six. If the list runs on and on, you might make it too difficult for the participant to make an accurate choice.

- **Give participants a pass.** In some cases, your participants might not have an answer to your question or the question may not apply to them because they don't use a particular product or service. In such cases, it's important to give them a way to respond with an "I don't know" or a "not applicable" so they aren't frustrated or confused about how to answer.

- **Avoid redundant questions.** Don't fall into the temptation to ask the same question in a different way in the same survey. It's tempting to repeat yourself or hyperfocus on one area of a product or service feature. But this can annoy your participants.

- **Avoid ambiguous questions.** Ambiguous questions can be understood in two or more possible ways. There are few better ways to skew your survey results than being ambiguous.

- **Ask a single question.** Don't ask more than one question at a time or ask about more than one concept in a single question. The respondent may end up answering half the question, and you may not know which half.

- **Avoid the "if, then" syndrome.** "If this, then that" questions can get pretty complicated pretty quick. They also take the reader a long time to digest mentally and slow down the survey. This can lead to *survey abandonment* (when a person who began taking your survey decides not to finish it) or just plain inaccurate results.

For a more in-depth look at writing questions, check out Chapter 6.

Asking Too Many Open-Ended Questions

Open-ended questions — questions that seek to explore the qualitative, in-depth aspects of a particular topic or issue — can be a valuable asset to your online survey. Sometimes you just can't get the feedback you need with a rating scale or a multiple-choice scheme. Sometimes you need to let the respondent give you a piece of his mind in his own words. That's fine. But you know what they say about too much of a good thing.

While you're considering how much to use the open-ended question type, consider one more thing: You have to read them all and assess their insights manually. Also, the answers to open-ended questions don't show up in your stats.

Open-ended questions may yield valuable information, but they may also end up spawning a survey with a lot of blanks or half-baked answers that are just about as helpful. Generally, you should only use open-ended questions when you can't get the information you need any other way. Asking too many open-ended questions can burden your respondents and may lead to survey abandonment. To find out more about the proper use of open-ended questions, take a look at Chapter 6.

If you really want to take a shot at open-ended questions, guard your interests by asking a yes-or-no or multiple-choice question first and then offering a blank form where respondents can expound on their answer if they choose. If they really have a strong opinion, they'll share it. If not, you don't lose out on important data.

Sending Surveys on the Wrong Days

There are wrong days on which to send out your online survey. If you send your survey out on the wrong days, your response rates are likely to suffer, and sometimes dramatically. Sure, you may end up getting your would-be respondents to participate by sending a follow-up invitation a few days later — on the right day — but you'll wait longer for your results. But the good news is there are also right days.

If you're in an industry where you know the high and low points of the month, take that into consideration before sending your survey. Manufacturing companies, for example, often get squeezed to meet quota the last few days of the month. Same with sales firms. People will be too busy during those periods to focus on your online survey.

Friday, Saturday, Sunday, and Monday are the worst possible days to send your online survey. Here's why: On Fridays, most people are trying to wrap up their workweek. On Saturday and Sunday, people aren't working and your e-mail could get lost in the mass deletions that take place Monday morning.

And, of course, Monday is the first day back in the office, and most people are too busy to think about responding to your survey.

Sending your survey on a Tuesday, Wednesday, or Thursday is ideal. If you can't get your survey ready to roll in the middle of the workweek, hold it until the following week.

Using Too Much Industry Jargon

Using too much industry jargon can send your would-have-been survey respondents clicking away — and fast. What might seem like common every-day language to you and your peers might seem foreign to your readers. If they can't figure out what the heck you're talking about, they can't offer you an accurate answer.

If you're dead set on avoiding the trap that is industry jargon, consider these tips as you develop your questions and instructions. You'll be glad you did.

✔ **Don't use acronyms.** If you want your answers ASAP, don't use acronyms, AKA, a word formed from the initial letters of several words in a phrase, or your survey might end up DOA.

Do you need a survey glossary?

Your industry jargon is probably as natural to you as acronyms like RBI are to a baseball statistician. But your specialized industry terms might not always be crystal clear to your respondents. Still, sometimes that terminology, or jargon, is the only suitable way to describe what you mean.

In those cases, it's a good idea to develop a *survey glossary* — a list of definitions of terms used in an online survey — for those respondents who aren't completely familiar or may only be vaguely familiar with the products, services, or concepts you are asking questions about. A good example is the retail industry, which has strange names for display units, such as wobbler, end-cap, and bottle glorifier.

Many online survey software vendors accommodate for survey glossaries within the technology. Vovici, for example, underlines each keyword in the questionnaire. If the respondent hovers over a keyword, the glossary will be displayed. Others allow you to turn keywords into hyperlinks. When a participate clicks the link the glossary page will pop up. The goal is to avoid any possible confusion that would derail the accuracy of your online survey and to reduce survey abandonment rates from people who are frustrated by language they don't understand.

✔ **Cut your word usage in half.** After you write your question, rewrite it in half as many words. That trick helps you to remove any buzzwords that have no real value and might confuse the reader.

✔ **Test your questions.** Before you release your survey to the public, get someone from outside your industry to read through the questions and peg any jargon or otherwise unfamiliar terms.

Building Surveys That Go On and On

You probably have at least one friend or co-worker who just won't stop talking. They go on and on and on — and on. You love them, but you just don't have time to engage in a 30-minute conversation every time you meet. You may even be hesitant to start a conversation with this person because you know how long it's going to take. The same holds true for the online survey world.

Building surveys that go on and on and on — and on — raises survey abandonment rates faster than just about anything else. Unlike a real-life conversation where you may not want to hurt someone's feelings by cutting the conversation short, people will bail on your online survey in an instant if they see no end in sight.

Surveys that run more than ten minutes are too long in most cases. If your survey takes more than ten minutes to complete in the test run, consider splitting the questions into two different surveys or eliminating noncritical questions.

Let your participants know in advance just how much time they're going to have to commit to taking your online survey — and be realistic. Don't think you can fool people by telling them it's a five-minute survey when it's really a 15-minute survey. You'll violate their trust, and they might not even start your next online survey, much less complete it with valuable insights.

If your online survey absolutely must be long, be upfront about it and give your would-be participants good reasons why you couldn't launch several smaller surveys instead of one long survey, With longer surveys, offering incentives may boost response rates. In addition, many survey software vendors offer a save-and-continue feature that allows your respondent to save their progress and come back to the survey later.

Falling into Question Bias

Question bias, wording that influences the respondent to answer with a preference toward a particular result, is an ugly online survey trait. It's ugly because it skews your survey results. If you fall into the question bias trap, you've allowed your verbiage to take your survey hostage. The responses are all but useless.

You can't avoid bias if you can't see the path that leads you toward this destructive survey questioning method. It's safe to say that most people who are developing questions aren't falling into the bias trap on purpose. They just don't realize how their words are predisposing respondents to lean one way or another. Consider the following tips for preventing question bias:

- **Avoid double-barreled questions.** A *double-barreled question* combines two or more issues in a single question, such as "Do you think babysitters should have more contact with parents? And do you think they should deal more with the mother?" Respondents will have difficulty gauging what you're measuring with this type of question. What's more, they might want to answer "yes" to one part and "no" to the other.

- **Avoid loaded questions.** A *loaded question* is also known as a trick question because it contains an assumption of agreement. For example, "When you read for fun, do you prefer to read fiction or nonfiction books?" This assumes the respondents enjoy reading, which might not be the case. If they don't read for pleasure, they can't possibly answer truthfully.

- **Avoid leading questions.** A *leading question* is one that suggests the answer or reveals the interviewer's opinion. Leading questions, as their name suggests, try to lead the respondent to the desired answer. For example, "Would you use X product, which has been known to cause allergic reactions in children?"

- **Avoid double negatives.** A *double negative* occurs when you use two negatives so that they cancel each other out and become a positive. For example, "Do you agree with the following statement? Parents should not be required to give their children immunizations."

If the respondent gives a negative answer, she's saying she does not think parents should not give their children immunizations. That means they think parents should immunize their children. That may or may not be an accurate response depending on whether the respondent caught on to the double negative.

Beware of sensitive issues

If you don't want your innocent online survey to cause a firestorm of customer backlash, beware of how you handle sensitive issues in your questionnaire. Avoid questions that might offend or otherwise spark controversy in your surveys. However, if you must ask questions about controversial issues as part of your survey, do so without bias and with plenty of cultural sensitivity. In other words, be politically correct.

It's vital that your survey is accurate and that your respondents and others who are analyzing the survey are confident that you took every precaution to avoid leading or loaded questions, or potentially offensive phrasing. Defensive respondents don't always provide accurate answers. Even simple surveys about internal business practices can lead to controversy. So, again, beware of sensitive issues.

Forgetting Past Survey Initiatives

Maybe you've never heard the phrase survey-happy. It describes a phenomenon in which marketers send too many surveys too frequently that ask too similar questions.

When you set out to deploy your next survey, look back over your last few surveys to jog your memory about the survey objectives and the results. Sure, there may be some questions that you have to ask each and every time to establish usage of a product or service. By the same token, you might also choose to do the same exact survey each quarter to measure some aspect of customer satisfaction. But sending similar surveys too frequently might make it appear as if your organization doesn't have its act together.

You can overdo online surveys. Sending a customer survey feedback each time your customer contacts you is overkill, for example. Use online surveys strategically so you don't wear out your customers. Breaking up your customer list into groups and sending surveys to one group at a time can prevent what's known as *survey fatigue*.

Failing to Follow Through with Results

Failing to follow up and follow through is a weakness that could damage your relationships with your online survey participants. When you launch a survey, people expect you to act on the results you find. If you are conducting a customer service survey, for example, your participants expect you to identify areas of improvement and takes steps to offer better customer service based on the results. Failing to offer insights into what you learned from the survey and how you plan to remedy any issues sends the signal that you aren't going to do anything at all.

In addition, following up with your customers demonstrates that you actually care about the time they've spent giving you feedback. Who would want to respond to a survey if he knew his answers would just drop into a black hole, never to be heard from again?

Chapter 18

Ten Online Survey Best Practices

*B*est practices. Everybody loves them. They mean other people have found proven methods to do things — and those methods can save you a lot of headaches. Best practices can improve the quality of your survey, which, in turn, can improve the quality of your responses. Best practices can also save you time and money by boosting your productivity and efficiency. They prevent you from having to reinvent the wheel. Indeed, there are plenty of benefits to using best practices. It's up to you to take advantage of them.

Of course, online surveys aren't age-old, and the best practices are still evolving. What's more, you might discover that some of your best practices clash with what your counterparts in other organizations are doing. You have to identify, document, and validate best practices for yourself. But isn't it nice to know there's a body of online survey best practices to draw from? Maybe you can contribute to it when you become an online survey pro.

In this chapter, we share with you the top ten best practices online survey gurus are employing today. Sure, there are many others. But if you can start with these ten, which range from question development to distribution strategies, you will be well on your way to finding success with your online surveys.

Doing the Prep Work

Some have said that every hour of preparation can save you four hours in execution. Some have gone so far as to say it can even save you weeks or months. That might be an overstatement in the world of online surveys. But the axiom holds true: Those who do their homework get better grades. In other words, if you take the time to prepare your survey in advance you can get better response rates — and probably better responses — than if you throw together your survey in a hurry.

Preparation is key. Take the time you need to develop questions that illicit answers you can actually use. Look at other surveys in similar industries, if you can, to get some tips. Read materials on how to develop questions and how to structure surveys. Yes, this book offers plenty of advice in that regard, but take the continuing education approach and stay on top of the latest trends and best practices.

Have you ever taken an online survey? Take a moment to consider what you liked and didn't like about it and work the former into your survey development.

Again, preparation is key. Before you rush into your online survey software account to start building your survey, build a draft offline. You can create a full draft of your survey in Microsoft Word — or the word processor of your choice — and circulate it around to your colleagues to get feedback before you endeavor to Web-enable your survey. Pay close attention to the order of your questions, the questions themselves, and the choices you offer in multiple-choice queries.

Always launch your survey internally to make sure your best-laid plans don't go to waste. Even with the most in-depth preparation, simple mistakes (like typos, putting too many questions on one page, or making the survey too long to keep the respondent's interest) can derail your success. Do a test drive with internal staff and get feedback.

Keeping Your Survey As Brief As Possible

What's the first thing that crosses your mind when you discover that new best-selling business book your boss wants you to read is 600 pages and counting? Dread is a typical response. Sure, the book might be full of information that's going to put you over the top, but the length of the manuscript is so intimidating that you might never pick it up. Although your online survey won't rival *War and Peace,* a survey with 60 pages might have similar results to a 600-page business tome.

Put your most important survey questions toward the beginning of the survey. That way, if the respondents drop out before the end, at least you might be able to salvage some insights from the trail of answers they left behind.

The point is that you need to keep your survey as brief as possible while also getting all the results you need to collect the clues to the market research puzzle you set out to solve. If you're having trouble keeping the survey brief, take these steps:

1. Go ahead and do a brain dump. Ask every question you can possibly think of. You can even ask your colleagues to do the same.

2. Weed out every question that doesn't have anything to do with the key objective of your survey. (Don't discard them, though, because you might be able to use them for a separate survey in the future.)

3. Review the questions to make sure that they're pertinent to the task at hand. If your survey is still too long, go through Step 2 again.

Remember, the goal is to get completed surveys. Shorter surveys have higher response rates than long, drawn-out questionnaires that seek to know everything the respondent ever thought of concerning your product, organization, customer service, and so on. If you want your respondents to take part in another survey, whether related or unrelated, you can always plant that seed at the end of your survey with an invitation to click through to another survey or a heads-up that you might be sending out another questionnaire on a different topic soon.

Using a Survey Template

If you don't have a clue how to build a survey, don't worry. You can use survey templates. Online survey software companies typically offer free survey templates that you can copy and modify. You can even import example questions from those templates into your own surveys.

You can find many different template types from which to choose, including marketing templates, customer satisfaction templates, services templates, community templates, human resources templates, and academic/research templates. Templates are designed to give you a running start on building your survey. (To find out more about the pros and cons of survey templates, see Chapter 5.)

Organizing Your Survey Like Dr. Spock

Do you remember the original *Star Trek* television series? Whether you saw the blockbuster movie, watched the show back in the 1970s, or you're enjoying reruns today — or even if you never watched it at all — you're probably familiar with the character called Dr. Spock. Spock didn't give emotional responses to anything. He assessed everything in life according to logic. When it comes to organizing your online survey, you would do well to take a Dr. Spock mentality. That is to say, you need to get logical when it comes to the structure of your survey.

Put on your customer-colored glasses and look at your online survey from the respondent's point of view. What would you want to see first? Probably the survey's intention. If you're collecting responses that will help guide the development of a new product or service, let your respondents know. If you're looking for insights into a branding campaign, let them know that, too. Communicating the goal of your study helps them align their thought processes from the get-go. (That's an added bonus for catering to the respondent's curiosity about how the data will be used.)

As you continue to walk along the lines of logic, be sure to break your survey up in a page order that makes sense. Good old-fashioned common sense can take you a long way. For example, if you were conducting a story about orange juice, you'd want to group all the questions about packaging together, all the questions about taste together, all the questions about dietary concerns together, and so on. Dividing your survey pages in accordance to groups of questions also makes taking the survey less intimidating. Instead of a laundry list of questions that appears to be never ending, the survey uses a logical grouping that encourages the respondent to continue through to the end.

Making Your Questions Interactive

Society is increasingly interactive. Reality television shows let you call in and vote on who will become the next winner on *American Idol*. Cellphones have touch screens that let you play video games on the fly. Cars have navigational systems that you can talk to — and they talk back. Why should an online survey be any different? With enterprise-level online survey software, it doesn't have to be. Online survey software — okay, maybe not the freebies, but the paid stuff — lets you tap into the power of *branching*, a feature that lets you jump to a specified question based on responses to previous questions. In essence, branching serves up different sets of questions to different people.

For example, pretend you have a different set of questions for men and women. The first screen asks the respondents to choose "Male" or "Female" and then gives subsequent questions based on the sex of the respondent. A jeweler's survey might ask men about watches and women about necklaces and earrings.

Here is another example. Imagine you're conducting a survey on fitness. Your first question might ask the respondent whether he or she goes to a fitness center to work out regularly. If the answer is "yes," your next question might ask how regularly, then another question after that might ask what equipment the respondent uses most. If the answer is "no," however, you would have no need to ask those particular questions. The survey might jump ahead to a question about outdoor activities or home exercise programs ala Richard Simmons.

Using the "Other" Option

If you've ever taken a survey of any kind, you know that even the most creative list of multiple-choice answers doesn't always offer the option that best describes your feeling on a subject. That's the beauty of using the "other" option (see Figure 18-1), which allows the respondent to type in an answer. Why box your respondents into the choices that you thought of when there might be an equally valid choice — or even an odd-ball choice — that you might never have considered?

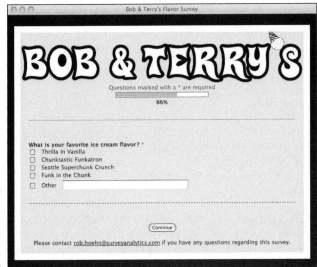

Figure 18-1:
The "other"
option in a
survey.

Not only do you get more accurate responses by offering an "other" option, but you also get insight into what other choices you may want to include in future surveys. If you notice a major trend in the "other" category, you might consider adding that option on the next iteration of your survey. (To find out more about how to develop solid questions, read Chapter 6.)

Don't use the "other" option too often. If you add an "other" option to each question, people are bound to use it more frequently than you'd like. Analyzing open-ended questions takes more time than analyzing a report that shows the number of responses for each "A,B,C,D" answer. It's also possible that you won't be able to discern much from the open-ended answer or that the person really didn't answer the question.

Building a Library of Questions

If you start sending surveys out even semi-regularly, you'll begin to notice that you use some of the same questions and answer options in all your surveys. If you get it right the first time in terms of question development, choices, and spelling, why do the same work twice? Folks call that "reinventing the wheel."

You can save time by identifying those questions and adding them to your online survey software's question library. The question library becomes your template library of questions that you can reuse across all your surveys. (To find out more about the question library, see Chapter 5.)

Promoting the Survey on Your Web Site

You've spent thousands of dollars developing a Web site — and probably thousands more promoting it — so it should go without saying that you would promote your survey on your Web site. But it doesn't go without saying. Often, people forget about this strategic venue.

When it comes to promoting your survey on your own Web site, you have a couple of options. You can use a pop-up window to get readers' attention and invite them to take your survey. That pop-up window should briefly communicate the purpose of the study and any incentive you might be offering, as well as how long it will take. You can also post a link on your Web site in strategic locations. The home page might be the best option, or you can place it on other product or service pages on your site that relate to the online survey you're conducting.

Many online survey software providers offer widgets that aim to make it easier for you to post a survey on your Web site. If you're wondering what in the world a widget is, it isn't one of those hypothetical manufactured products Harvard Business school professors always speak about when giving examples of how to become an industry tycoon — at least not in the Web 2.0 world.

Short for *window gadget,* a *widget* is a mini–Web application that you can put on your Web page, blog, or social media site that allows you to embed information. Some widgets tell you what time it is. Other widgets scroll the latest news headlines. Still other widgets track eBay auctions.

In the context of online surveys, you can find widgets to display a one-question survey (or *poll*) right on your Web site (see Figure 18-2). You can also find widgets that display the results of a survey and widgets that allow your visitors to sign up to your e-mail list.

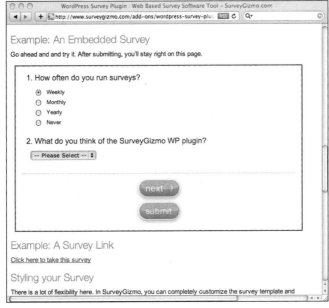

Figure 18-2:
A Survey-
Gizmo
WordPress
survey
widget.

If you decide to place a widget on your Web site, be sure you test it somewhere that doesn't see droves of traffic. Unfortunately, widgets don't always
work the way you thought they would when you installed them, so test it
somewhere behind the scenes to make sure it does what it's supposed to do.

Posting Progress Indicators

When you're doing your online shopping, don't you appreciate it when the
merchant offers you a progress bar as you go through the shopping cart
process? It sort of calms your anxiety because you know in advance how
many hoops you have to jump through in order to seal the deal. Studies have
even shown that progress indicators reduce shopping cart abandonment.
It's always nice to know how long you've gone and how long you have to go.
(That's why people put counters and timers on treadmills!)

Most online survey software makes it easy for you to add a progress bar to
your survey. It doesn't tell the respondents exactly how many pages are left,
but it indicates on a bar how far along they are in the process (see Figure 18-3).
You can even specify the location or remove the progress bar if you want to.
Progress bars are a good way to reduce survey abandonment the same way
they're helpful in reducing shopping cart abandonment.

A progress indicator

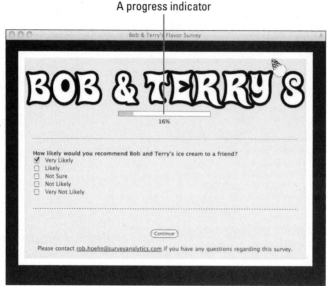

Figure 18-3:
A progress
indicator in
a survey.

Minding Your Manners

After your respondents spend their valuable time offering you their opinions, be sure to return the favor with a thank you. It's the least you can do. After all, without your respondents your survey wouldn't be a survey at all. You don't need to get fancy. Just a simple "thanks" will do. Another common courtesy is to provide the respondents with a link or some other way to see the survey results. As you do these things, you're taking steps toward building relationships with your respondents that will be fruitful for your future surveying endeavors.

You can say thanks many ways in the online survey world. One of the most common techniques is a special Thank You page at the end of the survey. If you want to be extra nice — and if you have the respondent's e-mail address — you can also send a follow-up Thank You e-mail as well (see Figure 18-4). Both options usually can be configured within the survey tool and in some cases are enabled by default.

Figure 18-4:
A simple
Thank You
page at the
end of a
survey.

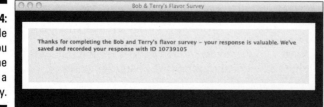

Glossary

abstract: A short summary of the management report.

affirmative consent: The practice of someone deliberately choosing to receive e-mail from an organization.

aided recall: Also called *awareness,* this is a technique used to aid memory. This technique involves using something that stimulates remembering, for example, a picture or words. Reading or showing the respondent the possible answers to a specific question.

anonymous survey URL: A URL in your e-mail invitation that allows the respondents to remain anonymous.

attitude research: A survey conducted to obtain information on how people feel about certain products, ideas, or companies.

ballot stuffing: When an individual responds to your survey more than once.

banner table: An element in an online survey report that gives you a picture of the data that corresponds to individual survey questions.

bar chart: A chart that uses bars to show frequencies or values for different categories.

basic frequency analysis: An analysis that offers an overall insight based on percentages and averages.

bidirectional information: A two-way information exchange that benefits both sides.

blacklist: A list of e-mail addresses that are blocked from sending e-mail. This is also known as a *blocklist.*

branching: Also called *skip logic,* branching is a feature that lets you jump to a specified question based on responses to previous questions. In essence, branching serves up different sets of questions to different people.

CAN-SPAM Act: Controlling the Assault of Non-Solicited Pornography and Marketing Act. The law established requirements for organizations that send commercial e-mail.

check box questions: Also known as *multi-select-based questions,* check box questions let users choose more than one answer option for the same question.

closed-end questions: *Dichotomous questions, multiple-choice questions, ratings,* and *ranking questions* are sometimes referred to as closed-end questions. These are basically any questions that don't involve open-ended or free form text input boxes.

comment box: Comment boxes are customary to online surveys. This is essentially an open-ended text box with multiple lines to allow the respondent to comment.

completed count: The completed count is all respondents that have gone through the entire survey and clicked the Finish button on the last page of the survey.

completion rate: This is equal to the number of completed survey responses divided by the number of started survey responses.

conjoint analysis: A popular marketing research technique used to determine what features a new product or service should have and how it should be priced.

Conjoint Simulator: A tool that lets you predict the market share of new products and concepts that might not exist today and measure the gain or loss in market share based on changes to existing products in the given market.

constant sum question: A question that permits collection of "ratio" data, meaning that the data is able to express the relative value or importance of the options (for example, option A is twice as important as option B).

contingency question: Also called a *filter question,* a contingency question helps you determine whether a respondent is qualified or experienced enough to offer the insights you need in your online survey.

continuous data: Quantitative data that is measured in intervals on a number line.

convenience sampling: A probability method of sampling in which natural segments or groups are clear within a target population.

cookie: A small text file stored on a user's computer by a Web browser. Cookies are used to enrich the Web browsing experience by saving the user's state after they leave a Web site.

cross-survey reports: Reports that aggregate data across multiple surveys.

cross tabulation analysis: An analysis that offers insights into how two variables interact and shows a distribution of how users responded to both of them.

customer loyalty surveys: Surveys that seek to determine how loyal a customer is to your brand.

customer satisfaction surveys: Surveys that seek to determine whether your customers are satisfied with your products and services, or even your customer service itself.

data cleaning: The process of detecting, correcting, and removing data from your online survey results that's inaccurate, corrupt, incomplete, or irrelevant.

demographic questions: Questions used to identify characteristics such as age, gender, income, race, geographic place of residence, number of children, and so on.

demographics: Population characteristics such as age, gender, income, race, geographic place of residence, number of children, and so on.

dichotomous question: Generally a yes or no question, such as "Have you ever purchased a product or service from our Web site?" The respondent simply answers yes or no.

double-barreled question: A question that combines two or more issues in a single question. This type of question makes it difficult for the respondent to gauge what you're measuring.

double negative: A double negative occurs when you use two negatives in the same sentence.

drop-down menu: A menu of options that appears below the item when the user clicks it.

drop-out analysis: Tracks at what point your participants dropped out of the survey.

drop-outs: Respondents who start a survey but don't complete it.

e-mail firewall: A piece of hardware on a software application that's programmed to identify and blog e-mails that appear untrustworthy.

e-mail reminder: A resend of your survey invitation to people who have not completed the survey.

embedded dynamic controls: Interactive components that can be placed in the body of an e-mail newsletter.

employee attitude surveys: Surveys that offer a series of multiple-choice items grouped along one or more dimensions of the organization.

employee exit interview: A survey that seeks to determine an employee's reasons for joining the organization, the department or business unit in which the employee worked, and the reasons for leaving.

executive summary: A short document that summarizes a longer report so that readers can draw conclusions without reading the entire document.

filter question: Also called a *contingency question,* this is a question that helps you determine whether a respondent is qualified or experienced enough to offer the insights you need in your online survey.

forced response: When the respondent is required to answer your thought-provoking question before he or she can move on to the next question.

frequency analysis: A basic calculation on how often a particular choice is selected.

group: One or more filters on your data set.

grouping and segmentation analysis: An analysis that lets you create filters to group respondents based on demographics or responses.

harvesting bots: Software that scans Web pages, postings on forums, and other sources to gather e-mail addresses.

histogram: A chart that typically shows the quantity of points that fall within various numeric ranges.

hosted solutions: Web-based software that requires you to log on to an ASP's Web site to create, launch, and analyze your reports. Also called *on-demand solutions.*

hybrid survey: A survey in which you use more than one technique to gather responses.

interval scale question: See *staple scale question.*

JavaScript: A scripting language most often used for client-side Web development.

judgment sampling: A nonprobability method of sampling that includes a sample based on your gut instincts.

junk mail box: Also called a *spam filter,* a junk mail box is a folder that stores what your e-mail provider thinks is spam, whether it is or not.

leading question: A question that suggests the answer or reveals the interviewer's opinion. Leading questions try to guide the respondent to the desired answer.

line chart: A two-dimensional scatter plot of ordered observations where the observations are connected following their order.

loaded question: Also known as a *trick question,* a loaded question contains an assumption of agreement.

malware: Software designed to infiltrate or damage a computer system without the owner's knowledge.

management report: A summary report of the survey data covering the highlights or key findings.

methodology: The collection, the comparative study, and the critique of the individual methods that are used in a given discipline or field of inquiry.

MicroPoll: QuestionPro's terminology for a quick, single-question poll.

multiple-choice questions: Questions with answers that consist of three or more mutually exclusive categories.

multiple-select question: A question that allows participants to select more than one option.

mutually exclusive responses: Responses for which the respondent cannot choose more than one answer.

nonprobability samples: Samples that don't give every person a chance to be selected and are nonrandom.

nonrespondent bias: The bias resulting from limiting the survey analysis to the available data.

online survey: A survey in which you collect survey data electronically from your target audience over the Internet.

open-ended question: A question that seeks to explore the qualitative, in-depth aspects of a particular topic or issue.

opt-in e-mail: The practice of someone deliberately choosing to receive e-mail from an organization.

opt-out: An option that allows people to ask you not to send them future e-mail messages.

ordinal scale questions: See *rank order scaling questions.*

page break: A break in the survey that sends you to the next page.

panel company: A company that gives you a list of people who are willing to participate in surveys like yours.

participant statistics: A group of analytics related to the level of participation in your survey. These usually include participation rates at various points in your survey such as *started, viewed,* and *completed.*

permission-based e-mail marketing: E-mail marketing in which you have permission from the recipient to send the message.

phishing scam: An e-mail or Web-based scam that sets out to gather personal information from victims to use in identity-theft rings.

pie chart: A chart that shows a percentage value as a slice of a pie.

pivot question: The question you use to segment the rest of the survey.

probability samples: Samples that give every member of the population a chance of being selected in the sample and involves random selection of that general population.

qualitative questions: Questions that explain perceptions or opinions using text instead of numbers.

quantitative questions: Question types that include multiple-choice, rank order, and constant sum.

question bias: Wording that influences the respondent to answer with a preference toward a particular result.

question separators: Tools used to break the survey into multiple pages for a better look and feel.

quota sampling: A nonprobability method that combines stratified sampling and either judgment sampling or convenience sampling.

radio button: A circular button on a Web page that can be selected by the respondent.

random sampling: A probability method in which each member of the population stands an equal chance of being chosen for survey participation.

rank order scaling questions: Questions that allow a certain set of brands or products to be ranked based on a specific attribute or characteristic.

rating scale questions: Questions that require a person to rate a product or brand along a well-defined, evenly spaced continuum.

reach: The proportion of the audience (target group) that chooses a particular option.

real-time summary reports: Reports that provide basic statistical analysis on your survey questions as they come in.

relationship surveys: Surveys that measure the satisfaction of customers who have an ongoing relationship with your organization.

respondent: The person who completes the survey.

respondent reports: See *participant statistics*.

respondent tracking URL: A URL in your e-mail survey invitation that allows you to track the activities of your respondents.

response-based pricing: A pricing model that's based on how many responses you generate.

response rate: The proportion of those who actually participate in a survey.

Response Viewer: A real-time view of your database. You can use the Response Viewer to view, edit, or delete individual responses.

RSS feed reports: Various types of reports that are offered in an RSS-based (XML-based) format.

RSS reader: A software program that aggregates data from Web sites.

sample: A group of people that fit a particular demographic who are willing to take your survey.

sample bias: Data that's skewed because the selection of a sample is not representative of the target population.

sampling error: The error that inevitably arises when you don't observe the entire population.

satisfaction survey: A survey designed to measure consumer satisfaction.

scatter plot: A plot that displays the relationship between two factors.

semantic differential scale: A scale that asks a respondent to rate a product, brand, or company based on a seven-point rating scale that has a bipolar adjective at each end.

shopping cart abandonment survey: A survey that seeks to determine why people abandon shopping carts and registration pages and gives you the opportunity to make improvements to your site.

simple frequency analysis: The simple act of counting all the responses for each answer in a question and comparing the totals against each other.

skills inventory: A survey that measures and rates the skills of the people within your organization.

skip logic: Also called *branching,* skip logic is a feature that lets you jump to a specified question based on responses to previous questions. In essence, branching serves up different sets of questions to different people.

snowball sampling: A probability method of sampling where you choose participants at consistent intervals, such as every fourth person in a group.

spam: Unsolicited e-mail, or junk mail.

spam false positives: A legitimate message that is mistakenly marked as spam.

spam filter: A software program that examines incoming mail and sorts spam into a separate folder.

spam index: A measure of how likely your online survey e-mail invitations are to be classified as spam.

spotlight report: A report that lets you share the survey results with each respondent so that he can see how his answers compared to the rest of the respondents' answers.

staple scale question: A question that asks a respondent to rate a brand, product, or service according to a certain characteristic on a scale from +5 to –5, indicating how well the characteristic describes the product or service.

started number: The total number of respondents that have started the survey.

survey abandonment: When a person who began taking your survey decides not to finish it.

survey glossary: A list of definitions of terms used in an online survey.

survey invitation: The e-mail your respondent receives to ask him to complete your survey.

system variable–based filtering: Grouping surveys based on variables.

table: A set of data arranged in rows and columns.

terminated via branching: If you have set up branching in your questions to terminate the survey for specific criteria, the number of terminated respondents will be displayed.

time-based grouping: Creating segments of data based on time, such as when the survey was completed.

tracking studies: Studies that track consumer behavior over long periods of time.

transactional surveys: Surveys that measure the customer's satisfaction in relation to a particular transaction.

TURF (Total Unduplicated Reach and Frequency) analysis: A statistical model that can be used to answer questions such as "Where should we place ads to reach the widest possible audience?" and "What kind of market share will we gain if we add a new line to our model?"

validation errors: Errors that occur when users do not respond to required items.

validity: Whether the survey measures what it intends to measure.

variables: Used to store additional information that's passed to the survey to create a more personalized survey experience. Also called *hidden questions*.

viewed number: Total number of users who click the link to access the survey.

Web-based software: Software that's hosted on a Web server. That means you access it through your favorite Web browser.

Webinar: A Web conferencing tool used to conduct live meetings or presentations online.

whitelist: A list of e-mail addresses that are known, trusted, or explicitly permitted.

widget: A mini–Web application that you can put on your Web page, blog, or social media site that allows you to embed information.

Index